DAVID BOWIE AND THE SEARCH FOR LIFE, DEATH AND GOD

DAVID BOWIE AND THE SEARCH FOR LIFE, DEATH AND GOD

Peter Ormerod

BLOOMSBURY CONTINUUM
LONDON · OXFORD · NEW YORK · NEW DELHI · SYDNEY

BLOOMSBURY CONTINUUM
Bloomsbury Publishing Plc

50 Bedford Square
London
WC1B 3DP
UK

Bloomsbury Publishing Ireland Limited
29 Earlsfort Terrace
Dublin 2
D02 AY28
Ireland

BLOOMSBURY, BLOOMSBURY CONTINUUM and the
Diana logo are trademarks of Bloomsbury Publishing Plc

First published in Great Britain 2026

Copyright © Peter Ormerod, 2026

Peter Ormerod has asserted his right under the Copyright,
Designs and Patents Act, 1988, to be identified as Author of this work

For legal purposes the Acknowledgements on p. 222 constitute
an extension of this copyright page

Photos © Pictorial Press Ltd/Alamy; St Mary's church photo © author photograph; Steve Hickey/Alamy Live News; RAPH GATTI/AFP via Getty Images; ZUMA Press, Inc./Alamy Live News; Gie Knaeps/Getty Images; Koh Hasebe/Shinko Music/Getty Images; Michael Ochs Archives/Getty Images; RGR Collection/Alamy; Gie Knaeps/Getty Images; Gie Knaeps/Getty Images; Gabe Palacio/Image Direct/Getty Images; Georges De Keerle/Getty Images; Toby Melville/PA Images/Alamy; Michael Putland/Getty Images; Henry McGee/MediaPunch/Alamy; Evan Agostini/Getty Images

All rights reserved. No part of this publication may be: i) reproduced or transmitted in any form, electronic or mechanical, including photocopying, recording or by means of any information storage or retrieval system without prior permission in writing from the publishers; or ii) used or reproduced in any way for the training, development or operation of artificial intelligence (AI) technologies, including generative AI technologies. The rights holders expressly reserve this publication from the text and data mining exception as per Article 4(3) of the Digital Single Market Directive (EU) 2019/790

Bloomsbury Publishing Plc does not have any control over, or responsibility for, any third-party websites referred to or in this book. All internet addresses given in this book were correct at the time of going to press. The author and publisher regret any inconvenience caused if addresses have changed or sites have ceased to exist, but can accept no responsibility for any such changes

A catalogue record for this book is available from the British Library

Library of Congress Cataloguing-in-Publication data has been applied for

ISBN:	HB:	978-1-3994-2282-6
	TPB:	978-1-3994-2284-0
	EBOOK:	978-1-3994-2283-3
	EPDF:	978-1-3994-2281-9

2 4 6 8 10 9 7 5 3

Typeset by Lumina Datamatics Ltd
Printed and bound in the U.S.A. by Lakeside Book Company, Harrisonburg, VA

To find out more about our authors and books visit www.bloomsbury.com
and sign up for our newsletters
For product safety related questions contact productsafety@bloomsbury.com

CONTENTS

Introduction   1

1. Choirboy   7
2. Buddhist   17
3. Occultist   27
4. Messiah   49
5. Lost   63
6. Vanquisher   85
7. Gnostic   105
8. Denier   119
9. Holy Man/Shaman   137
10. Doubter   163
11. Lover   181
12. Magician   197

Conclusion   217
Acknowledgements   222
Notes   223
Index   241
A Note on the Author   249
A Note on the Type   250

INTRODUCTION

In a blue room looking out over a fading industrial landscape in the northernmost part of the English Midlands, I was weeping and I didn't know why. It was 1996, shortly after 6 p.m. on Wednesday, 27 March. My brother, eight years older than me, had a lot of old albums in his room, and I would sometimes listen to them. Some I liked more than others, but none had done anything like this to me. The album was *Hunky Dory* by David Bowie.

I was 17 and, like most boys my age in the town I grew up in, I kept a tight lid on any emotions. But it was as if frozen wastes were being melted by the rising of a sun. The first rays were cast by the opening tones and hums; within a few minutes, I was lost in it, and found in it. Now, 30 years later, here we are.

I have long struggled to make sense of why David Bowie could make me cry when little else could. For a while, I assumed that I just really loved his songs. But I started to suspect something else was going on. Yes, the album's hopscotching between safety and danger, its clarity and confusion, its delicate surefootedness and gentle rebellion – this all appealed. As a teenager, I had always felt rootless, always an observer from the periphery, and *Hunky Dory* felt like a message from that place. But there was another dimension I had overlooked.

Hunky Dory draws on a whole realm of religion, spirituality and philosophy, sometimes hinted at, sometimes shouted about. By the end of the first side, I had heard prophecies of a coming race, been told that my species was obsolete and that it was time to make way for *Homo superior*. There were references to split selves and eternal impermanence, to something called The Golden Dawn, to someone called Crowley, to a *bardo*, whatever that is, to the salvation of faith, which is simultaneously beguiling and bullshit, and to death and the sublime knowledge that comes with it. I had absorbed it all without really noticing it. It took me years of listening to Bowie to realize that this stuff was important.

Two months before I heard *Hunky Dory* for the first time, Bowie had been presented with the Brit Award for Outstanding Contribution to Music. Few recipients could be more deserving. In the latest edition of *1001 Albums You Must Hear Before You Die*,[1] Bowie has more albums than anyone else, nine in total, ranging in style from glam rock to soul to ambient electronica to avant-garde jazz, spanning 45 years. Then there was Bowie live, whether performing as an electrifying otherworldly demi-god in the English provinces or as a stately master of stadiums around the globe. There's no way of separating his music from the iconography, the imagery, the constant invention and reinvention, the clothes, the make-up, the reconfiguration of gender and sexuality, the newly boundless sense of possibility, the *hair*, for goodness' sake.

Bowie inspired and influenced not only numerous bands and individuals but whole movements and genres. A list of acts shaped in some way by Bowie would at the very least include Madonna, Prince, U2, the Sex Pistols, Simply Red, Depeche Mode, Kate Bush, Joy Division, Gary Numan, ABC, Duran Duran, Nick Cave, The Smashing Pumpkins, Spandau Ballet, The Smiths, Simple Minds, Culture Club, Soft Cell, The Cure, Pet Shop Boys, Suede, Pixies, Blur, Lady Gaga, Arcade Fire, Oasis, Siouxsie and the Banshees, Pulp, Nine Inch Nails, Radiohead, Manic Street Preachers, Placebo, Nirvana and The Killers. He brought new audiences to figures as diverse as Brian Eno and Tina Turner, and sang the praises of the Velvet Underground and the Stooges and their respective frontmen Lou Reed and Iggy Pop, who influenced countless acts in turn. Look, and you will see him; listen, and you will hear him. Bowie is everywhere.

By the time I discovered Bowie, it seemed the work had essentially been done. He was routinely called 'the chameleon of rock'.

Journalists would obligingly refer to his 'ch-ch-changes'. Bowie's apparent lack of definition was coming to define him. But he saw things differently. That year, 1996, he was asked on Dutch television if any thread ran through his body of work. His answer may sound surprising. 'A search for a spiritual foundation,' he said. 'I keep coming back to it.'

I was unaware of this interview until a few years ago, but I had already begun to wonder if there was something deeper joining the dots – something that endured despite the shifting personas and genres. My father was a priest in the Church of England, and while such parentage can often be enough to turn any child into the most virulent atheist, my own faith has somehow survived. I knew that Bowie had written a hymn; I had heard of his dalliances with what was called 'black magic'; I remembered seeing him pray onstage at Wembley. All of this seemed incidental: he was surely just a restless artist who liked trying new things out of curiosity or boredom or in search of a quick buck, and the spiritual stuff was a mere accessory. But the more I read, and the more I watched, and the more I listened, the more I asked myself if I had got it the wrong way round: rather than the spirituality being incidental to the music, what if it was *essential* to the music?

When you look at Bowie's career in this way, it becomes illuminated anew. Songs whose vibrancy may have been dulled by their ubiquity now rediscover their spark; those that have retained their power become almost overwhelming. Yes, there is change, but through it all there emerges an epic worthy of ancient eras and forgotten words, lived in our time by a man from Bromley.

It is important to ask what Bowie meant by that phrase, 'a search for a spiritual foundation'. The word 'spirituality' is prone these days to be used liberally and recklessly, deracinated for a secular age; it can be lumped in with faddish terms like 'wellness', and is in danger of coming to mean nothing more profound than something like 'inner mood'. Bowie was quite clear, however, that he was talking about matters of God, in the weightiest, deepest and most meaningful sense. Again in 1996, he was asked if he thought there was a God. 'Yes I do,' he said, 'but I don't think the man with the white beard on a cloud as a personification is enough for me.'

His search, then, may be understood at its most modest as a quest to discover a kind of God that made sense to him, and at its most bold, as a quest to discover nothing less than the *reality* of God. This means it ventures at times beyond the sort of language and ideas we might expect from a rock star. There are many examples of standard religious imagery and vocabulary in Bowie's work, as well as direct references to the occult and the esoteric. But beyond this is where his broader metaphysical beliefs find their wings, and where his most moving and possibly life-changing work lives.

There are earthly matters to contend with too, times of sweat and grit and blood. Bowie had little time for organized religion, which he saw as a force for oppression, warping and corrupting the beauty of that which it claimed to venerate. He was horrified by the propensity of humans to fall prostrate before those who stand as messiahs. He could rage against God, and sang of the failing of his faith.

Bowie was a master of ambiguity, and there are few, if any, wholly right or wrong ways to read his lyrics or hear his music. Some of his artistic choices were purely intellectual, experimental and cerebral; others were motivated by his desire for money and fame and status. And this book is not so crass as to claim Bowie for a particular faith or spiritual tradition: while I would be delighted to report that Bowie was a dedicated churchgoing man throughout his life, handing out the hymn books, helping with the coffee, arranging the flowers and mowing the lawns, my loyalty here is to reality.

But oh, what a reality. The story I uncovered took me to extraordinary places and affected me in unexpected ways. Yes, Bowie's career spanned 50 years of remarkable change, but his quest for a spiritual foundation inspired his creativity and fired his imagination throughout. It powered some of his greatest songs and shaped his defining works. It pushed him, pulled him, called him onwards.

From his simple childhood experiences of church through to the profound spirituality of his final record, via Buddhism, occultism, witchcraft, messiahs and Kabbalah, it is all here. Along the way are encounters with a whole cast of extraordinary men and women. It's a story of anguish, escape, epiphany, revelation and, above all, love.

I

CHOIRBOY

All great journeys begin somewhere. Odysseus had Troy. Neil Armstrong had Cape Kennedy. For David Bowie, it was Bromley. He was not born there, but this story starts there, in a place where the conventional meets the supernatural.

Today, Bromley feels like a normal suburban town. It lies in the hinterland: head a few miles north and you're definitely in London; head a few miles south and you're definitely not. It is generally a light and open place – there are chunks of fiercely concrete architecture from the mid-twentieth century, but their effect is softened by the town's many Victorian cupolas, spires and arches. The modernist and the traditional seem to get on fine. This is where Bowie went through his first great transformation. He arrived in Bromley as a boy called David Jones in 1953 and left as a man known as David Bowie in 1969, having watched the pop revolution unfold from the front row.

There is a place in Bromley where you can see Christ enthroned in glory, encircled by adoring cherubs. Angels play in an orchestra fit for paradise, with harps, horns and cymbals. The saints of all the ages gaze on, rapt, as do the prophets of ancient days: here is Noah, there, Elijah and Moses. Overhead, in the highest heights, is a burst of flame, and out of it flies a dove.

This towering vision in stained glass is what David would have seen as he walked in procession to the choir stalls at St Mary's Church. St Mary's is a sturdy stone-grey building with a graceful, light and white interior. It is both grand and welcoming, and in that sense, archetypically Church of England. The congregation might be smaller today than it was when David Bowie was young, but the bells still ring every Sunday to call the faithful to worship. There was a time when the boy David came here every week to sing in a uniform of surplice, cassock and ruff. He was ten years old and of quietly unusual appearance: short, swept, fairish hair, narrow-shouldered but broad of face, with ears that still curled out like a toddler's but eyes that suggested he had already seen more than many ever see – eyes of infinite curiosity, eyes that ask who you really are.

This was 1957. The Church of England was in fine health and the local MP was Harold Macmillan, who was also the Prime Minister; he famously declared that year that 'most of our people have never had it so good', such was the relative prosperity of post-war Britain. The Jones family lived about ten-minutes' walk from St Mary's, and they appeared to live out Macmillan's claim. In 1953, they had moved out of Brixton and up in the world, from a tight terrace to something larger and more respectable, with a little garden and fresher air. John Jones, the man of the house, worked in the publicity department of the children's charity Dr Barnardo's. His wife Margaret, known as Peggy, had been a waitress at a cinema and was now a housewife.

Meanwhile, David was making friends. He met another boy who sang in St Mary's choir, called George Underwood, and they would remain close for the rest of their lives. They sang in church on Sundays and at funerals and weddings. But at this point in the story, David's singing had very little to do with God or faith. 'Joining the church choir had nothing to do with religion in my house, or David's for that matter,' George told me. 'My parents wanted me to socialize.' David sang in the choir for less than a year. 'I don't think his heart was in it,' said George. Worship at St Mary's had changed little for decades, with the liturgy from the centuries-old *Book of Common Prayer*, and the congregation and choir singing from the ubiquitous *Hymns Ancient and Modern* ('modern' in this instance being a relative term), accompanied by a grand organ.

David may not have known or cared, but he was experiencing the final years of a golden age of Anglicanism. One way of assessing the state of faith is to count the number of people taking the bread and wine of Holy Communion: across Great Britain, in the Church of England, the Church in Wales and the Church of Scotland, more people were taking communion in 1956 than in any year since 1939. The number fell only slightly in 1957, from 2.4 million to 2.35 million. But by the end of the 1960s, this figure had sunk to 1.9 million.[1] During that decade, the number of people in England taking communion at Easter, the holiest festival in Christianity, fell by 24.5 per cent.[2] The Church of England's most recent figures for attendance on a typical Sunday, a subtly different measure, are from 2024, when they stood at 582,000.[3] David the choirboy thus encountered the C of E at its post-war zenith.

The Joneses may have looked like the perfect suburban '50s family, but there were tensions and fractures. As a young man, John Jones, a quietly spoken Yorkshireman, had wanted to break into showbusiness. He received an inheritance of £3,000 in 1933,[4] on his 21st birthday; he spent two-thirds of it trying and failing to make a star of his first wife, Hilda, and the rest of it on a West End piano bar, which closed within a year. When it all fell apart, John was left ill and miserable. His second wife Peggy's family, meanwhile, had a history of mental illness, and her eldest son, Terry, from a previous relationship, was diagnosed with schizophrenia. David was born in 1947, before John and Peggy were married – indeed, while John was still married to Hilda – and such a state of affairs was widely regarded as unseemly in 1940s Britain. Other children noticed that there was something cold and somewhat unhappy about David's home.

This blend of conventional and unconventional extended to matters of faith too. Looking back many years later, Bowie said, 'My own father was one of the few fathers I knew who had a lot of understanding of other religions. He – this is an abuse of the word – "tolerated" Buddhists or Muslims or Hindus or Mohammedans, whatever, and he was a great humanitarian in those terms. I think some of that was passed on to me, and encouraged me to become interested in other religions. There was no enforced religion, though – he didn't particularly care for the English religion – Henry's religion. Oh God!'

By 'Henry's religion', David Bowie meant the Church of England. This is a telling insult, associating the supposedly sacred institution with human power and vanity – referring to the fact that the Church of England was founded partly so Henry VIII could get a divorce and marry his mistress. A hostility towards organized religion – interpreted as a system of oppressive structures, unbending dogmas, debauched hypocrisy and dehumanizing exploitation – became a fundamental force in Bowie's spiritual explorations. He was raised to question the notion that there was one true Church, one official creed. But whether through indoctrination, inspiration or intuition, he evidently held a kind of faith that withstood this hostility: a faith that there was *something*, and that this something was worth looking for. It was not just that there were other religions worth exploring. For Bowie, there would be other ways to experience the divine that required no priests or doctrines or hymns or prayers or special buildings.

But the great revelation in David's early life didn't require faith or spirituality – in fact, all he needed was a radio or a record player. One day, he turned the dial and found a man yelling wildly over piano, sax and double bass. For David, this moment was an epiphany. 'My heart nearly burst with excitement. I'd never heard anything even resembling this. It filled the room with energy and colour and outrageous defiance. I had heard God.'[5]

That song, 'Tutti Frutti' by Little Richard, came out in the UK in 1957. Its release happened to coincide with the start of the long decline of the Church of England. An identical phenomenon occurred in America, where churchgoing peaked around the same time.[6] This is surely a case of correlation rather than causation, but the synchronicity is delicious. Rock and roll was converting the young. Here was something new to believe in. Here was salvation. Here was *life*.

Then there was Elvis Presley. 'I saw a cousin of mine dance when I was very young,' said Bowie. 'She was dancing to Elvis's "Hound Dog" and I had never seen her get up and be moved so much by anything.'[7]

Bowie's fellow choirboy Geoff MacCormack felt it too. He became another lifelong friend, and lent his talents as a singer and songwriter to various Bowie albums and shows. 'Some of the 78 rpm discs that David had in his small collection were, without exaggeration, life changing,' he recalled. 'It was as if some secret joy had escaped from the gods that had hitherto been withheld.'[8]

You could call it a holy spirit. The children lost it; the children used it; the children, well, *boogied*.

Something had to give. The tension between the old and the new was too much. It was 1966, and David Jones had become a singer called David Bowie; he chose the surname because of 'the idea that the Bowie knife was sharpened on both sides so it cuts both ways'.[9] The first song he recorded under his new alias sliced into the past and slashed a way forward.

It was called 'Can't Help Thinking About Me', and it found the young Bowie torn between competing terrors. There was the life to come, with all its uncertainty and danger; and there was the life he was living, which was intolerable. In the song, he yearns for the security of his childhood, but knows he cannot turn back. There are three vivid memories: his quaint fear of school; his friends; and going to church on Sundays.

His sense of insecurity was understandable, given all that had happened in the previous decade. There was band after band, book after book, idea after idea at this time, and they all tell us something about the man he became.

From a young age, and inspired at least in part by his older half-brother Terry, who lived fairly detached from his family, David was ravenous for all the world and all its weirdness. One of his favourite early reads was *Strange People*, an avowedly factual account of clairvoyants, ghosts, psychic detectives, lost civilizations and the like; he never lost his fascination with the shadowy world of the paranormal. At the age of 14, he became enthralled by the actor and musician Anthony Newley, in part because of his unusual desire to sing in an almost affectedly English accent, which would become a hallmark of Bowie's own voice. Around that time, David acquired a saxophone, having been inspired by watching films of Little Richard and by reading Jack Kerouac's novel *On the Road*, which bounds along to the beat of jazz. In a fight over a girl, George Underwood punched David's left eye, damaging it for life. At 15, with big hair and bigger dreams, David joined his first band as a sax player, got into the raw and rollicking sounds of British rhythm and blues (R&B), hit the clubs night after night and started writing songs. He left school at 16 with one O level, in art.

That band, called The Konrads, turned out not to be a surefire route to fame and got rejected by Decca Records. David fell into a junior job at a commercial art studio in Old Bond Street, helping to create advertisements. He formed a new and more raucous band, the King Bees, and this time he was the frontman. They signed a record deal, recorded a single titled 'Liza Jane', and David left his job to focus on music. The band even made it on to the television shows *Ready Steady Go!* and *The Beat Room*, but the single failed to chart.

So David quit the King Bees and joined the R&B act The Manish Boys as their singer. They played clubs beloved by the Mod scene, which was around its peak at the time. David, having supposedly been mocked publicly on account of his flowing locks, founded the International League for the Preservation of Animal Filament, quickly renamed The Society for the Prevention of Cruelty to Long-Haired Men; what it lacked in members it made up for in publicity, and he was interviewed on the BBC television programme *Tonight*. Davie Jones & the Manish Boys started getting bookings outside London and earned a place on a tour, opening for an evening of acts that included Gerry & The Pacemakers, Gene Pitney, Marianne Faithfull and The Kinks.

Some of the crowds loathed them, but just a few weeks later, early in 1965, The Kinks' producer Shel Talmy took an interest in one of David's songs, the slinkily frisky 'Take My Tip'. With the addition of a session guitarist named Jimmy Page – yes, *that* one – they recorded it for EMI's Parlophone label, which also published The Beatles' records. 'Take My Tip' was released as the B-side to the band's cover of the blues number 'I Pity the Fool'; the single flopped.

There followed a manufactured row between David and the producer of the BBC Two show *Gadzooks! It's All Happening!*, concerning the length of David's hair, winning a good deal more column inches for him. A rift developed between David and his bandmates: he wanted his name to be displayed more prominently, and they did not. Davie Jones & the Manish Boys played their last gig in April that year.

A band called The Lower Third let it be known at the coffee bar La Giaconda that they wanted a singer. David auditioned, got the job and got a proper haircut; of course, the ensemble's name would now be Davy Jones & The Lower Third. They looked and sounded convincingly Mod and came to the attention of a manager called Kenneth Pitt, who suggested that David change his name so as not to be confused with the lead singer of the Monkees, Davy Jones. But success remained elusive: they failed an audition for a BBC show,[10] and the label Pye refused to release what might have been a hit[11] because of a reference to drugs. They recorded two more songs for Pye, one of which was 'Can't Help Thinking About Me'. It was released as a single on 14 January 1966. Going to church on Sundays? It must have felt like several lifetimes ago.

Those nine years can be distilled into three words: ambition, impatience and belief. Wanting it, wanting it now, pursuing it relentlessly. And if it cannot be found? Well, don't waste any time and just try another way, because it's there somewhere. Those three words also fuelled what was to follow; inchoate and embryonic as all this was, everything was essentially here, in the way that the acorn contains the oak tree.

Indeed, a cynic may say that this is all he ever did, that he was a man who leapt from look to look and sound to sound out of nothing more than pathological vanity and material self-interest. Yet there is a crucial distinction to be made between the serial band-hopper of the mid-sixties and the artist he became. The younger David pursued money, stardom and sex. But even when he had all the money he wanted, all the stardom he wanted and all the sex he wanted, still he searched, never settling. He evidently sought something else.

'Can't Help Thinking About Me'[12] inaugurated a theme in Bowie's work which concerned the strange and often nostalgic relationship between then and now. In that respect, his songs from this time were not unique: The Beatles evoked a kind of prelapsarian age on their 1967 album *Sgt. Pepper's Lonely Hearts Club Band*, as did The Kinks on their 1968 album *The Kinks Are the Village Green Preservation Society*. But in the case of Bowie, this theme was to return in various forms across five decades. And what made him unusual at this point was the frequency with which he evoked a sense of past naivety by drawing upon simple expressions of faith. At some level, it was as if he shared the anxiety of the Church of England: both found comfort in the practices of yore, or at least in what they represented, but both had to face a new age.

David Bowie's first album as a solo artist came out in 1967. It was called *David Bowie*, and it's an album which also looks back to childhood; in one song, 'There Is A Happy Land', which shares its name with a hymn,[13] Bowie described a place populated by children. It names various boys: one wants to buy a kite; another has chickenpox; another can now ride a bicycle; another enjoys singing prayers and hymns. In another song, 'When I'm Five', recorded in 1968, there is a further reference to churchgoing and a naïve prayer offered to Jesus. It's sung from the perspective of a four-year-old, and an accompanying film shows Bowie singing with hands together like a dutiful schoolboy. These songs from the time before Bowie's stardom all associate early childhood with an unsophisticated Christian faith – and thus imply an association between unsophisticated Christian faith and childhood.

Having reflected on his parents and his younger self, the narrator of 'Can't Help Thinking About Me' concludes that he will have to leave his past in a Neverland, a realm of eternal infancy. For Bowie, even if there was some comfort in that simple Christianity, it needed putting away with those other childish things: it could not contend with the adult world. He had already seen too much.

In the 1950s, the Church of England had not been a monopoly exactly, but its ways were the norm. David Jones knew it in its pomp. His friends thought he had little regard for the role of choirboy. But perhaps he took more from his experiences at St Mary's than was immediately apparent. He was certainly left with no great hatred of Christianity; rather, he would forever be deeply curious about it, giving every impression that he detected in it something of impossible value. As things fractured, as one became many, as the globe spun more rapidly, the C of E became less sure about its place in the world, and so did David. The idea of going to church on Sundays and all that it implied – routine, ritual, rigmarole, respectability – was in some ways repellent to him. Yet there was also an inescapable attraction. Such opposing forces would buffet him for decades.

2

BUDDHIST

For the first 23 minutes of David Bowie's debut album, almost everything is domestic and parochial: curious bachelors, brass bands, town gardens, rhubarb fields. Then suddenly, after four short bursts of a horn, we are taken to Tibet. The music is elegant, graceful and spacious. It's as if the curtains have been flung wide on the world – a new light is pouring through. The song in question is 'Silly Boy Blue', and it is about Buddhism.

Anglicanism was out, but spirituality was in, and Buddhism had promise. Jack Kerouac's *On the Road*, published in 1957, had already helped turn young David on to jazz. But the Beat Generation, including Kerouac's cohorts Allen Ginsberg and Gary Snyder, also loved Buddhism: Kerouac followed *On the Road* with *The Dharma Bums*, a novel in which his characters spurn hedonism and seek transcendence. The idea of dharma (roughly, the moral law that upholds the universe) is at the heart of Buddhism, and Buddhism is at the heart of the book.

Buddhism became hip in the 1960s, but for David the allure was deeper. Buddhism acted as a counterpoint to the organized religion of his neighbours in Bromley, with no place for conventional ideas of God: there is no great authority figure in the sky. To a Buddhist, the self is not a fixed entity; all is in a constant state of change. The dead are neither condemned to an eternal Hell nor exalted to an everlasting Heaven; they can spend time in various realms and be reborn into new bodies on earth. Fusty old Anglicanism this was not.

There was a further fascination. David was enthralled by *Seven Years in Tibet*, the memoir of an explorer named Heinrich Harrer. Published in 1952, it gives an outsider's view of the land in the 1940s, before it was invaded by the Communist Chinese People's Liberation Army; China annexed Tibet in 1951. After David read it, his interest in Buddhism acquired a political dimension. Bowie later said he was impressed by Harrer's being 'one of the very first Westerners to ever spend any time in Tibet; in fact, one of the very first Westerners actually to go into Tibet and discover for himself this extraordinary existence and this incredibly sublime philosophy'.[1]

Daily life was unsteady for David. While his first album was being recorded in the north London neighbourhood of West Hampstead, he was living in central London with Ralph Horton, one of his former managers. Success was in no way guaranteed. Indeed, all the evidence so far suggested it was unlikely. His father had taken risks, followed his heart and lost a fortune. Were David to fail, the consequences would be miserable, but on he went, surviving on nascent talent, charm and looks (Horton's interest in David was widely considered to be personal as well as professional). The British headquarters of the Buddhist Society happened to be only a few minutes' walk away from Horton's flat in Warwick Square; David looked in.

He gave an account of the visit in 2001. 'Sitting in front of me at the desk was a Tibetan lama. And he looked up and he said: "You're looking for me." He had a bad grasp of English, and in fact was saying "who are you looking for?" But I needed him to say "you're looking for me."'

The lama was called Chime Youngdong Rinpoche. His own story melded the spiritual and the political. He 'had just come over from Tibet and led his own followers over,' recalled Bowie. 'A majority of them, sadly, were shot by the Chinese as they made their exit from Tibet down into India. He started off with I think something like 2,000 followers – and ended up with 50 or 60. Because the helicopters would come out there and shoot them.... But he fortunately came through and really tried to guide me into some kind of informed opinion about Buddhism.'²

According to tradition, Siddhartha Gautama, known as the Buddha, lived 500 to 600 years before Jesus. He was born into an aristocratic family whose home was in the foothills of the Himalayas. One night, when he was aged 29 and frustrated with domestic tedium, he left his wife and newborn son and set out in search of what was called the holy life. Relying on the generosity of others, he learned the ways of asceticism – the renunciation of earthly pleasures – and meditation. He went on to practise increasingly intense spiritual disciplines, but these proved as unsatisfying as his previous existence of privileged indulgence. Seeing the wisdom of a middle-way between those extremes, he sat beneath a large tree, meditated and, over the course of one night, gained enlightenment. Soon, he began preaching, and over time there developed a rich body of teaching known as dharma, examining suffering, death, life and the nature of reality.

Different forms of Buddhism took hold at different times and in different places. Tibetan Buddhism is a form of Mahāyāna Buddhism, Mahāyāna meaning 'great vehicle' in Sanskrit. 'It is considered by its adherents to be great because it is the best way to reach liberation,' says Dr Paul Fuller, a Lecturer in Buddhist Studies at the University of Edinburgh. 'Part of the great vehicle is Tantric Buddhism. Tantric practices are unconventional practices – for example, polluting substances or harmful practices or forms of behaviour, of which sex is the most obvious – used in order to reach liberation more quickly than practising ethical behaviour, for example.' Tibetan Buddhism is also particularly ritualistic, with 'lots of chanting of syllables [mantras] and lots of deities embodying wisdom and compassion'. For various reasons, it was right up Bowie's street.

Bowie's first, eponymous album is strange and strangely charming; it is hard to think of any other record it resembles. It doesn't look quite how it sounds: the cover shows Bowie wearing a distinctly narked expression, like he's just been interrupted while trying to have a deep conversation, and it makes his feathery Mod hairdo look almost intimidating. The only suggestion of the album's whimsy and playfulness comes in the lettering of his name. Much of the record could be dismissed as lightweight eccentric novelty, and Bowie himself would all but disown it within a couple of years. But 'Silly Boy Blue' carries a gravitas and grandeur absent elsewhere; encountering it on the album is rather like flicking straight from a minor Ealing comedy to a David Lean epic.

In this song, the instruments evoke a faraway scene. A cello flows like a wise river; a horn calls as if summoning pilgrims from across a valley; a gong shimmers like sun through rain. Bowie sings of Lhasa, the capital of Tibet, and of its mountains and of the lanes leading to the Potala Palace –the winter home of the Dalai Lama, the spiritual leader of Tibetan Buddhism, until China took over the site in 1959. He refers to a 'chela', a Buddhist disciple, and the concept of an 'overself', which, for a chela, is his 'essential being, the all-important residue which is left when he succeeds in banishing the thought of his identification with the physical body and the intellect'.[3] But as its title[4] suggests, the song is not all earnest and reverential: it is addressed to a student who is struggling to learn these ancient ways, who defies his teacher and whose soul cannot escape the pull of gravity, however much he wishes it to, and however hard he tries. The instrumentation becomes more western: drums and guitars join in, albeit respectfully. By the end, the narrator treats the boy with warm pity: he is a gift, but a reincarnation of a better man, and he faces a long journey home. Perhaps the song's singer might sympathize: 'I wouldn't say that I was a very good Buddhist,' said Bowie many years later.[5]

'Silly Boy Blue' is David Bowie's first important song. He was far from stardom at this point, but he was gaining some attention, and it is not surprising that this song featured in his first BBC radio session, recorded in December 1967. Bowie also played it in his second, recorded in May 1968, this time accompanied by chants of 'Chime Chime Chime' to honour his teacher.

The song would return occasionally throughout Bowie's career, and would have a rebirth of its own in the twenty-first century. In 2000, Bowie recorded an album called *Toy*, on which he revisited some of his earliest songs*; 'Silly Boy Blue' was the only track from his debut album to make the cut, and those chants of 'Chime' returned. The next year, he performed it at a benefit concert at Tibet House in New York, joined by a troupe of Buddhist monks.

The emergence of Buddhist influences on Bowie was actually less sudden than the album implies. Two years earlier, he had released 'Baby Loves That Way', recorded with The Lower Third; its backing vocals were intended to sound monastic. He told *Melody Maker* in 1966: 'I want to go to Tibet. It's a fascinating place, y'know. I'd like to take a holiday and have a look inside the monasteries. The Tibetan monks, lamas, bury themselves inside mountains for weeks and only eat every three days. They're ridiculous – and it's said they live for centuries.'

'Silly Boy Blue' is not the only song from this period to arise from Bowie's spiritual interests. 'Karma Man', recorded in 1967, takes place in a bustling fair or fete: there is a coconut shy, and families enjoy ice cream. They are unaware that transcendence lies just yards away, in an unvisited tent. The song revolves around a cross-legged a man in saffron robes, with a tattoo on his side of the Wheel of Life, a Buddhist symbol depicting the cycle of life, death, rebirth and suffering. 'Slow down,' sings Bowie repeatedly: it sounds like an exhortation to follow the example of the Karma Man and take life at a different pace, live it differently, open it up. 'As far as I'm concerned the whole idea of Western life – that's the life we live now – is wrong,' said Bowie in 1966.[6] 'At the moment I write nearly all my songs round London. No, I should say the people who live in London – and the lack of real life they have. The majority just don't know what life is.' But the lyrics are ambiguous, and perhaps the person being told to slow down is the Karma Man himself; perhaps his influence is feared.

---

* *Toy* was not released until 2021.

In 'Did You Ever Have a Dream', recorded at the end of 1966, Bowie wrote about the phenomenon of astral projection. It spans ages, cultures and spiritual traditions, and typically involves the sensation of one's consciousness becoming detached from one's body and being directed around the physical world or through spiritual realms. The tone of the song is almost comedically dismissive of its topic. But astral projection evidently feels very real to many who have experienced it – Bowie included. He said in 1993: 'I was studying Mahāyāna Buddhism, which is very deeply involved with astral projection. With his [Rinpoche's] meditation methods I often felt that I got three or four feet, maybe even further, outside my body and I was absolutely and totally aware of it.'

Bowie also found meditation an aid to songwriting, to the point where a bandmate found him so deeply in a trance that he 'appeared to lose consciousness'.[7] This can be seen as an early example of Bowie's desire to silence the rational mind during the creative process to allow greater freedom to the subconscious, a desire that shaped much of his subsequent work. He wasn't alone in finding creative inspiration in Buddhism: it was something he shared with the man who would become one of his most significant collaborators.

BOAC Flight 506 from New York landed in London late one night in April 1967. On the aeroplane was a 23-year-old from Brooklyn called Tony Visconti. He had four guitars and no visa. Among his obsessions were British music and the quest for enlightenment. Tony and his wife Siegrid had become familiar with *The Tibetan Book of the Dead*, a fourteenth-century text grounded in Buddhism; they knew it via a translation written especially for LSD trips. Eventually, the couple decided to keep the transcendental and ditch the pharmacological. Out went acid; in came Eastern spirituality. Visconti had dreams of making records in London, and among the first songs he worked on with David Bowie was 'Karma Man', a song about a Buddhist, produced by a Buddhist, written by a Buddhist.

It is fair to say, however, that not everyone was convinced by Bowie's apparent Buddhist turn. Eastern spirituality was fashionable among young artistic types: John Lennon had already brought *The Tibetan Book of the Dead* to the masses in 1966 with The Beatles' song 'Tomorrow Never Knows'; George Harrison was playing the sitar and singing about Hindu philosophy the following year;[8] Pete Townshend of The Who was writing under the inspiration of the Indian spiritual guru Meher Baba; the singer-songwriter Donovan was becoming an evangelist for a practice known as Transcendental Meditation. It is easy to see how, to an older generation, it could all look faddish; and Ken Pitt, Bowie's manager at the time, was suspicious of Bowie's fondness for Buddhism. 'I don't think he was really that interested,' said Pitt. 'It became part of his future publicity to say that he was.'

One particular episode encapsulated, for Pitt, the gap between Bowie's understanding of Buddhism at that time and the reality. 'I do remember him meeting a Buddhist monk at my Curzon Street office. To say that David was gobsmacked is an understatement,' said Pitt. 'David himself was going through a slovenly, almost dirty phase. That was because he'd read that one of the tenets of Buddhism was that you shouldn't concern yourself with false exterior images. Then this amazing creature walked in who was wearing a lovely yellow gown, a shaven head and beautiful leather sandals with a jewel between his toes. He was also drenched in glorious perfume. It was very funny.'[9]

But other sources attest that Bowie was pursuing Buddhism with zeal. Late in 1967, he went as far as spending time in a new Buddhist monastery in Scotland. It was an old hunting lodge renamed Samye Ling by the two Tibetan lamas who ran it; Samye is the name of the first Buddhist monastery built in Tibet and can be translated roughly as 'beyond conception', while Ling means 'place'. With its regime of rituals and meditation, it is known for encouraging initiates to sleep upright, in order to make meditation easier.[10] There, Bowie was apparently on the brink of becoming a monk.

As he put it: 'I had stayed in their monastery and was going through all their exams, and yet I had this feeling that it wasn't right for me. I suddenly realised how close it all was: another month and my head would have been shaved – so I decided that as I wasn't happy, I would get right away from it all.'[11]

Bowie returned to London, and spent months gigging and living in a desultory fashion throughout 1968. But a rare highlight came in June at the Royal Festival Hall. His friend Marc Bolan had invited him to perform as an opening act for Bolan's band Tyrannosaurus Rex. Having possessed a remarkable sense of poise since childhood,[12] Bowie had developed an interest in mime, and had lessons from master of the art, Lindsay Kemp. That night, Bowie performed a routine he had devised and written called 'Yet-San and the Eagle'. It was set to an instrumental version of 'Silly Boy Blue' adorned with supposedly authentic Tibetan sounds, played on instruments that included saucepans. Visconti narrated the story, which depicted China's invasion of Tibet and told how, in Bowie's words, 'though the Tibetans may be struck down, their spirit would fly for eternity'. Peaceable as it all sounds, it was too much for some. 'He portrayed the Chinese going into Tibet and banning everything, including kissing,' Visconti wrote. 'David had just learned how to turn his back to the audience and pretend he was two people kissing, then he tapped himself on the shoulder as if he was a Red Guard. This was the point at which the audience lost it; Communist sympathizers booed.'[13] Chime Youngdong Rinpoche had been watching; Bowie later said of himself that he was 'trembling with anger and went home sulking'.[14] But a reviewer from the *International Times*, the counterculture's house journal, was impressed: 'David Bowie, although one or two drags were heckling him, received the longest and loudest applause of all the performers, and he deserved it.'[15]

Still, there was no sign of a change in Bowie's fortunes. The album had failed to chart, he had moved back home, and he was finding his parents ever more frustrating to live with. Then a chance encounter brought into his life a new and significant figure, Mary Finnigan. He moved into her flat in the neighbouring town of Beckenham in April 1969, and his landlady soon became his lover. Few people have a clearer insight into the Bowie of the late 1960s, and Finnigan – a psychedelic hippie at the time with her own interest in Buddhism — has no doubt about the sincerity of Bowie's enthusiasm.

'Quite a few people, some of them quite famous, who went to Samye Ling when it first opened, went there for a rest,' she told me.[16] 'We used to call it the Shrine and Dine. David went there with a more serious intention than that. And if you had a serious intention when you went to Samye Ling, it was very supportive of that and it gave you the opportunity to do it seriously... I only have his word for it but he did say that he had some breakthroughs.'

His personality reflected Buddhist principles, but it is hard to discern to what extent the principles informed the personality, says Finnigan. 'He had a very egalitarian attitude towards people. He didn't like elitism at all, of any description, either the social or intellectual. And he was very astute in the way that he related to people. He had a very good insight into human nature, and how to behave, and generally speaking was very courteous.'

Finnigan believes that Bowie's future direction was informed by one Buddhist notion in particular: the illusion of the separate self. 'All these different personalities are a reflection of there not being anything substantial to the self, to identity. The idea that we're all separate individuals is entirely insubstantial. So you can play with it. David was manifesting different layers of illusion, which is what actors do. More than anything else, he was an actor.'

Finnigan was instrumental in creating and running Beckenham Arts Lab, a regular night showcasing musicians, dancers and more; for a few months, it became the centre of Bowie's world.[17] In August 1969, Finnigan, Bowie and friends organized the first Beckenham Free Festival, a day when the countercultural stole into the suburban. Bowie wrote about it in the song 'Memory of a Free Festival', released that year, in which he equated the experience with the Zen Buddhist concept of Satori, a kind of sublime enlightenment.

By 1970, however, he said he was no longer a Buddhist, 'though a lot of the basic ideas are still with me'.[18] And they would remain so. Bowie's impassioned 'Buddhist phase' may not have lasted long, but to consider it therefore trivial would be a mistake. As we will see, Bowie's career was full of enthusiasms that were no less sincere for being short-lived. 'I was a terribly earnest Buddhist at that time, within a month of becoming a Buddhist monk,' Bowie told one interviewer.[19] 'I was a Buddhist on Tuesday and I was into Nietzsche by Friday,' he told another more flippantly.[20]

Perhaps both can be true.

And Bowie always spoke about Chime Youngdong Rinpoche with great affection. Bowie said in 1997: 'The one thing that he left me with was a sense of transience and change, which actually became fundamentals to my life and my approach to it – and not holding on to anything, not considering there is anything that will last through one's entire eternal life, living or dead. And it makes letting go very easy – material things or physical things. And looking for the source of one's own being becomes much more important. And I guess that's been sort of my own personal journey – trying to sort out where my spiritual bounty lies, where my thread to a universal order lies. That can become a life's search. And I think that's, as a writer, probably what I involve myself in more than anything else.'[21]

Buddhism, then, was not only part of the journey – it enabled it. It gave Bowie a sense of freedom. It was not just an arty affectation or an admission ticket to the in-crowd. There is little evidence of his sustained involvement in devotional practices; having deprecated his own qualities as a Buddhist, he laughingly defined a good Buddhist as 'somebody that even tries'.

But he took to his heart its deeper wisdom. Buddhism had broken in, and would never leave.

3

OCCULTIST

'It's been a recurrent qualification of my work from the day I started writing,' said David Bowie in 1994. 'A very early example, I suppose, is "Space Oddity".'[1] Bowie was talking here about spirituality. The song he cites may seem unlikely: it mentions no angels or demons; there are no references to ideas or practices from any religion; there is no clear pattern of redemption, no path towards enlightenment. Quite the opposite. The official line is that something is wrong. There is a mention of God, but only in passing, in platitude, perhaps in vain.

Yet 'Space Oddity' is integral to Bowie's spiritual quest. Perhaps it *is* the quest. Initially derided as a grubby exercise to make some easy money off the moon landing, it ended up framing his career. It would be its prologue and its epilogue, its overture and its finale. It would lie deep and rise high; it would lurk, it would loom, it would haunt, it would dazzle. For a while, it seemed 'Space Oddity' would be the one hit of a one-hit wonder, but if it had been, it would have sufficed: a song of science fiction for a young man, a song of reflection for a mature man, a song of desperation for a dying man, a song of acceptance for a man finding rest. And its immediate effect was to take him somewhere else: to a place of spiritual murk and confusion, of secrets and mysteries and shady paths. The atmosphere around some of his resulting music is so thick it can almost be smelled.

'Space Oddity' is unique. It seems to have come from nowhere, and there was nothing quite like it thereafter. But as with all things Bowie, there is a danger that its otherworldly subject can lead us to forget the more earthly circumstances that led to its creation. Indeed, the tension between the two – the terrestrial and the extra-terrestrial, the known and the unknown – lies at its heart.

Bowie essentially wrote the song to order, and it came after a period of some struggle. He had accomplished barely anything of note since his first album came out in 1967, and from a commercial perspective, that record itself was hardly an accomplishment. He released no music at all in 1968, fluttering between cabaret, acting and mime. There was the occasional recording session, the occasional radio session. But he had split from his record label and was back living with his parents again. Feeling pressure from his father to make money, he got a job operating a photocopier at a firm specializing in printing legal documents, and also found work as a cleaner.[2]

It was a time of drift and muddle. Plans were forming vaguely for a second album that soon faded from his dreams; judging from the demos that have emerged, it would have sounded beefier than his debut but remained hidebound by provincial preoccupations.[3] More daringly, he wrote a musical about a man who throws a party for his own suicide, but it died before getting anywhere near a stage.[4]

Bowie was looking less like a gently psychedelic Mod. He grew his hair, which made him appear more vulnerable and elfin, and dressed simply. He was romantically involved with the mime master Lindsay Kemp and with the costume designer Natasha Korniloff, and then, powerfully, life-changingly, with the dancer and singer Hermione Farthingale. He later said that 1968 was the year he had a 'silly flirtation with smack', which he 'never really enjoyed'.[5]

Bowie ended 1968 with a series of performances in small venues as part of his new musical trio, Feathers. He was joined by Farthingale and the guitarist and singer John Hutchinson, known as Hutch. Bowie had already been racking up the genres – rowdy R&B, bluesy rock, modish pop, music hall, comedy, novelty, cabaret and more, all since 1964 – and here was another one – namely, folk. Even by this point, his musical adventurism was evidence of an openness to experience that was becoming mirrored in his spiritual wanderings.

Feathers was hardly the big time. But there was the promise of something new: a short film, a kind of musical anthology in which Bowie would perform dramatized versions of his songs. The idea came from Ken Pitt, who was still convinced his man was a star, if only the rest of the world would pay attention.

Balancing optimism with realism, Pitt assessed the songs so far assembled for the project. He knew something was missing, so he asked Bowie to write 'a very special piece of material'. One day, Bowie got stoned and watched the epic science fiction film *2001: A Space Odyssey*; what ensued not only met the brief, but zoomed far beyond it.

Directed by Stanley Kubrick and based on a story by Arthur C. Clarke, *2001: A Space Odyssey* was released in 1968, and it is easy to see why it would have resonated so deeply with Bowie, stoned or not. It is an adventure, a quest, infused with mystery; its name tells us everything about its blend of the ancient and the futuristic, and its exploration of the place of the human, 300,000-year-old *Homo sapiens*, in a world that seems ever more alien to human life. The further it ventures into outer space, the deeper it ventures into inner space.

'Space Oddity' traces the same trajectory, but in five minutes. To strong tunes and catchy refrains, it relates the story of what could be merely a simple tragedy: an astronaut loses contact with earth and slips out into the cosmos. But there is much more.

We can start with its first two words. *Ground*: stability, firmness, the known. *Control*: power, authority, the denial of individual will. Of course Major Tom wants to escape. The melody in this opening section spans only three semitones; it is pretty much horizontal. After the cacophony of lift-off there is exhilaration, and the tune immediately leaps by nearly an octave; and then a more placid floating; then a further burst of adrenaline as Major Tom proclaims his freedom; then an ecstatic kind of stasis; then no words as the music swirls and spirals and spins in sublime disorientation.

Major Tom had gone a long way. So had David Bowie. In 1967, a critic in the *Financial Times* described him as 'a young pop-singer whose songs tend to follow ambition beyond the boundaries of his talent'.⁶ No one could ever say that again.

Yet we may ask quite what Bowie meant when he said the song reflected in some way a kind of spirituality. We could say with some justification – or at least a dash of poetic speculation – that the song depicts a voyage of the soul and an affirmation of the spirit. That may be it; if so, fine. But there may be another aspect to all this, and an answer may lie in that word *control*.

We are never sure who is in charge. Ground Control issues the orders, but the spaceship follows its own course, and there is nothing Major Tom can do. The song is the first overt examination of what appears to be part of Bowie's basic understanding of the universe: a sense that there are forces that control us.

This idea pops up again in some curious places. In 1975 he released a song called 'Win', in which he feels someone else is driving. In 2003 we get 'She'll Drive the Big Car': a male passenger is in the back seat; the driver is thinking of steering the car into the river. That same year, he released a song called 'Your Turn to Drive'.

There is a song where Bowie does the driving himself. It does not go well: the song is called 'Always Crashing in the Same Car'. Perhaps it is better, then, to submit to the will of this faceless driver. Describing the sensation of success in 1974, Bowie likened it to 'that feeling you get in the car when someone accelerates very, very fast and you're not driving'.⁷ Reflecting on his younger self, Bowie said in 1996: 'I was driven then. I have a drive now.'⁸

Driven. There he is in 1974 on the BBC, in the back of a limousine. Early on in this documentary, he is smiley and affable; later, he is haunted and possibly hunted, panicked, paranoid. Those images of Bowie burned themselves into the cinematic imagination of the director Nic Roeg; he cast Bowie for a film he shot the following year, which again shows Bowie in the back of a limousine, driven.

'I've always felt like a vehicle for something else, but then I've never really sorted out what that was,' he said in 1973. 'I think everybody, at one time or another, gets that kind of feeling; that they aren't just here for themselves and more often than not they turn to the Bible and agree that it's probably Jesus and God and all of that section of religion. There's a feeling that we are here for another purpose. And in me it's very strong.'[9]

There is a force here, an unknown and unnamed force; obeying it may bring terror but denying it will bring annihilation. This force has its own momentum and its own ways, he seems to be saying. Lying beyond the reach and grasp of human power is a scheme of things.

Major Tom's story could be described as a leap of faith: the man defies reason on the way to an unknown destination in the belief that the trip will be worthwhile. Bowie was immersing himself in philosophy, and pertinent here is the work of Søren Kierkegaard, with whom the phrase 'leap of faith' is especially associated.

There are philosophers about whom Bowie spoke at length. Kierkegaard was not one of them. In the countless interviews he gave over 40 years, Bowie said his name only once, in a comedy interview with a puppet.[10] But Kierkegaard's ideas add some depth to Bowie's description of 'Space Oddity' as 'spiritual'.

Born in Denmark in 1813, Kierkegaard was a Christian philosopher and theologian, and a key figure in the development of existentialism. The term is broad, but the *Stanford Encyclopedia of Philosophy* notes its 'emphasis on freedom and the struggle for self-creation,' its 'engagement with the relationship between faith and freedom and the incomprehensibility of God' and its 'penetrating analyses of anxiety and the importance of self-realization'. Given all this, it is natural that existentialism became a preoccupation of Bowie's.

In Kierkegaard's book *Fear and Trembling*, published in 1843, he fixates on a story from the Bible. It tells how Abraham and his wife Sarah in their old age were blessed with a son named Isaac, and how God promised that Abraham's descendants would be as numerous as the stars in the sky and bring blessings to all the nations on earth. But God later commands Abraham to kill his son; Abraham proceeds in accordance with God's will, going as far as binding Isaac and drawing a knife to slay him. It can be understood as a tale of blind obedience taken to an extreme: if God wants Isaac dead, so be it. But Kierkegaard sees Abraham acting instead from a belief in God's earlier promise, trusting that Isaac will somehow be restored to him. To Kierkegaard, Abraham is willing to do something he knows is wrong in order to serve a greater purpose; Kierkegaard calls this the 'teleological suspension of the ethical'. It so happens that an angel of God stops Abraham at the point of the killing; the son is spared, Abraham is commended, and he is known for subsequent millennia as the father of faith, revered in Judaism, Christianity and Islam.

Major Tom leaves behind his beloved wife and proceeds in defiance of convention, received wisdom and human instinct. He makes that leap not knowing what lies on the other side, but because he feels driven to do so, and he trusts in something that cannot be seen. 'No one has the right to... suppose that faith is something inferior or that it is an easy matter,' writes Kierkegaard, 'when in fact it is the greatest and most difficult of all.'

Major Tom reports floating peculiarly. Kierkegaard, on the other hand, had reason to regret his own inability to make the leap: 'I can swim in life, but for this mysterious floating I am too heavy.' He sees the ideal believer, Abraham, as a 'knight of faith': such a figure must be solitary, 'in cosmic isolation'.

Back on earth, the ground was unsteady. Days after Bowie recorded the first version of 'Space Oddity' in February 1969, Farthingale left him. The experience seems to have disturbed Bowie to an extent that some may class as trauma. Romantic relationships would prove difficult for years, maybe even decades. 'I was in love once, maybe, and it was an awful experience,' he told *Playboy* magazine in 1976. 'It rotted me, drained me, and it was a disease. Hateful thing, it was.'

He wrote a song of anguish called 'Letter to Hermione', and recorded it for his second album, which was released in November

1969. The split came after Farthingale was offered a part in the film *Song of Norway*; Bowie would wear a T-shirt bearing the title of that film in a music video over 40 years later.

To intense heartbreak was added deep grief. On 5 August that same year, at the age of 56, Bowie's father died of pneumonia at the family home in Bromley. There had been tensions between them: 'My father tries so hard,' Bowie had said a few months earlier, 'but his upbringing was so difficult that we can't communicate. He and all his friends were in the army during the war – an experience I can't imagine – and he takes naturally to iron discipline.'[11]

But time and increasing maturity had been bringing them closer. As Bowie reflected in 1993: 'It was at a point when I was just beginning to grow up a little bit and appreciate that I would have to stretch out my hand a little for us ever to get to know each other. He just died at the wrong damn time, because there were so many things I would have loved to have said to him and asked him about. All those stereotypical regrets when your father dies and you haven't completed your relationship. I felt so... Damn! Wrong time! Not now, not now!'[12]

Then there was the strange, wayward journey of the song itself. Bowie's initial recording of 'Space Oddity', for his short film, has a certain homemade charm, but it is far from the interstellar epic the world has come to know. That latter version was recorded on 20 June, and just five weeks later, man landed on the moon. Visconti, despite having already established a close bond with Bowie, wanted nothing to do with 'Space Oddity': 'I thought the song was a cheap shot to capitalise on the first moon landing... What I didn't realise at the time was that the music was just window dressing for a subtler subject.'[13]

This deeper dimension was not lost on the orchestral arranger Paul Buckmaster, whose work on 'Space Oddity' led to a career spanning five decades and collaborations with the likes of Elton John, The Rolling Stones, Guns N' Roses and Taylor Swift. Recalling his conversations with Bowie, he said: 'We had some wonderful, intellectual discussions. The first ones we had had a lot to do with a pop science-fiction mysticism.'[14]

'Space Oddity' was released as a single on 11 July. Evidently having heard only the first few lines, the BBC played it during its otherwise upbeat broadcast of the moon landing on 20 July. Success, then, for the marketing ploy, such as it was. But there was no scramble to the record shops to buy it the following day, or the following week, or the following month. In fact, it had still barely sold any copies even by September. It seemed destined to be remembered only as a novelty, if not a folly, if not a flop, if indeed it were to be remembered at all.

Yet the A&R man at Bowie's new record label, Philips, kept the faith. The song kept being plugged to radio stations, and finally made it off the launch pad, entering the charts at number 48 on 6 September. It fell out again the following week, but then went back in at 39, then climbed to 25, which led to Bowie's first appearance on *Top of the Pops*. Its ascent peaked at number five, on 26 October. Mission accomplished. It was Bowie's first hit.

Yet matters did not proceed as one might expect, either for the song or for its writer. 'Space Oddity is the first tenuous link in a long chain that will make David Bowie one of the biggest artists, and one of the most important people, British music has produced in a long time,' wrote Penny Valentine in *Disc and Music Echo*.[15] She was right, and the song brought Bowie a degree of fame, but 'Space Oddity' proved something of a false start: his next hit was nearly three years away, and would require quite a transformation on his part.

'Space Oddity' was perhaps the lightning before the thunder. This works in the song's favour: it is somehow cut adrift, temporally and musically, not being an example of any particular phase of his, not connected to any particular image; there is no defining performance of it, no landmark video. It is just there; it could almost be by someone else,[16] but of course it could not be.

Bowie's relationship to the song became more peculiar over time. As one might expect, he performed it frequently in his early years of stardom. But despite it being one of his most popular songs, he dropped it from his set after 1974, and it did not return until 1983.[17] He omitted it from his 1987 tour, but it opened his 'greatest hits' shows in 1990. Thereafter, it would appear rarely, as if its signal could be received only intermittently and at special times: to close his 50th birthday concert in 1997, and at an evening in support of Tibet in 2002. He played snippets of it at some shows in 2004, but this was for laughs, as a tease, as if the song had by then become simply too much. Yet it would return, again, in his last works, when the scale of the moment could accommodate it. This song of fate, this spiritual song, would realize its own destiny. Outer space, inner space: who's flying this thing?

In some important ways, David Bowie was quite normal. It is common, at least up to this point, to find him described as polite, funny, somewhat shy, even diffident. He enjoyed reading, and being alone in his room. He had a certain flair, but he was not especially outrageous. His earliest interviews reveal a primness, his voice light and careful and enunciated delicately. His clothes could be unusual, as could his hair; but his character was not that of a typical hellraiser or oddball.

And while he is often thought of as a man who shaped his times, it is worth remembering that his times shaped him. By the late 1960s, it was not especially unusual for a person of curiosity to be found reading about the occult. The less ordinary part is where he would take it, and where it would take him; but for now, he was just another young fellow in love with the strange.

In 1969, Bowie joined an unusual kind of club: every Tuesday evening, its members would gather in Hampstead, meditate, and look for UFOs.[18] He had long been fascinated by the Fortean and the arcane; after 'Space Oddity', this fascination reached new heights and depths.

Over the previous few years, interest in the esoteric[19] had exploded like a burst of tie dye. *The Morning of the Magicians: Introduction to Fantastic Realism*[20] was published in French in 1960 and translated into English in 1963; it is a work of quasi-history, telling of alchemy, lost civilizations, UFOs, secret cabals, 'magic socialism', 'Hitler and political esoterism', 'Martians at Nuremberg' and the like. It offered a seductive alternative to mainstream thinking and proved enormously influential in the counterculture, prefiguring today's army of 'truthers' and conspiracy theorists.

An array of writers and theorists known collectively as the Earth Mysteries Movement repopularized the 1920s notion of 'ley lines' – supposed alignments between ancient sites. The esotericist John Michell argued in his 1969 work *The View Over Atlantis* that ley lines guided alien spacecraft. In the 1950s, a man named Gerald Gardner devised a version of witchcraft named Wicca, which came to prominence in the 1960s. All of this was entirely understandable, even natural: disillusionment with previous generations and their institutions was profound and widespread, while the emergence of psychedelic drugs led to experiences that defied reality as it had hitherto been described.

Amid all this, it was not surprising that one figure in particular would come once more to public attention. His name was Aleister Crowley, and his image can be found in millions of perfectly sensible homes around the globe: he stands tall, between the Hindu guru Sri Yukteswar Giri and the actress Mae West, on the cover of *Sgt. Pepper's Lonely Hearts Club Band*. But Crowley, born in 1875 in the Warwickshire town of Leamington Spa, was known during his lifetime as 'the wickedest man in the world'. By the time Bowie discovered him, he was almost mainstream.

Crowley's parents were fundamentalist Christians; it is fair to say he rejected their faith. He joined the Hermetic Order of the Golden Dawn in his early twenties, the order being devoted to the magickal arts: that *k* denotes ritual of a supposedly genuine supernatural kind, rather than mere trickery. It was founded in London in 1887: at its peak in the 1890s, it had as many as a hundred members, among them the poet William Butler Yeats. The order had close similarities to

Freemasonry: there were elaborate ceremonies involving robes and liturgies, and various grades through which initiates could rise. They would begin by studying practices that included astrology and tarot divination; ascending to the next grade would introduce one to magic such as alchemy and astral travel. The final grade comprised the Secret Chiefs, mysterious figures who essentially governed the universe. All this was allied to a mystical philosophy that drew what might be considered a chain of links between mankind and the divine;[21] and there were orders of angels, and complex diagrams explaining the relationships between different emanations of divine energy.

In 1904, while in Cairo, Crowley claimed to hear a voice belonging to a messenger of the Egyptian god Horus. He transcribed what the voice told him. The result was *The Book of the Law*, which contained a commandment that would long outlive Crowley: 'Do what thou wilt.' The idea was that one would align oneself with one's will through ceremonial magick. This formed the basis of Thelema, a new religion invented by Crowley. He would later promote what he called 'sex magick', the ritualistic use of sex for allegedly spiritual purposes. Crowley became a notorious figure, and he embraced moralistic opprobrium, calling himself 'the Beast 666'. He did not in fact consider himself a satanist, but he did profess a hatred of Christianity.

Of course, by the 1960s, Crowley could be championed as a subversive, a mischief-maker, a man of playful danger and bizarre spirituality, so his ideas were more than welcome. As were those of the great German philosopher Friedrich Nietzsche. Although Nietzsche died in 1900, his thinking had lived on quite spectacularly through the twentieth century. As Nietzsche fell ill in the 1890s, his sister Elisabeth took charge of archiving and promoting his work; she developed close connections with the Nazi regime in the 1930s, to the extent that Hitler attended her funeral in 1935. Nietzsche's work ended up being celebrated by the Nazis,[22] and Hitler went on to exploit Nietzsche's ideas to bolster the concept of an Aryan super-race. The fascist Italian leader Benito Mussolini was arguably even more of a Nietzsche devotee. These grim associations meant that Nietzsche was deliberately overlooked after the Second World War,[23] before undergoing a resurgence in popularity that was sparked in part by the publication of an acclaimed biography in 1965,[24] and in part by his popularity with such influential French intellectuals as Jacques Derrida. God is dead, Nietzsche had written, and they were rather taken with the idea.

So: Crowley, Nietzsche, alien spacecraft, suppressed truths, magickal Nazis, magickal sex. There was a lot of it about, and Bowie couldn't get enough; but although his mind was in mysticism, his body was in Beckenham. After moving out of Mary Finnigan's place, David moved in with a woman called Angela Barnett in September 1969, living in a home ten-minutes' drive and a world away from his childhood home in Plaistow Grove. David and Angela – better known as Angie – had got together earlier that year while dating the same man. Their new residence was a large ground-floor flat in a shambling and decadent Victorian mansion called Haddon Hall. The place became an informal hang-out for their friends and collaborators; Tony Visconti moved in too, with his girlfriend, Liz Hartley. 'While it was a splendid setting for a commune,' Visconti wrote, 'we all had the distinct feeling it was haunted. And it was.' He and Angie claim separately to have seen a figure they named Mrs Grey.

'David and I both liked to think of ourselves as "visionary" people looking at the world and the universe as completely uncharted territory,' remembers George Underwood, referring to this time. 'David would read books about alchemy, magic – various esoteric subjects. I was also keen on all subjects that required imagination to fully understand. We would talk for hours about different possibilities of how we came to exist, quite often at Haddon Hall.'

David and Angie were married at Bromley Register Office on Friday 20 March 1970. The ceremony was low-key, their clothes anything but. David's mother was not invited, but turned up anyway; photographs from the day suggest she was made welcome.

Yet these remained uncertain times, and Bowie's recording career had stalled. The first single after 'Space Oddity' was 'The Prettiest Star', an ode to Angie, with Marc Bolan on guitar. It sold pitifully. Next was a re-recording of 'Memory of a Free Festival'; it did nothing. Away from the studio, however, there was a kind of coalescence; the scene around David looked quite chaotic, but shapes were forming.

On 3 February 1970, Mick Ronson, a municipal gardener and keen guitarist from Hull, saw Bowie perform at the Marquee in Wardour Street. Ronson and Bowie met at a club afterwards, and Ronson joined Bowie's band the next day. Bowie had been helping to run what was called Beckenham Arts Lab, a regular night at the Three Tuns pub, since May 1969. Peter Frampton, Steve Harley and Rick Wakeman were among the musicians it attracted, and Bowie's penchant for blending art forms led to the involvement of visual artists, poets, dancers, puppeteers and the like. It was sound, earthy, vaguely hippie stuff. Now, things were about to get electric.

Bowie had a new band. Its first performance gave birth to glam rock on Sunday, 22 February 1970 at the Roundhouse in Camden, north London. No longer was it plain old David Bowie on vocals, Tony Visconti on bass, Mick Ronson on guitar and John Cambridge on drums: now they were Spaceman, Hyperman, Gangsterman and Cowboyman. They grumbled that they had nothing decent to wear, so Angie Bowie and Liz Hartley made new outfits. Goodbye down-to-earth clobber; hello leotards, silver crocheted briefs, gold lamé, diaphanous scarves, superhero attire. The earnest and the honest be damned: this band was called The Hype.

It could be interpreted as just another act of artistic itinerancy. But there was a more significant force at work. 'When the hippies came along with their funny tie-dyes and things, it all seemed naive and wrong,' said Bowie a few years later. 'It didn't have a backbone. I hate weak things. I can't stand weakness. I wanted to hit everyone who came along wearing love beads.' He expressed his fury in 'Cygnet Committee', a track on his second album, which was released in November 1969 and, like his first album, was titled *David Bowie*. 'Cygnet Committee' is a song of rage, in which he despairs not only at the fragility of hippie idealism, but also at the ease with which it can turn destructive, and how love can be twisted to lethal effect, sanctifying killing. Such desecration evidently outraged Bowie, who, in the song, sees a beautiful ideal corrupted by human weakness and vanity. This has a clear analogue in Bowie's hostility towards organized religion; the outrage comes from the same heart.

John Cambridge left just a few weeks after the Hype gig, following an unhappy recording session. Ronson suggested a replacement: Mick Woodmansey, who was also from Hull and had played for Ronson's former band, the Rats. The core was now assembled of the band that would make Bowie's next album, *The Man Who Sold the World*. They began their work in London that April.

The air that Bowie breathed was now thick with spirituality and philosophy. We can hear this on 'The Width of a Circle', the first song on *The Man Who Sold the World*. In the second part of the eight-minute track, Bowie sings of having an erotic encounter with God, or maybe Satan; despite the voices exhorting him repeatedly to flee, he cannot resist. Yet while this may sound exciting, in comparison with Bowie's later work it comes across as second-hand shock-rock, almost like a parody of Black Sabbath or Deep Purple.

The greater interest here lies in the first part of the song. Bowie said of the song a year later, 'I went to the depths of myself in that,' and it was to its opening minutes that he was surely referring. Here, Bowie sings of encountering a sleeping monster by a tree – and then realising that *he* was the monster. It suggests that Nietzsche had penetrated the innermost parts of Bowie's psyche. 'He who fights with monsters should be careful lest he thereby become a monster,' wrote Nietzsche in *Beyond Good and Evil*.[25] 'You yourself will always be the worst enemy you can encounter,' he wrote in *Thus Spoke Zarathustra*; 'You yourself lie in wait for yourself in caves and forests.'[26]

Various currents of Nietzschean thought flowed strongly through Bowie. At this point, it seems he was particularly interested in Nietzsche's idea of the *Übermensch*, effectively a new race or species of mankind. The *Übermensch* eschews Christian morality, or even what we might consider basic ideals such as mercy or compassion. Instead, he embraces supreme strength and supreme power, enabling him to master his life and the world, and he is animated by joy. The *Übermensch* also relates to another Nietzschean principle, the Death of God; its importance became more explicit later in Bowie's life. Lying beneath both of these is Nietzsche's reverence and zest for life itself, and this too made itself felt in the most meaningful way.

We are already witnessing the formation, the flickering into being, of a kind of constellation. The *Übermensch* – often translated awkwardly as 'Superman' – finds its clearest depiction in *Thus Spoke Zarathustra*. It begins with Zarathustra, a prophet, moving from a place of comfort and convention – his home on a lake – to the mountains, where he would spend ten years of solitude. It is a journey from safety into the unknown. He sometimes descends to share his wisdom with men, but he finds his greatest happiness up high, alone: 'I am a wanderer and a mountain-climber (he said to his heart), I do not like the plains and it seems I cannot sit still for long.'[27]

Thus Spoke Zarathustra inspired a musical work of the same name by the composer Richard Strauss, and this work is used to great effect in *2001: A Space Odyssey*. 'The Supermen', the song that closes *The Man Who Sold the World*, bears the imprint of Strauss's 'Also sprach Zarathustra' in its booming timpani, barely ever used again by Bowie. It is not entirely clear from the song whether Bowie misunderstood what Nietzsche was saying, or whether he had perceived a flaw in Nietzsche's thinking. In Bowie's song, these Supermen are wretched figures; cursed by eternal life, they yearn for death. The song also mentions 'supergods', who may be related to the Supermen; these supergods cry softly and they die softly. Nietzsche wrote in *Thus Spoke Zarathustra*: 'Thus – does a god laugh. Soft!'[28]

About halfway between 'The Width of a Circle' and 'The Supermen' is a song called 'After All', where the Buddha meets Crowley. Bowie juxtaposes the Buddhist notion of rebirth with Thelema's injunction to *Do what thou wilt*. Nietzsche has Zarathustra say repeatedly that 'Man is something to be overcome'; in 'After All', Bowie describes man as an 'obstacle'.

The cover of the album, in the UK at least, emphasized that this artist was different. Bowie is wearing a gleaming dress of silk or satin – a man's dress, he insisted. It is fastened across his chest, around which it clings closely, before it billows out elegantly from his hips. He reclines on a glistening chaise longue, his hair cascading down, one hand absent-mindedly teasing the crown of his head, the other pinching a playing card with the least possible effort. It is a scene of decadent listlessness: red curtains and a dressing screen create an Edwardian sense of the Oriental, while more playing cards are strewn on the floor. Hovering to his right is the name David Bowie, under which is written *The man who sold the world*. The lack of capital letters makes it read like a description of the man on the cover of the album, and it looks like you have played him at a game you will never win. Why has he sold the world? Maybe because, in this deal, he bought your soul.

Yet for all this enigma and provocation, and however much Bowie mused over the ways of the spirit and the nature of being, the world outside retained its indifference and its sharp edges. The album took a month to record, but there was no record label to publish it. Eventually it came out, first in the USA, in November 1970, and then in the UK, in April 1971. The album 'sold like hotcakes in Beckenham, and nowhere else', said Bowie.[29]

Once the album was finished, the record label judged it to have no obvious singles, so Bowie tried to write one. The result, which stood alone, outside any album, was 'Holy Holy'. It rather reeks of Crowley's sex magick, the singer extolling the holiness of the sexual act as he propositions his woman. There is mention of a righteous brother, a term describing members of the Golden Dawn.

Bowie sings of favouring evil and devils over angels. The music has a vaguely martial, ritualistic quality; a press release called it 'the first haunted song', and the recording does possess a somewhat abnormal aura.

Vagueness, uncertainty, dabblings, sparks. David Bowie was already four years and three albums into his career, but all was still nascent. Yet what makes this phase frustrating is what makes it fascinating. In other words: anything could happen.

And then it did. Perhaps it was because he was starting to compose on his piano, rather than his guitar; perhaps it was because Marc Bolan was becoming successful, and Bowie was jealous; perhaps it was because he was growing in confidence, having been named 'Brightest Hope' by *Disc and Music Echo* in 1970; perhaps he had been inspired by a promotional trip to the USA;[30] perhaps, after years of trying, he was finally mastering his art. Whatever the reason, Bowie was starting to write brilliant song after brilliant song after brilliant song. What had been glimpsed in flashes or obscured by haze was now undeniably *there*, tangible, illuminated crisply and with full vividness. The result of all this was Bowie's first classic album, *Hunky Dory*.

David Bowie had sung songs of confusion before, and they sounded confused. He was singing songs of confusion again, but now they sounded certain. However far he might have come in life since *The Man Who Sold the World*, it seems like his mind remained just where it had been. All that filled it before filled it still: that tangle of esoterica and occultism, cobwebbed terrors, nightmarish visions. You could call it a morass; he called it 'Quicksand'.

'The chain reaction of moving around through the bliss and then the calamity of America produced this epic of confusion – anyway, with my esoteric problems I could have written it in Plainview or Dulwich.' Thus wrote Bowie about this song, 'Quicksand', in his initial notes on the album.[31] He added in a press release: 'There's a time and space level just before you go to sleep when all about you are losing theirs and, whoosh, the void gets you with its cacophony of thought – that's when I like to write my songs.'[32]

Its origins may be crepuscular, but its subjects are lit brightly, as if extracted from the crevices of the imagination and placed in a scientist's laboratory. After some reflective but confident strums, the words begin. In the first five lines there is mention of Crowley, the Golden Dawn, and Himmler with his Nazi mysticism. Then there is the battle inside Bowie between the light and the dark; he describes himself as a kind of frustrated child of Nietzsche, one who would be an *Übermensch* but is tied to the ways of *Homo sapiens* and remains distracted by the salvation promised by faith, which he simultaneously derides. Then a sprinkling of Buddhism with a mention of *bardo*, the transitional state between death and rebirth. And then, to a melody that may be as beautiful as any he wrote, he sings of the knowledge and freedom that comes with death; and then this dense and wordy song dissolves into wordlessness. The intellect can do only so much; there comes a point where one must let go.

'Quicksand' is the sixth track on *Hunky Dory*. The second track is 'Oh! You Pretty Things'; here we have madness, Nietzsche and the author Edward Bulwer-Lytton. The son of an army general, Bulwer-Lytton was born in London in 1803, studied at Cambridge and visited Paris and Versailles before settling back in England and marrying an Irish woman, Rosina Doyle Wheeler, in 1827. His first novel, published that year, was not a success; but his second, *Pelham*, which was published in 1828 and concerned the adventures of a dandy, proved popular. He and Rosina lived extravagantly, so his books needed mass appeal, and they won it: he had more readers than Charles Dickens. But his melodramatic style irked the critics of his time, and he has since become associated with bad literary taste.[33]

His appeal to the young Bowie, however, was obvious, for Bulwer-Lytton had a penchant for blending science fiction and the occult. In 2013, Bowie published a list of a hundred books he regarded as being particularly important to him. Among them was *Zanoni* by Bulwer-Lytton. Its eponymous protagonist is a 'cultivator of the occult sciences' who has lived for 2,000 years and would be immortal were it not for the fact that he has just fallen in love. Zanoni is a brother in an order known as the Rosicrucians, a mysterious seventeenth-century European sect whose members supposedly possessed secret knowledge and who studied such fields as alchemy, Christian mysticism and a form of Jewish mysticism known as Kabbalah. Here, the border between fantasy and reality begins to blur, if it has not already evaporated: the Hermetic Order of the Golden Dawn was derived from the Rosicrucians, but the Rosicrucians themselves may never have existed, the writer of the order's texts declaring that they were intended as parody.

'Oh! You Pretty Things' refers fleetingly to another Bulwer-Lytton novel, *The Coming Race*, which was published in 1871. It tells of godlike subterraneans who have achieved mastery over themselves, and who derive power from a wondrous form of energy called Vril. *The Morning of the Magicians* claimed that a 'pre-Nazi' group known as the Vril Society existed in interwar Berlin, its members apparently trying to harness supernatural powers for dark political ends.

The song starts off a bit like 'Martha My Dear', Paul McCartney's ode to his sheepdog.[34] It is an early example of a trick Bowie came to master: smuggling disquieting lyrics and troubling ideas into cheery tunes. It begins with a scene of quiet domesticity: breakfast, coffee and a log fire. But before the end of the first verse, the sky cracks open and a hand stretches down. We are told that the nightmares have come, and they aren't planning to leave. Another kind of human is on the rise and is ready to supplant us. Old *Homo sapiens* has had his day; it is now time to welcome *Homo superior*. Bowie made all this sound delightfully inoffensive; psychic terror has never worn a prettier mask.

Into all this fed Bowie's personal circumstances. He wrote the song when Angie was pregnant with their son, and it is not a stretch to surmise that the conclusion to *2001: A Space Odyssey* remained imprinted on his mind: the vision of the 'Star Child', in utero. 'Then he waited, marshalling his thoughts and brooding over his still untested powers,' wrote Arthur C. Clarke of this figure. 'For though he was master of the world, he was not quite sure what to do next. But he would think of something.'[35]

Much else could be said about *Hunky Dory*, which is so easy to listen to but so hard to fathom. A similar quality is evident in its cover, which is clear and occluded. Bowie looks like a film star from the golden age of Hollywood – not Cary Grant or Jimmy Stewart, but Marlene Dietrich. He gazes upwards with an air of assurance. It is a photograph made to look like a painting, a monochrome image coloured by George Underwood with uncanny unrealism. On the back, Bowie calls himself 'the actor'. The album title may need a question mark.

Recorded at Trident Studios in central London, with Trevor Bolder replacing Tony Visconti on bass, Ken Scott producing, and Rick Wakeman's baroque piano perhaps its defining texture, the constituent parts of *Hunky Dory* can be identified and are finite; but they relate to each other in ways that are seemingly infinite, like reflections of mirrors. There is one more song to consider for now: it is called 'Life on Mars?'

A lonely girl argues with her parents and goes to the cinema. All she sees on the screen is a parade of clichés. But while the words tell us one thing, the music tells us another: this is immense, sweeping, intoxicating. Logic fractures, strange images emerge. Then one of the greatest accidents in all popular music: after the intended grand denouement falls away, it reveals beneath it a muffled sound, a previous recording of the piano accompaniment. This dies, and a telephone rings; we are back on earth.

It is a song of descents and ascents: the harmonies in the verses fall; before the chorus, they rise; in the chorus, they orbit. As he sings of Mars, Bowie's voice escapes; the music is borne aloft, and then the cycle repeats. In 'Space Oddity', he rises; in 'Life on Mars?', she rises and falls. The distance between where we are and where we want to be, the distance between who we are and who we want to be, the desperation to defy gravity and be with the gods, or at least to see reality from their pinnacle, on the scrounge for secrets: this is what animated the soul of David Bowie, occultist.

4

MESSIAH

The idea of the 'rock god' was born in 1971 in an article in the *Edwardsville Intelligencer*, a newspaper in Illinois, USA.[1] But David Bowie had long believed in such beings, and now he was about to make one, become one, and kill one.

There was once a singer named Vince Taylor, whom Bowie had befriended in the mid-1960s. 'He had a firm conviction that there was a very strong connection between himself, aliens and Jesus Christ,' recalled Bowie in 1996.[2] 'Those were the three elements that went into his make-up and drove him. And one night he decided he'd had enough. So he came out on stage in white robes and said the whole thing about rock had been a lie and in fact he was Jesus Christ. It was the end of Vince, his career and everything else.'

Even before Vince Taylor, Elvis Presley and Little Richard had sent the younger generation into rapture. In 1957, the magazine *Melody Maker* first used another holy word, declaring: 'Rockers-and-rollers fought to lay hands on their idol.' The object of their devotion was Bill Haley: 'One girl, crushed to impotence, swung a despairing face toward us. "If only I could touch him," she gasped.'[3] Two thousand years earlier, a woman said of Jesus: 'If I only touch his cloak, I will be made well.'[4]

Ziggy Stardust, Bowie's most famous creation, emerged in 1972. The process took the best part of a year. By the time *Hunky Dory* was released in December 1971, *The Rise and Fall of Ziggy Stardust and the Spiders from Mars* – the album ostensibly telling his story – was mostly recorded. The vision, however, was as crucial as the sound, and the vision was as yet inchoate, embryonic. Bowie had at least cut his hair: those swishing locks had been chopped by the end of that year, and a leaner look took shape.

There followed a curious few months, during which Bowie was supposed to be promoting *Hunky Dory*; but that album already belonged to a different world. Its opening track, 'Changes', was released as a single in January 1972, and the disc jockey Tony Blackburn named it Record of the Week on his BBC Radio 1 show, ensuring much airplay. It failed to chart, prolonging the streak of duds.

Whatever was driving Bowie hit the accelerator around then. January 1972 was pivotal in Bowie's career — and, by extension, in musical history. It was the month that Bowie, with Mick Ronson, Trevor Bolder and Woody Woodmansey, saw a new film, *A Clockwork Orange*. It was directed by Stanley Kubrick, whose previous film had been *2001: A Space Odyssey*. Just as its predecessor lodged itself into Bowie's imagination, so this latest work inspired him visually: the extraordinary outfits worn by the droogs, the film's gang of stylized thugs, led to the clothes that would eventually adorn Bowie and his bandmates. It was also the month that a photographer named Brian Ward invited a vibrantly attired Bowie to Heddon Street in London and took his picture under the sign of a furrier and inside a telephone box — the images would appear on the front and back of Bowie's next album, *The Rise and Fall of Ziggy Stardust and the Spiders from Mars*. It was also the month that Bowie told *Melody Maker*, 'I'm gay and always have been.'[5] And it was the month that Bowie and the band first performed in their new clobber. The musicians were not yet called the Spiders from Mars, but that is what they now effectively were.

February 1972 was pretty important too. Dennis Katz, the head of A&R at Bowie's record label, RCA Records, was unconvinced that any of the songs recorded so far for the new album would be a hit. So he asked him to write one, and he did; it was called 'Starman'. Then Bowie and the band made their first television appearance on the BBC programme *The Old Grey Whistle Test*. Then, at a pub called the Toby Jug in the London suburb of Tolworth, the Ziggy Stardust tour officially began.

Bowie dyed his hair red. Angie Bowie called it 'the single most reverberant fashion statement of the seventies'. She wrote: 'The new hairstyle triggered new experiments with make-up, and greater interest in clothes, and it wasn't long at all before young David Jones had transformed himself into a figure that was pure, one-hundred-percent, head-to-toe Ziggy: a lithe, redheaded, face-painted, very revealingly and very originally clothed polysexual stardust alien.'[6]

Then, late in April, it was time to release that song, 'Starman'. It was at once familiar and strange, like 'Somewhere Over the Rainbow' gone sci-fi, and it changed everything. The reviews were not so much glowing as incandescent; queues for concerts, hitherto often modest, now stretched around the block.

On 6 June 1972, the album arrived. Before you heard the record, you saw the cover. Soggy cardboard boxes, a sack of rubbish, a forgotten and rainswept street whose dankness seeps into your nostrils: behold, right there, your Messiah. This is how a classical nativity scene might look updated for the 1970s: mundanity and detritus glorified by a mere presence.[7]

The title – *The Rise and Fall of Ziggy Stardust and the Spiders from Mars* – suggests a coherent narrative. Yet the album provides none. What we have instead are images, snapshots, memories. It is like a scrapbook that has been compiled haphazardly, the odd vivid photograph pasted among apparently irrelevant cuttings. It represents an amalgamation and a culmination of much that had led him here. The record is perhaps his most famous, but try listening to it in the knowledge of all the spiritual adventurism that has gone before, and it sounds new again. And a fresh possibility presents itself: that it is even more to do with Jesus Christ than its allusions to messiahs might imply.

That *Christ* bit is really a matter of belief: it is essentially a Greek translation of a Hebrew word, *Messiah*. In Judaism, the Messiah is the awaited saviour; this figure is sent by God, but is not God. Christianity considers Jesus to be both Christ and God. And by the time the album was released, attempts had begun to reconcile Jesus Christ – that figure of childhood and the Church and the establishment – with popular culture.

There was the Jesus People movement, a blend of the hippie and the holy, which began in California in the late 1960s. By 1971, *Time* magazine was proclaiming on its cover 'The Jesus Revolution'. That year also saw the first staging of a new musical, *Godspell*, which told the story of Jesus in Broadwayish pop.[8]

And there was a more British effort: the rock opera *Jesus Christ Superstar*, written by Andrew Lloyd Webber and Tim Rice. It is unclear whether Bowie saw it – he typically loathed mainstream musical theatre – but he was certainly aware of it because the first woman cast as Mary Magdalene in the London production was Dana Gillespie, who had been a close friend since 1964. She also lent her voice to a song on the Ziggy Stardust album. *Jesus Christ Superstar* had started life as a concept album, released in 1970; among its musical contributors was Lesley Duncan, another of Bowie's long-term associates, and the writer of 'Love Song', covered by Bowie in 1969.[9] British readers of a certain age may also be intrigued by a story involving Floella Benjamin: before becoming a baroness and a beloved presenter of children's television, she performed in *Jesus Christ Superstar*; one night during the run, she attended a party at Bowie's house, and rebuffed his attempts to seduce her.[10]

Jesus Christ Superstar used rock to tell the story of Jesus. One could say the Ziggy Stardust album used Jesus to tell the story of rock. But the distinction may not be quite so neat, because the record is infused by Jesus, Christian imagery and matters of God to an extent that goes beyond easy symbolism.

The first song, 'Five Years', comes into vision slowly; then a blast of light from piano and guitar, and Bowie tells us where we are: a market square. People are in shock – in five years, the world will end. The market square may be just a market square, but for one versed in Nietzsche, there is another connotation: in his most famous parable, a market square is where the death of God is declared.[11] And when Bowie next performed in Aylesbury as Ziggy, he wanted the concert to be shown on a big screen in the town's market square,[12] thereby offering his own proclamation to those assembled. There are scenes of psychic disarray – one involves a policeman, a priest and a 'queer' – and the song ends with Bowie's abandoned, desolate howl, yelling the news repeatedly as if its import is yet to register.

'Five Years' bleeds into 'Soul Love'. Visions and concepts from Christianity abound. There is a priest; there is the Word, a term used in Christianity to refer to Christ and to Holy Scripture; there is God, whom the priest calls love; there is a baby and a cross, bookending the life of Christ. Then, once the song has ascended to its chorus, there is a dove, ablaze. Remember that window in that church in Bromley, in whose heavens were the dove and the flame: together, they are a symbol used commonly to depict the Holy Spirit. The song is also an early exploration of love as a spiritual force. In the song, love is as intimate as a boy and a girl talking, as moving as a woman grieving for her son, as transformative as the life of Christ. The work of love, and the question of what happens when love is absent or defiled, became a central preoccupation.

The next song, 'Moonage Daydream', is mostly intergalactic passion and knowing sci-fi schlock, a Roy Lichtenstein comic-book painting made musical. Yet even here there is a church: whether it's of 'man love' or of 'man, love' is up to the listener, but one way or another, it's holy.

Then a driving acoustic guitar opens 'Starman'. The song tells of a heavenly figure with a message of liberation for humankind. There is an echo of those first transcendent experiences of rock and roll for the young David and his cousin, Bowie's phrasing of 'let the children' evoking Jesus's words: 'Let the little children come to me, and do not stop them; for it is to such as these that the kingdom of heaven belongs.'¹³ What stays in the memory is how the song swoops and soars; but, as with the similarly celestial 'Space Oddity' and 'Life on Mars?', it begins on the ground, this time with the narrator at home, listening to the radio. It is a play between the domestic and the cosmic: the verses have an earthy churn to them, before the chorus shoots high and weightless. This is more than mere technique, more than an effective use of contrast – it is an example of a recurring motif, a kind of verticality, an upness and downness. Bowie may be associated in the public mind with songs about space and extraterrestrials, but these are songs about living on earth and striving for the heavens. As he told MTV in 1997 when asked about the aliens in his songs: 'For me it only represented spiritual search.'¹⁴

Side one of the album finishes with its first unremarkable song, 'It Ain't Easy'. It is a somewhat hoary number by an American named Ron Davies, who released it in 1970. Its inclusion on the album has long been a cause of bafflement among Bowie fans, not least as it was originally recorded for *Hunky Dory*. But the original radiates a kind of old-time religion; and while the music of Bowie's version lacks some of that spirit, the words still carry it.

The imagery of the song chimes with some of Bowie's deepest spiritual preoccupations. A mountain is ascended and the sea is surveyed. There is more ascending and descending between realms, with talk of getting to heaven and going down. And consciously or otherwise, there is another echo of *Thus Spoke Zarathustra*, as Nietzsche has Zarathustra, high on a mountain, deciding to impart his wisdom to humanity: 'I must *go down* – as men, to whom I want to descend, call it.'¹⁵

The second side of the album deals more with the mythology of rock and roll itself: performances, audiences, pretences; sex, death, salvation. It is here we find the song 'Ziggy Stardust'. The narrator is a bandmate – a disciple, maybe – recalling his frontman, his leader.

Ziggy, we are told, was The Nazz. 'The Nazz' is the name of a remarkable work of performance poetry by 'Lord' Richard Buckley, who was a major influence on the Beat Generation so admired by the adolescent David Jones. In the poem, whose storytelling style and use of the word 'cat' are aped in the song, the Nazz is Jesus of Nazareth. The song describes Ziggy as the confluence of the leper – the great biblical outcast – and the Messiah. Consider this from the Babylonian Talmud, a collection of ancient Jewish writings: 'What is [the Messiah's] name?... The Rabbis said: "His name is 'the leper scholar'."'[16] The song ends with Ziggy being killed, slain by those he came to save.

The final words on the album are Ziggy's own. 'If only I could touch him,' said the girl at the Bill Haley concert. 'Give me your hands,' says Ziggy.

***

Hunky Dory sold 11,000 copies in six months. *The Rise and Fall of Ziggy Stardust and the Spiders from Mars* sold more in two weeks. Angie Bowie recalled: 'The dynamic of those first months of real stardom was transcendent... We were all high on work, action, applause, and more work.'[17]

Angie Bowie's role as catalyst for the supernova has sometimes been cruelly overlooked, but cannot be overstated. She cajoled, organized, inspired, listened, charmed, dreamed, instructed, ordered, directed. She even worked the lights at the early Ziggy shows. She was essential to the phenomenon, integral to it. Yes, David Bowie was a solo artist; but, as the narrator of 'Five Years' says, he needed so many people. And at this crucial point in his career, Angie was foremost among them.

The tour was going spectacularly. As if more sensation was required, Bowie was photographed appearing to fellate Mick Ronson's guitar; meanwhile, 'Starman' was rising up the charts, earning an invitation from *Top of the Pops*. The performance was broadcast on 6 July 1972, and everything changed, again.

It may well be the most significant moment in the history of British music television. Half a century later, it startles and sparkles still: the supreme conviction of it, its insouciance, its playfulness, poise, seductiveness, directness, its welcome. To watch it is to be invaded gently, and then conquered.

If that is true now, it is easy to understand why the experience proved so overwhelming to so many in 1972. Campness was not new in pop, and Marc Bolan had sung on the programme some months earlier in silver jacket, pink trousers and glitter. But at a time when chart songs on television were a rare treat, when the UK's first Gay Pride march had taken place only five days earlier, when there were still laws against homosexuality, and when denim remained the fabric of choice for rockers, and machismo the prevailing attitude, at this time, to see a multicoloured but laceratingly sharp-looking Bowie draping a languid arm over the shoulders of a golden Mick Ronson, to see him pointing at *you* with such apparent force and discernment that you half expect the screen to shatter, all to the sound of a graceful singalong about a starman – well, some of us can remember how it felt, and the rest of us can only imagine.

'As soon as I heard "Starman" and saw him on *Top of the Pops*, I was hooked,' said Ian McCulloch of Echo & The Bunnymen, one of many who watched agog. 'I seem to remember me being the first to say it, and then there was a host of other people saying how the *Top of the Pops* performance changed their lives.'[18] Those other people included Adam Ant and Boy George. Then there were the future stars who attended those early Ziggy shows: Freddie Mercury; Ian Curtis, later of Joy Division; Steve Harley, who was inspired to form Cockney Rebel; Neil Tennant, later one half of Pet Shop Boys. Among those at shows later in the year were Chrissie Hynde, who went on to front the Pretenders, and Stephen Patrick Morrissey, who became known primarily by his surname, and formed The Smiths.

But someone had gone missing in this technicolour whirlwind. 'I'm rarely David Robert Jones any more,' Bowie said that August. 'I think I've forgotten who David Jones is.'[19]

The album that followed *The Rise and Fall of Ziggy Stardust and the Spiders from Mars* was called *Aladdin Sane*. The cover, one of the most genuinely iconic images in all popular music, shows Bowie's face split by a bolt of lightning.

Open the gatefold sleeve and he stands before you. Bowie had toyed with gender before; here, Aladdin Sane transcends it. Ziggy had his bandmates and a London street and a London phone box; Aladdin Sane stands alone, nowhere, imperious. His stance screams defiance, but his eyes whisper pain. Ziggy played guitar and wore one; Aladdin Sane plays nothing and wears it. He seems to have risen above music, humanity, everything. Ziggy played with time, but Aladdin Sane bestrides it like a god: the album has a song about him called 'Aladdin Sane (1913–1938–197?)'. Pay attention to those dates. He is a harbinger of cataclysm, maybe even a midwife to it. Watch out: he's back.

Aladdin Sane was less a stage character, more a psychic crisis. In case it is not obvious, his name is a pun. Bowie described him as 'Ziggy goes to America': various songs on the album were written there, and the record captures the disorientation that might be felt by a sensitive young man who was simultaneously wide-eyed and cynical. Bowie never officially performed *as* Aladdin Sane, whose appearance was a fairly mild evolution of the Ziggy look. But the music[20] is rougher and wilder; the title track is as avant-garde as he would get for a few years, the guitars properly grunt and snarl, and there is a genuine air of sleazy unease. It is another bravura effort, but with a more fragile bravado.

A sense of groundedness had been crucial to Bowie's work, a *terra firma* from which to leap. Previously, this had been lyrical or musical: an extraordinary song might start in an ordinary house, a high-flying melody might be earthed by an acoustic guitar. This was crucial to the idea of journey. Here, the groundedness remains, but it is communicated differently: written on the record label beside the name of each track is the place it was written. New York, Detroit, Los Angeles, New Orleans, London; it turns out these songs actually come from somewhere. The abstract is nothing without the concrete.

Aladdin Sane was a tremendous success commercially. It excited and electrified Bowie's fans: it was his first album to reach number one – despite all the reports of 'Ziggymania', its predecessor peaked at only number five – and it secured his place in British popular culture. But while it blazes with energy, that energy is generated in large part by anxiety. This shows itself in various forms: anxiety about war, about urban life, about getting old, about dying. This is not the work of a settled mind.

The record was released in April 1973. David, Angie and Duncan moved out of Haddon Hall the following month; what was once a place of steady if bohemian domesticity was now unlivable, with fans camping outside, and one even making his way in. The last proper Ziggy concert was two months later. By the end of the year, David had become troublingly addicted to cocaine.

'The first thrust of being totally unknown to being, what seemed to be, very quickly known – it was very frightening for me,' Bowie said the following year.[21] 'One half of me is putting a concept forward, and the other half is trying to sort out my own emotions… I got lost in it at one point. I couldn't decide whether I was writing characters, or whether characters were writing me, or whether we were all one and the same.'

It is easy to overlook, amid the apparently casual brilliance, that the man playing Ziggy was anxious. That is why Ziggy was created: to bestow the confidence of a star on a man who felt awkward on stage and thought he couldn't sing properly. By labour, by wizardry, by harnessing the power of myths and messiahs, Bowie had made it big. But it is worth reflecting here on a mime routine he devised in 1967, in which he played an unassuming young man who buys a mask.

He wears it for his parents, who are suddenly and uncharacteristically impressed by him; so then he wears it for the lads at work and his friends at the pub, and they like him too. He wears it for a theatrical performance; the audience applaud. Fame comes to him. 'It had a very strange effect on me though,' he says. He becomes more alarmed by it, even resentful. Then, one night at the London Palladium, he puts on the mask to wild acclaim; but he is unable to remove it, and he writhes in terror. The story makes the papers. 'Funny though,' ends the mime, 'they didn't mention anything about a mask.'

This time, Bowie got the mask before the mask got him. Just enough of him remained alert to the danger. 'I'm not what I'm supposed to be,' he said in 1972. 'What are people buying? I adopted Ziggy onstage, and now I feel more and more like this monster and less and less like David Bowie.' From the perspective of his great friend George Underwood, who worked on the album cover:[22] 'When David invented Ziggy Stardust, it did two things – it catapulted him into stardom and fame but nearly killed him.'[23]

So on the final night of his tour in July 1973, at the end of the show and to the surprise of almost everyone – including some of his band – Bowie killed Ziggy. He said: 'Of all the shows on this tour, this particular show will remain with us the longest, because not only is it the last show of the tour, but it's the last show that we'll ever do.' Bowie did this to save himself from the one who had saved him, to free himself from the one who had granted him freedom. He knew too well the danger.

There is a figure who stalked Bowie from the start. He casts a kind of messianic spell; he is deified in some way, and he uses his power to deceive or destroy. By the end of 1973, Bowie was working on a new theatrical piece, a musical adaptation of the novel *Nineteen Eighty-Four* by George Orwell, in which this figure loomed large. By now, the appeal of the story to Bowie may be obvious: it depicts the struggle of a man, Winston Smith, against a regime whose powers of oppression are seemingly infinite. Free thought is banned, individual expression is banned, sex is banned. Words are corrupted: the Ministry of Peace wages war; the Ministry of Love is a place of torture. Here already are familiar Bowie concerns, seen in everything from his fascination with Nietzsche to the experiences that found expression in 'Cygnet Committee'. But there is another aspect to Nineteen Eighty-Four that now becomes particularly relevant: the role of an all-powerful entity called Big Brother.

The populace is fed a constant message that it is being watched by Big Brother. There is an image of Big Brother, and it is everywhere. But no one ever actually sees Big Brother. Winston asks a member of the regime whether Big Brother will ever die. He is told: 'Of course not. How could he die?' An immortal, omnipotent being who may not even exist, being used to control the masses: to certain eyes and from a certain angle, this could look rather like organized religion.

Suitably inspired, Bowie went to work on Nineteen Eighty-Four: The Musical. Among the songs he wrote was 'Big Brother', which Bowie portrays as an object of religious devotion: the people view him as a saviour and as 'some brave Apollo'.

This figure shifts his shape throughout Bowie's career, but you know him when you see him. He appears in a subtly different form in 'Candidate',[24] also written for the musical; the song sets the words of a lascivious and narcissistic would-be leader to a buoyant and appealing tune. This time, he calls himself the Führerling, an intriguing term that Bowie may have invented, combining Hitler's title with a suffix usually used to create a diminutive: think gosling or duckling. A vicious tyrant, then, and cute with it.

He is there again in 'Somebody Up There Likes Me', written in 1974. The figure is described as the personification of divine benevolence. His coming was foretold in messianic terms, by the planets and by wise men. The music here is smooth, supple, infectious; the overall effect is one of insidiousness. Then, with the music growing denser and heavier as if a camera is zooming out to reveal the true picture beyond the frame, Bowie warns us to watch our souls and guard our hearts.

And he is there again in 2013 on Bowie's penultimate album, in 'If You Can See Me'. Here he is an all-powerful destroyer and thief who paints himself with holy words and slays all dissenters and burns their books.

All of this reflected and informed Bowie's attitude towards organized religion. And in 1973, it might well have reflected and informed Bowie's attitude towards himself, towards his own power, his thirst for it and his fear of it. The god-man was breaking up.

About 30 years later, Bowie became friends with the writer, actor and comic Ricky Gervais. 'I emailed David on his 57th birthday,' said Gervais.[25] 'It read: "57???? Isn't it about time you got a proper job? Ricky Gervais, 42, Comedian."' He replied: 'I have a proper job. "David Bowie, 57, Rock God."' At least by then he could laugh about it.

5
LOST

According to David Bowie, '1975 and 1976, and a bit of 1974, and the first few weeks of 1977, were singularly the darkest days of my life. It was so steeped in awfulness that recall is nigh on impossible – certainly painful.'[1]

It was a crisis that might have cost him his sanity, if not his soul, if not his existence. Various currents were forming a whirlpool, and Bowie was being sucked into the vortex. There was the fragility of his mind, made yet more vulnerable by the havoc unleashed by Ziggy Stardust. There was the fragility of his body, sustained mostly by milk and peppers: 'I was painfully emaciated,' he recalled. 'I was not even skin and bone. I was just bone with these veins wrapped around them. I think at some points I almost reached 80lbs.'[2] There was the cocaine – avalanches of the stuff. And there was that fetid brew of occultism and esotericism, of which there had been little evidence in 1972 and 1973, but which still swirled around Bowie's psyche, or whatever passed for it. All of this was about to take him to hell.

Bowie spent six months of 1974 performing as himself, for the first time in years. The 1974 tour was groundbreaking, melding rock and theatre in a mightily ambitious manner: there was a stage set of decaying skyscrapers, depicting Bowie's new dystopian creation, Hunger City; there was an elevated walkway, a crane that raised him high above the audience, an array of props and costumes, avant-garde and aggressive dance. Bowie no longer wore conspicuous make-up or flamboyant dress, yet he looked more alien than Ziggy ever had.

And however little there was on the outside, there sometimes seemed even less on the inside. He appeared, in the truest sense, haunted. 'My God, it looks like as if I've just stepped out of the grave,' Bowie said decades hence when reflecting on a recording of a concert.[3] 'That's actually how I felt. That record should have been called David Bowie is Alive and Well and Living Only in Theory.'[4] Halfway through the tour, which never left the USA, Bowie ditched the set, and the show became a kind of soul revue. This was curious, partly because it was an unexpected departure into a new style, and partly because Bowie's own soul seemed to be in a critical condition.

There had been two albums since *Aladdin Sane*. The first was *Pin Ups*, on which Bowie covered some of his favourite British songs from the 1960s; it had a bright and Ziggy-looking Bowie on the cover, and contained the last knockings of what remained of the Spiders from Mars. Spirited and brisk but uneven, it was another big hit, going straight to number one in the UK.

The second was another matter entirely. George Orwell's estate had refused Bowie permission to turn *Nineteen Eighty-Four* into a musical, but he kept some of the songs he had written for the project, and wrote some more with vaguely post-apocalyptic or otherwise troubled themes. The resulting album was *Diamond Dogs*, and it had a grandiosity and scale of vision that exceeded all his previous work. It also had 'Rebel Rebel', Bowie's last glam smash, and 'Rock 'n' Roll with Me', the song that hinted most clearly at what was to come. *Diamond Dogs*, its cover featuring a Ziggy-mulleted Bowie with disconcertingly canine features, was released in May 1974, and topped the charts. The distinctions between Bowie's various phases are rarely as clear as critics often suggest, but *Diamond Dogs* genuinely marked the end of an era: it was the last album he made while based in London and the last to have any glam stylings.

The Diamond Dogs tour began in June that year. Possessing a keen sense of place, the ear of a mimic and an openness to fresh experiences, Bowie found himself ever more influenced by American soul, funk and R&B. Black American music had enthralled him from afar in his childhood, but now he was immersed in it. He was asked about this by the BBC documentary maker Alan Yentob that August for a film that would be broadcast the following year, and gave a memorable answer in a fractured voice: 'There's a fly floating around in my milk. There's a foreign body in it, you see, and he's getting a lot of milk! That's kind of how I felt. A foreign body. And I couldn't help but soak it up.'[5]

In that same documentary, *Cracked Actor*, Bowie talked about an unusual aspect of his writing process. He would cut up lines of text, rearrange them and seek inspiration or revelation from the results. He borrowed the idea from the creative polymath Brion Gysin and the writer William S. Burroughs. 'I've used this method only on a couple of actual songs,' said Bowie. 'What I've used it for more than anything else is igniting anything that might be in my imagination. I tried doing it with diaries and things – I was finding out amazing things about me and what I had done and where I was going. A lot of the things that I've done, it seemed that it would predict things about the future, or tell me a lot about the past. It's really quite an astonishing thing. I suppose it's a very Western tarot.'

There was a break in the tour, and Bowie went to Philadelphia, to record at Sigma Sound Studios. This was the home of the 'Philly Soul' sound and was used by artists such as Wilson Pickett, the O'Jays and the Spinners. The resulting album was *Young Americans*; it came out in March 1975. And for two consecutive albums released less than a year apart, the difference between *Diamond Dogs* and *Young Americans* is about as pronounced as it gets.

On *Diamond Dogs*, Bowie had a new voice, something rounder, deeper, fuller, that sounded bigger than his own body; *Young Americans* is the album on which it matures. *Diamond Dogs* was officially produced by Bowie, but he needed help with mixing, so he called an old friend, Tony Visconti;[6] *Young Americans*, however, was a full Visconti production job, as is evident from the breadth and clarity of the sound. The musicians, meanwhile, included an array of players with full-funk bona fides, led by Carlos Alomar, formerly of the house band at the Apollo in Harlem and a previous member of James Brown's band. Backing singers – including Ava Cherry, Robin Clark and an up-and-coming Luther Vandross – brought warmth, energy and exquisite syncopation.

Yet while the style had changed, the substance remained. True, these songs lacked the *appearance* of nightmares, but beneath the gloss they had the *feel* of them: nervy, edgy, agitated, tense. The album's big single was 'Fame', an angry song written with John Lennon and Bowie's first number one in America; its subject is a false god that takes more than it could ever give. The title track is breezy and smooth, but its portrait of empty lives is above all a searing lament.

The following year, Bowie described *Young Americans* as 'the definitive plastic soul record. It's the squashed remains of ethnic music as it survives in the age of Muzak, written and sung by a white limey.'[7] There is a sense in which he was being unfair on himself: *plastic* suggests inauthenticity, and while it may have been a naked attempt to crack America, it also stands as an authentic representation of who Bowie was at the time. There is no lack of commitment, and it does not sound like the work of a dilettante at play.

Yet in another sense he was quite right, because the origins of soul music can be traced back to the Church, but you would not know it from hearing this album. Sam Cooke and Aretha Franklin were both children of Baptist ministers and started out singing in their church choir, as did Otis Redding; Ray Charles, who pioneered the genre, brought the 'yelps and yowls' and call-and-response of church singing to secular music;[8] and church life was foundational to Mahalia Jackson, perhaps the godmother of them all. But to Bowie, church had meant something different, and *Young Americans* makes that plain. It is soul music deracinated and etiolated, but this may be what gives the album its unique appeal. For all its professionalism and accomplishment, what is missing from *Young Americans* is what is most revealing about it. *Young Americans* is, however, crucial to what came next: it might be considered a kind of base layer, the establishment of new foundations, upon which would be built towering works.

By the end of 1974, Bowie was clearly in a bad way. He made an infamous appearance on *The Dick Cavett Show* on ABC in November in which he was plagued by an incessant sniff, and made strange shapes on the floor with his cane. Addressing Bowie, Cavett remarked: 'There's a lady who said "I don't know if I'd want to meet him – he'd make me very nervous. I have a feeling he's into black magic and that sort of thing," and other people see you as just a very skilful performer who changes from time to time from one thing to another.'

Bowie replied: 'Well... both of that is...' Cavett: 'All of the above?'

Young Americans reached number two in the UK and number nine in the USA when it was released in March 1975 (April in the USA), by which time things had begun to go very wrong. David Bowie was living in Los Angeles. The city has doubtless been a happy home for a great many people, but it has had its critics, and Bowie's experience would chime with theirs. In *On the Road*, Jack Kerouac called it 'the loneliest and most brutal of American cities'. Aldous Huxley said it was 'nineteen suburbs in search of a metropolis'.[9] Bertolt Brecht, in his poem 'Contemplating Hell', wrote that his brother thought Hell was like London, whereas 'I, who do not live in London, but in Los Angeles, find, contemplating Hell, that it must be even more like Los Angeles'.

By the time Bowie moved there, Los Angeles had also emerged as the capital city of what might be called 'alternative spirituality', teeming with occult bookshops, astrologers, tarot readers and the like. One day he called his wife in some panic to tell her that he was with a warlock and two witches. He said they wanted his semen in order to conceive a child of Satan. 'I'd heard David speaking from some pretty cold, strange places, both by telephone and in person,' wrote Angie some years later, 'but this sounded different, worse than I'd heard before.' She dismissed the spooky aspects as 'just puffed-up, superheated, secondhand bullshit' but said that 'the spiritual degradation demonstrated by his story (true or false) was really sad'.[10]

There are other stories like this, and they can sound sensational. But there may be something more true in that word *sad*. David Bowie was lonely, and scared and sad. 'From the way he sounded, he might just as well have been off in the emptiness of some awful cold black hole,' remembers Angie, who promptly went to his aid.

Shortly after that episode, David spotted an old photograph of him and Angie and panicked to the point of having a seizure, because her arm looked black. 'In his scheme of things,' wrote Angie,[11] 'this meant that the witches were going to kill me as a way of getting to him.' Following the advice of a white witch, she calmed him by scattering herbs and reading to him from *The Tibetan Book of the Dead*, 'kept handy since his Buddhist monk-wannabe days'.

It needs to be stressed that Angie is a practical woman and that she had a sighing scepticism regarding matters of the occult. She was perturbed, however, to note that a violent storm was raging outside David's window, even though this was a sunny late afternoon. The experience 'cast a persistent, troubling shadow on the notion that cocaine paranoia was David's only enemy'.

David, Angie, Duncan — better known by then as Zowie, his middle name — and his nanny, Marion, were living in Doheny Drive, a sun-kissed Beverly Hills boulevard lined with palm trees. The house had an indoor pool; David said he had seen Satan rising from it. He demanded an exorcism and performed it, in accordance with the instructions of the white witch. Angie reports that the pool began to thrash inexplicably. After about 15 minutes, it calmed; but Angie kept watching.

'I saw what I saw. Nothing can change that,' she wrote.[12] 'On the bottom of the pool was a large shadow, or stain, which had not been there before the ritual began. It was in the shape of a beast of the underworld... It was shocking, ugly, malevolent; it frightened me.'

Years later, Bowie was asked if he remembered the mark: 'on the bottom of the pool? Yeah, and I bet it's there to this day. I do remember that because it was such an indelibly real thing at the time.'[13]

Geoff MacCormack, that great friend from Bowie's early days in Bromley, related another paranormal occurrence. At the house in Doheny Drive, he said, 'David suggested we conduct an extra-sensory perception test, using me as the medium'. Concentrating hard, MacCormack wrote down four words: *pyramid*, *windows*, *children*, *tree*. He had no idea what this could mean. The two of them proceeded to search the room for anything these words might relate to. They were just about to give up when David found something wedged in the back of a drawer. David 'looked at it open-mouthed and wide-eyed.' He had found a card bearing the image of a pyramid-shaped Christmas tree, 'adorned with little windows that, when flipped open, revealed the happy, smiling faces of children'.[14] Pyramid, windows, children, tree. '"Shit," he said.'

MacCormack saw something else that evening that baffled him. Bowie had written out something he called the Isolaric Alphabeth; that spelling of the latter word is typically associated with Hebrew, whose alphabet has mystical dimensions, but Bowie seemed to have created his own set of characters. The word *Isolar* is one that Bowie appears to have invented: decades later, he said it was a blend of *isola* – Italian for island – and solar. ('If I remember correctly,' he added. 'I was stoned!') Bowie's penchant for flippancy aside, the word evidently possessed a powerful meaning for him: the official names of his tours in 1976 and 1978 were, respectively, Isolar and Isolar II, and Isolar was the name he gave his music publishing company in the mid-1970s.[15]

This was a terrifying time to be David Bowie. He was interviewed in May 1975 by the journalist Cameron Crowe for the magazine *Rolling Stone*. All was proceeding in a fairly straightforward manner, until: 'Suddenly – always suddenly – David is on his feet and rushing to a nearby picture window. He thinks he's seen a body fall from the sky. "I've got to do this," he says, pulling a shade down on the window.

A ballpoint-penned star has been crudely drawn on the inside. Below it is the word "Aum". Bowie lights a black candle on his dresser and immediately blows it out to leave a thin trail of smoke floating upward. "Don't let me scare the pants off you. It's only protective. I've been getting a little trouble from... the neighbours."[16]

***

If an occultist is making a magic circle, and for any reason wishes to seal it with the Kerubim of the Elements instead of the Archangels, as is more commonly done, and feels himself unequal to the task of drawing a presentable eagle, the symbolic form of the Kerub of Air, he will use the Zodiacal sign for Scorpio.

So runs a fairly typical passage from *Psychic Self-Defence*. Written by the British occultist Dion Fortune and published in 1930, it had become by now one of Bowie's more treasured belongings. The book is written in measured tones, and Fortune presents herself as an entirely reasonable woman, one who is skilled in the magickal arts but is no lunatic. She might be described in layman's terms as a practitioner of white magick, and explicitly opposed to black magick.[17]

Fortune described various forms of psychic attack, and how they may be diagnosed and thwarted. Her ideas drew upon an array of spiritual beliefs, including Kabbalah, a Jewish mystical tradition that attempts to explain the relationship between God and mankind, between the eternal and the temporal, between heaven and earth. She also discusses the immense power of the five-pointed star.

Psychic Self-Defence is not just a handbook – it contains numerous astonishing and unsettling stories. One tells of an encounter with a malevolent spiritual presence that sent a man 'plunging through a ten-foot-high window to the ground below'. This raises questions about what Bowie saw, or thought he saw, during his interview with Cameron Crowe. And it is notable that this tale and the book's most detailed account of Kabbalah appear in a chapter entitled 'The Risks

Incidental to Ceremonial Magic', which suggests that Bowie's intellectual interest in occult ritual may at some point have become more practical.

Draw circles, make stars: this is what Bowie did. The photographer Steve Schapiro captured him a few months earlier outlining the Tree of Life, a kind of Kabbalistic map, by his feet and on his walls. 'I drew gateways into different dimensions, and I'm quite sure that, for myself, I really walked into other worlds,' Bowie told the *New Musical Express* in 1997. 'I drew things on walls and just walked through them, and saw what was on the other side!'

Jewish mysticism was the 'foundation of modern Western occultism', according to Fortune. In her 1935 book *The Mystical Qabalah*,[18] she calls the Tree of Life 'the best meditation-symbol we possess because it is the most comprehensive' and the 'ground-plan of the Western Esoteric Tradition'. It consists of ten or eleven circles, each representing an aspect of the Divine – such as mercy, judgement and wisdom – connected by paths showing how they relate to one another. For Fortune, it was a key to ancient and hidden truths: 'It is well known to mystics that if a man meditates upon a symbol around which certain ideas have been associated by past meditation, he will obtain access to those ideas.'

Fortune also believed that there was a force greater than any power of darkness. That force was God. In combat with demons, Fortune recommended using forms of words that invoke God, as understood most clearly in a Christian context. One practice involves creating a 'magic circle', a special space that may be drawn or simply visualized, and saying: 'To Thee, O God (touching his solar plexus) be the Kingdom, (touching his right shoulder) and the Power (touching his left shoulder) and the Glory, (clasping his hands) unto the ages of the ages. Amen.' For another, Fortune tells the reader to say: 'By the power of the Christ of God within me, whom I serve with all my heart and with all my soul and with all my strength... I encompass myself about with the Divine Circle of His protection, across which no mortal error dares to set its foot.'

It was around this time that Bowie started to wear a cross. He was pictured with two: one rather bold and grand and on his chest, the other more modest and resting just below his neck. The former he used that year for an experiment involving a technique called Kirlian photography, which, it was claimed, captured auras: Bowie photographed it next to his fingertip before and after taking cocaine, the second image showing a more vivid and frazzled outline. The latter cross he would wear for much of his life thereafter. 'I just felt I'd been pretty godless for a few years,' he said in 1978.[19] 'It became part of a new positive frame of mind that I have about trying to re-establish my own identity for myself – for my own sanity.'

Bowie later described this time as 'an intense period of trying to relate myself to this search for some true spirit'.[20] His recollections of 1975 were not always reliable, but this one sounds about right.

Some moments in Bowie's career seem uncanny. In 1975, he was cast as the lead character in *The Man Who Fell to Earth*, a film directed by Nicolas Roeg and based on the 1963 novel of the same name by Walter Tevis. It is about an extraterrestrial from a drought-ridden planet who visits Earth in search of water, acquires great wealth and becomes a celebrity. He attends church (in a moment of pleasing irony, the alien at one point stumbles through the hymn 'Jerusalem'; George Underwood remembers this being a favourite during David's time in the choir at St Mary's, Bromley) and encounters human life in a variety of forms. Finally, unable to return home, he ends up isolated and alcoholic. His name is Thomas Jerome Newton.

By the mid-1970s, it had become quite common for singers to act in films. Elvis Presley had been in 31 of them; The Beatles had been in at least two and as many as five, depending on who is counting;[21] David Essex had been in *That'll Be the Day*; Mick Jagger had been in *Performance*, also directed by Roeg. But *The Man Who Fell to Earth* is not just another rock-star vehicle: it became integral to Bowie's career, and to Bowie's life more generally. Like 'Space Oddity', it stayed with him until the end; he would circle back to it, as if in an orbit, or perhaps in a spiral. It was not written by him or directed by him; it featured none of his music; he was cast only because Roeg had happened to see him in *Cracked Actor*, the BBC documentary. Yet it now seems almost as essential a part of his work as any song or any album.

'My one snapshot memory of that film is not having to act,' said Bowie in 1983. 'Just being me was perfectly adequate for the role. I wasn't of this earth at that particular time.'[22]

The spiritual motif of verticality that runs through Bowie's work is evident in the film's title, and in a scene about the myth of Icarus,[23] and in the name 'Newton', evoking the man who discovered the laws of gravity. There are also echoes of Zanoni, the titular character from Edward Bulwer-Lytton's novel: like Newton, he is an alien figure of mysterious powers brought low by earthly temptations.

By the time shooting began in June, Bowie had started writing an autobiography. It made little conventional sense. One of the few people to have read any of it is Cameron Crowe; in a piece for *Rolling Stone*,[24] he described it as 'a series of sketchy self-portraits and isolated incidents apparently strung together in random, probably cutout order'. He added: 'Despite David's enthusiasm, one suspects it may never outlast his abbreviated attention span.'[25] The autobiography had an unusual name: *The Return of the Thin White Duke*. These would be the first words of his next record.

Nicolas Roeg, the director of *The Man Who Fell to Earth*, was something of a prophet. 'He told me after we'd finished it would take me a long time to get out of the role and he was dead right,' said Bowie.[26] 'After four months playing the role I was Newton for six months afterwards.'

The sum does not quite add up – Bowie was speaking there in March 1976, less than ten months after the film's release – but the sense is clear. Bowie carried into his next project an essence of Newton: detached, masterful, yet vulnerable. This was by no means a stretch, but was a vital element of what would become an astounding artistic statement.

Bowie started work on his new album in October 1975 at Cherokee Studios in Los Angeles. He had a new bassist, George Murray, and was joined again by Carlos Alomar and the drummer Dennis Davis, both of whom had played on the *Young Americans* album. Those three musicians would be the force and the funk of Bowie's band for the rest of the decade. Full-on rock guitarist Earl Slick and Bruce Springsteen's pianist Roy Bittan completed the formidable line-up.

They and producer Harry Maslin had time to think and to experiment, to craft and to cut loose. Recording sessions were inspired and untamed: one started at 7 a.m. and ran for 26 hours, brought to an end only because another artist was booked for the studio; Bowie simply headed to another studio and kept working until midnight.[27] His creativity was ablaze; yes, the album introduced a new character, the Thin White Duke, but this was not a question of affectation or artifice. Indeed, the record is defined in part by a quite devastating honesty: he was baring everything, even the unseeable. 'It's the nearest album to a magick treatise that I've written,' he said later.[28] 'It's an extremely dark album.'

The album is called *Station to Station*. So is its first song, which lasts for ten minutes and begins with the sound of a train charging from speaker to speaker. The band begin to assemble what becomes a grinding, pulverizing sonic machine, churning and rattling and howling with ominous momentum. It goes on and on and on and on; arpeggiated guitar figures add a touch of humanity, but these sound eerier with each inevitable repetition, as if conjuring some force from the deep. Then, atop a suddenly lilting, drifting, flowing acoustic guitar, come the first words, intoned by a chorus of Bowie's voices. They proclaim 'the return of the Thin White Duke'. Like Aladdin Sane, this character transcends time: this is our first encounter with him, yet we are told he has been here before, that he is somehow already familiar to us, a kind of forgotten spectre.

The band resume their mechanical motif, and Bowie sings with a beguiling blend of intimacy and potency words that evoke those of Prospero in *The Tempest*: 'We are such stuff as dreams are made on.' In Shakespeare's play, Prospero is a magician and a duke, shipwrecked on an island. Bowie sings of dredging and overlooking an ocean, and of being lost in his circle; what one might conjecture is a magic circle, or a circle on the Tree of Life.

He alludes to the flashing of colours. The Hermetic Order of the Golden Dawn developed a technique called 'tattva vision', which was derived from Hindu mythology and involved a systematic flashing of colours to aid clairvoyance. The key line, however, speaks of flashing *no* colour, and this is worth noting, because it will become relevant.

Then he sings of moving magically from Kether to Malkuth. Kether is the pinnacle of the Kabbalistic Tree of Life. In *The Mystical Qabalah*,[29] Dion Fortune wrote: 'Kether is equated with the most transcendent form of God that we can conceive, whose name is Ehieh, translated in the Authorized Version of the Bible as "I am", or, more explicitly, the Self-Existing One, Pure Being.' Malkuth sits at the base: Fortune describes it as 'the Kingdom of Earth', representing merely 'sensory brain consciousness', the most primitive form of awareness. To move from Kether to Malkuth is to descend from the heights to the depths, from spirit to matter; it is to fall to earth. When performing this song on stage, Bowie would invariably illustrate this through gesture, first raising his hand and then lowering it in a straight line. Up and down, once again.

Then we hear the name of the song. 'The Station to Station track itself is very much concerned with the Stations of the Cross,' said Bowie in 1997.[30] He also tells us that 'all the references within the piece are to do with the Kabbalah'. It seems difficult to reconcile those two statements: the song can surely only be about one or the other. But there is no reason to doubt the broader claim, at least concerning the title. The Stations of the Cross are typically used as an aid to solemn prayer and meditation for Christians; they comprise a series of images depicting scenes from the moment of Jesus' arrest to the laying of his crucified body in the tomb.[31] The relevance of this to the song is rather obscure, and it is made no clearer by the repeated use of train sounds and the use of the word *drive*, which, when put together, suggest something rather more to do with locomotives than with the suffering and execution of Christ. There may, however, be a deeper connection between the Tree of Life and the Stations of the Cross: both are a kind of scheme or system imbued with spiritual meaning, elucidating a path or journey from one way of being to another. Although the stations usually end before the resurrection, they could be interpreted as illustrating at least part of a movement from earth to heaven, from Malkuth to Kether.

The chorus of vocals sounds again, as does the gentle guitar. There is an incantatory quality to this. The layered vocals suggest communal chanting, while the structure follows a liturgical pattern familiar from the *Agnus Dei*, a Christian prayer which is typically sung in acts of worship: *Agnus Dei, qui tollis peccata mundi, miserere nobis; Agnus Dei, qui tollis peccata mundi, miserere nobis; Agnus Dei, qui tollis peccata mundi, dona nobis pacem.* It can be translated as: Lamb of God, who takes away the sins of the world, have mercy on us; Lamb of God, who takes away the sins of the world, have mercy on us; Lamb of God, who takes away the sins of the world, grant us peace. At this point in 'Station to Station', there is a similar chant: three lines that all begin the same way, 'The return of the Thin White Duke', and continue with a short poetic description. The first two lines are identical, the third is different. It is unclear whether this similarity to the *Agnus Dei* is intentional, but it suggests a knowledge of liturgical rhythms and their hypnotic power.

We are told that this figure makes 'white stains'. *White Stains* is the name of a collection of poems by Aleister Crowley. Many are sexual, and the title is an obvious allusion to male ejaculation. Steve Schapiro's photographs of Bowie drawing the Tree of Life show his dark clothes bearing white diagonal stripes, which he had painted himself. 'He talked a lot about Aleister Crowley, whose esoteric writings he was heavily into at the time,' Schapiro recalled. Bowie was 'immersed in his own world and everything seemed to have some secret meaning'.[32] William S. Burroughs, in his 1959 novel *Naked Lunch*, describes semen as 'thin white rope'.

The song shifts into something more closely resembling conventional rock, with a long melody that peaks and plummets in search of something, and words evoking a landscape familiar from earlier spiritual excursions: there are mountains and more mountains, and there are soaring birds. Then we hear as clear a statement of Bowie's personal mission as he ever made in song: 'Got to keep searching'. He asks where this search will take him, where he will place his belief, how he might touch love.

The section ends with a reference to fortune, and to the men who protect us. It is tempting to speculate that this is about Dion Fortune, and the protection she offered. Dion Fortune was not a man, but there is a suggestion in an interview from 1997 that Bowie thought she was male, perhaps owing to her ambiguous forename: 'There was a guy called Edward Waite who was terribly important to me at the time. And another called Dion Fortune.'[33] Arthur Edward Waite was an English mystic and a member of the Golden Dawn who devised a deck of tarot cards with the illustrator Pamela Colman Smith; the Rider–Waite deck was first published in 1909 and has since been used widely for divination. Crowley wrote: 'The only theory of ultimate interest about the tarot is that it is an admirable symbolic picture of the Universe, based on the data of the Holy Qabalah.'[34] A note Bowie made in 1975 suggests his prayer ritual involved the Rider-Waite tarot deck, numerology, and *Psychic Self-Defence*.

A few lines later, there is a moment of ecstatic release – it's not drugs, maybe it's love – and the song plays out in incandescent fashion. We are repeatedly told, or warned, or reassured, that it's 'too late'. There is no going back. We are somewhere new. The song seems locked on a fresh course: where it was initially trapped circling in the shadows, it is now on an inescapable ascent. On stage, it always ended with a reprise of those opening lines, but on the recording it fades out, as if there is no way of halting it. Higher and higher.

The next song, 'Golden Years', is one of Bowie's slickest cuts from the seventies. Hear it on daytime radio and it's airy and catchy, upbeat and blissfully optimistic. It has a simple message: life may feel tough for you but, trust me, things will turn out well. However, 'Golden Years' is on *Station to Station*, so it should come as no surprise that there is more going on.

Bowie sings most of the song to a friend or lover, whom he addresses as 'angel'. But sometimes he addresses someone else, some divine entity, about her. This becomes clearer in an earlier draft of the lyrics, in which he pleads with the Lord to 'save her little, lonely soul.'[35] Maybe the singer is less confident than he sounds; maybe this angel is really in need of spiritual protection. It makes the song's later proclamation of belief in the Lord sound less trivial and more vital. Angie Bowie has long claimed the song was written for her.

And then from the depths of crisis comes a cry for salvation in the song 'Word on a Wing'. Bowie called it a 'signal of distress' and a 'call for help'.[36] '"Word on a Wing" I can't talk about,' he said in 1980. 'There were days of such psychological terror when making the Roeg film that I nearly started to approach my reborn, born again thing. It was the first time I'd really seriously thought about Christ and God in any depth, and "Word On A Wing" was a protection... The passion in the song was genuine.'[37]

It begins with a single note of synthesized strings and a gentle welcome on the keys, which leads into a simple and utterly lovely rising refrain on the piano, matched by a simple and utterly lovely rising refrain on the guitar. Bowie's unadorned, unaffected voice enters just a few inches away, and sings conversationally to one who has become newly real to him, one who has walked into his life out of his dreams, one who has been born again for him. His name is sweet; as a beloved old hymn puts it: 'How sweet the name of Jesus sounds in a believer's ear!'

The words here are naïve and guileless. Bowie asserts that believing is entirely compatible with thinking, that questioning has its limits. An earlier draft has the line 'Astonishingly simple, amusing to the learned';[38] St Paul wrote that 'we preach Christ crucified', which was 'foolishness' to the supposedly wise.[39] Pretty much every line of the song 'Station to Station' is laden with depths of meaning, but with 'Word on a Wing' there is barely anything to interpret. He kneels and prays to the Lord, and sings of his efforts to be part of God's 'scheme'. Those who find comedy in the typically gargantuan egos of rock stars may also smile wryly at how, in the same song, the Divine is repeatedly assured that Bowie feels he can now *shape* that scheme. 'Word on a Wing' is also the first song to mention Bowie walking beside his God, an image that will recur in later years.

While the words are disarmingly straightforward, the music is not. Bowie's vocal starts off as relaxed and tender; a quite bewildering multitude of other Bowies join in along the way; the song ends at an almost desperate pitch. Much of 'Word on a Wing' follows a basic harmony of three chords, but the melody seems untethered from them in an effortless flow; the chords underpinning other sections, meanwhile, are complex and sophisticated. The instrumentation is subtly remarkable too: at one point, Earl Slick, having played with dutiful discipline, suddenly finds a note that wrenches the soul.[40] As the song ends, there is no doubt that we have been taken to church: an organ resounds, joined by what sounds like a chorister.[41] Throughout, Roy Bittan plays his piano with touching sympathy and sincerity. It builds to an intensity that almost feels too much. But good taste be damned: it all adds to the sense that David Bowie – cool, detached, ironic David Bowie – really means this. And no wonder: it was to him a matter of life and death.

"'It was also around that time that I started thinking about wearing this (fingers small silver cross hanging on his chest) again, which is now almost a left-over from that period," he said. "I wear it, I'm not sure why I wear it now even. But at the time I really needed this. Hmmm (laughs), we're getting into heavy waters… but yes, the song was something I needed to produce from within myself to safeguard myself."'[42]

The final song on *Station to Station*, 'Wild is the Wind', was not written by Bowie, but makes for a natural ending to the album. An intense love ballad written by Dimitri Tiomkin and Ned Washington for the 1957 film of the same name, and sung memorably in the 1960s by Nina Simone, Bowie's version has a desperation like 'Word on a Wing', only of a more smouldering kind. He later cited it as one of his favourite vocal performances, and it is a masterclass in relaxed control, his expression of the word 'wild' becoming by the end as untamed yet unforced as the wind of which he sings. It is as if he had come to know its strength and effect; he knew what it was to be disorientated and intoxicated by an invisible force.

Even after all this, there are yet more dimensions to explore. In one, we find Led Zeppelin, and what they meant for Bowie. 'David just *hated* them,' wrote Angie Bowie. 'He regarded the Zep as offensive throwbacks to pop's primitive past,' she claimed, and said he was 'much offended by their blues base and big, bad, balls-out bump-and-grind stage show'.[43]

'Rock has always been the devil's music,' Bowie told *Rolling Stone* in 1975. And he meant this in a bad way. 'It will occupy and destroy you… It lets in lower elements and shadows that I don't think are necessary.'[44]

The human focus of Bowie's concerns was Jimmy Page, Led Zeppelin's guitarist. Page was working as a session musician when he played on one of Bowie's earliest recordings;[45] during the sessions, Page gave Bowie a riff he later used for 'The Supermen'. By the mid-1970s, Page had become one of the titans of rock, and was himself a devotee of Aleister Crowley, going so far as to buy Crowley's former house near Loch Ness in Scotland.

Bowie was apparently terrified of Page. 'He thought Jimmy was in league with Lucifer, and was out to get him,' wrote Angie Bowie. That business with the witches and the warlock who wanted Bowie's semen? 'He was convinced that the human arch-agent behind it all was none other than Jimmy.'[46]

Shadows, primitivism, a 'bump-and-grind stage show': Bowie's next tour would be an enemy to all of this. Led Zeppelin were in hock to the bluesy American musical canon; but for Bowie, it was time for what he called the *European* canon. The show opened with footage from *Un Chien Andalou*, a seminal 1920s surrealist film by Luis Buñuel and Salvador Dalí; blaring from the speakers were the sounds of Kraftwerk, the German pioneers of electronic pop. The show looked stark, its style inspired by the revolutionary German playwright Bertolt Brecht. On stage, Bowie smoked Gitanes, the potent French cigarettes.

Darkness would be obliterated by a barrage of blinding white light, although this would throw its own vast shadows; and judging from Bowie's work, this play of light and dark was a preoccupation of his. The cover of the *Station to Station* album was monochrome, showing Thomas Jerome Newton leaning aristocratically into a kind of chamber; his outfit for the Isolar tour was black and white, and its staging followed the principles of *chiaroscuro*, the balance of light and shade in art.[47] He had sung years earlier of a struggle within him between the dark and the light;[48] that feeling now had a violent urgency. For these shows, often regarded as the finest of his career, Bowie inhabited the character of the Thin White Duke, backed by most of the band that had recorded *Station to Station* to exhilarating, coruscating effect. Bowie never sounded better or looked better. Whatever had brought him here or sent him here, called him here or driven him here, here he was, at the summit.

The Isolar tour ran from February to May in 1976. David Bowie had appeared in public barely at all the previous year; but when he did, it was memorable. On one occasion, he presented the award for Best R&B Vocal Performance, Female at the Grammys.[49] His comportment was part reptilian, part vampiric; he had the demeanour of a being struggling to translate its thoughts into human speech. The winner was Aretha Franklin, of whom he was a fan. Her response was: 'Wow, this is so good I could kiss David Bowie! I mean that in a beautiful way.'

Bowie told *Rolling Stone*: 'The Grammys were very significant for me. It was like walking a tightrope. There were mostly ageing middle-class showbusiness people in that audience. It was a question of entertaining them or coming off like just another rock singer. I really did feel I was David Bowie and not a rock singer. It was very strange. Strange, strange, strange.'[50]

In November, he performed 'Golden Years' and 'Fame' on *Soul Train*, the American television programme that became legendary for its promotion of black music. It started badly: he was unprepared and forgot his words. Following a rebuke from the production staff, a suitably chastened Bowie recovered his professionalism and performed in a manner that earned him kudos among an audience he was keen to impress. He sang later that month on the *Cher* show, with Cher; they duetted on a medley so suffused with showbiz kitsch that it could serve as a parody, but there is a perverse enjoyment to be derived from it.

Yet his final broadcast of the year was arguably the most revealing. He was interviewed by Russell Harty for British television. Harty was a fascinating man himself, with a buttoned-up appearance that made him resemble a backbench MP, and possessing a perpetual air of either amusement or bemusement and more than a hint of delightful indecorousness. He was only 13 years older than Bowie, but there was a clear generation gap, and he treated Bowie like a lovably wayward nephew. They had worked surprisingly well together in an interview in 1973, but now they were in different studios, in different countries, and seemingly in different galaxies. There were moments of connection between them, but these emphasized how disconnected they were: Bowie often rejected or failed to understand Harty's questions, Harty certainly failed to understand many of Bowie's answers, especially one that included the phrase 'eclectic manifestations', and the interview sputtered. Harty looked and sounded like a mildly camp broadcaster from Lancashire in his mid-forties, which he was; Bowie looked like he was made of alabaster and copper and sounded like he was communicating for the first time, having read about the process somewhere. Attempts at levity misfired; attempts at gravity disintegrated. But there was an odd affinity too – 'I am a fan of yours,' says Bowie at one point – and the offbeat nature of the encounter lent itself to unusual lines of questioning. 'Are you still aware of forces apart from satellites that are moving around this globe, this planet – or around you, David Bowie?' asked Harty. 'Of course, yes.'

'What kind of eclectic manifestation do you have of this?' 'A mountain. Or. A tree. Is a manifestation of forces that we are not capable of dealing with.'

'Do you go to church?' 'No.' 'Do you pray?' 'Yes, of course.' 'But do you pray to mountains and to trees and to those physical manifestations, or to some kind of spirit?' 'I don't think I would like to get into that over a 20-minute interview.'

Station to Station, the album, and the tour that followed, might be seen as the end of something, the culmination of Bowie's musical, spiritual and theatrical interests. What comes next is a sharply jolting change of direction, and there would never again be a character as defined and realized as the Thin White Duke.

But the phase that was ending looks forward, too; it anticipates. One of David Bowie's favourite pictures of himself was taken by John Rowlands in 1976. It shows Bowie on stage in the guise of the Thin White Duke, adopting the pose of the archer. Now the archer is rich in symbolism: as a choirboy and, falteringly, as Newton, Bowie sang about a 'bow of burning gold' and 'arrows of desire';[51] there is a Greek archer god, Apollo, to whom Bowie likened Big Brother from *Nineteen Eighty-Four*; the Hebrew Bible at times portrays God as an archer; the literature of alchemy draws often on the symbolism of archery; the lower portion of the Tree of Life has been described as the 'heavenly bow and arrow'; and in an essay on archery for the pagan magazine *White Dragon*, Anthony Roe wrote: 'The arrow is a symbol of the intercommunication between Heaven and Earth... The divine archer is the one who walks between the worlds.'[52]

There was Earth, and there was Heaven, but now Bowie knew there was somewhere else too. In 1996 he quoted the words of a Native American theologian, Vine Deloria Jr. 'Religion is for those who believe in hell,' he said. 'Spirituality is for those who have been there.'[53]

6

VANQUISHER

David Bowie was in an old place, a place of torment. But he was also in a new place, a place of healing. It may not always have looked like that, but whether as an answer to a prayer or through sheer will to survive, he was climbing out of the pit, up to somewhere else. And maybe he had undergone a conversion when he was down there, for the man who rose to earth sounded startlingly different. It was as if words had been burnt off, exposing a raw spiritual essence. In its bruised and scorched way, what emerged was a declaration of victory.

In the summer of 1976, Bowie left Los Angeles. He described it as 'the most repulsive wart on the backside of humanity'.[1] He needed restoration and peace, so Angie Bowie suggested a château near Blonay in Switzerland. She, he, Zowie and Marion moved in.

But, according to Angie, David hated it: 'It wasn't his scene at all.'[2] The couple were soon living separate lives: when she was there, she said, 'he wasn't, and vice versa'. Their marriage had reached an irreparable point. They were on the road to divorce.[3]

That summer, David began work on *The Idiot*, a new album by Iggy Pop, at a recording studio in a château near Paris. David described these months in France as 'a dangerous period for me. I was at the end of my tether physically and emotionally and had serious doubts about my sanity.'[4] In August, Bowie and Pop moved to Berlin, where they shared a flat in the unglamorous district of Schöneberg and lived as earthly a life as possible.

Bowie and Pop had long been friends; Pop had been the confrontational frontman of the American proto-punk band the Stooges before going solo, and he had inspired Bowie's song 'The Jean Genie'. Bowie produced *The Idiot* and co-wrote all the songs; there is a widespread impression that Bowie was essentially directing the project, with Pop providing the lyrics and vocals.

The Idiot sounds like a blend of Bowie's immediate past and immediate future: there is the icy abrasiveness of his previous tour and the clipped claustrophobia of his following album, which was recorded in the last few months of 1976, straight after *The Idiot*, mostly at the same studio, and called *Low*.

This fresh venture of Bowie's had deep roots. He retained the rhythm section from *Station to Station*: Carlos Alomar on rhythm guitar, George Murray on bass guitar and Dennis Davis on drums. The producer was Tony Visconti, with whom Bowie had first worked in 1967. A new collaborator was Brian Eno, who had been a founding member of Roxy Music and came into public consciousness in 1972. Bowie had long been enamoured of Eno's solo work, especially in ambient music, a genre Eno essentially invented. Since the days when Bowie wrote songs while meditating, he had sought to bypass the more rational and cerebral human faculties and open up paths to the subconscious, which he felt was a better way to avoid cliché and create work of originality. In this, Eno was an ideal companion: he had long championed chance as a tool for creativity, and had helped devise a method that he called 'Oblique Strategies'. This consisted of a set of cards on which were printed phrases that included *Honour thy error as a hidden intention*, *Breathe more deeply* and *Disciplined self-indulgence*. The cards would be drawn at random, disrupting established patterns and setting artists and musicians on new paths. Bowie was also enthralled by cutting-edge German bands like Kraftwerk, Can and Neu!, who sounded like they hailed from an entirely distinct musical tradition, as though they had never heard a Rolling Stones record. It all made for an album that was radically different from what had gone before.

Up until *Low*, Bowie made it easy for us. His spiritual paths and fascinations were often made explicit in his lyrics. When he was particularly interested in Buddhism, he wrote about Buddhism; when he was particularly interested in occultism, he wrote about occultism; when he was particularly interested in Kabbalah, he wrote about Kabbalah. Sometimes references to spirituality and specific traditions and practices would be more oblique, but it was not a struggle to find them.

In the case of *Low*, however, this becomes a challenge, because the most immediate and striking change is a lack of words. The album has 11 songs, but only five have lyrics, at least in the conventional sense. And where they appear, they tend to be sparse and terse; we have travelled far from the verbosity of *Station to Station*. There is no explicit mention of any god, or any devil, or any demons, or any messiahs, or any churches or temples or prophets or mystics. And yet a case can be made that *Low* is as profoundly spiritual as any work of Bowie's career.

The working title for *Low* was *New Music: Night and Day*. This new music was not merely a new album: it was a new way for music to be made, to be thought about, to be imagined. There were new ways of working, new sounds, new voices, new ideas. The first track, 'Speed of Life', is a statement of intent: it is unquestionably *new*, the drums up in your face and sounding like no other drums, synthesizers squealing and sighing, and the lyrics – well, there are no lyrics. It just fades in, intrigues, excites, and fades out. It completes its work in two minutes and 48 seconds.

There is a sense of freshness here, albeit of an urban, neon-lit variety, a kind of nocturnal dawn. Yet still the past lives, and it is there in the album's next track, 'Breaking Glass'. The first words we hear Bowie sing are about breaking glass and drawing on the floor. Bowie said in 2001 that this refers to 'both the cabbalistic [sic] drawings of the Tree of Life and the conjuring of spirits'.[5] He may well have had in mind a passage from Fortune's *Psychic Self-Defence* which reports a visitation from a malevolent force that shattered a window and smashed mirrors, leaving the 'floor and top of my bed... strewn with broken glass'.[6]

This is the only clear acknowledgement of what had gone before. There is instead a new theme emerging: of the five tracks most closely resembling conventional songs, four are concerned with enclosed spaces. The third track on the album, 'What in the World', tells of another seclusion, that of a girl who never leaves her room. Then we arrive at the album's most famous song, 'Sound and Vision':[7] here is a room of electric blue, a place of blinded windows, devoid of stimulus, where the singer sits alone, waiting. It may be a passive and lonely existence, but the song celebrates it; this is introversion at its most joyous.

Next is 'Always Crashing in the Same Car'. No room as such this time, but a place within a place: a car in an underground car park. The song is about the night when, in David Bowie's words, 'everything kind of came to some kind of spiritual impasse'.[8] Faster and faster he sped, around and around. Pushing his foot down to the floor. Faster and faster, as he tried to kill himself.

He let go, in final submission to the forces of momentum and oblivion. 'And as I let go, I ran out of petrol. I just slowly came to a stop. I thought, "This is the story of my life."'[9]

He revealed that this was not his only attempt at suicide. And as he said: 'The full story is rather alarming. It involved a coke dealer whose car I saw on the Kurfürstendamm in Berlin one day. And I'd gotten it into my mind that he'd screwed me over a deal... I was so crazed I started ramming him in the Kurfürstendamm. In daylight, 12 o'clock in the day. And I rammed him and I rammed him and I could see he was absolutely mortally terrified for his life. I'm not surprised. I rammed him for a good five to ten minutes. Nobody stopped me. Nobody did anything. And I got out of it and thought, "What am I doing?"'[10]

The final decipherable lyric on the album speaks of escape but offers none. The solitude celebrated on 'Sound and Vision' has curdled into loneliness on 'Be My Wife': the narrator has lived everywhere and left everywhere. Now he wants a woman to share his life.

And that is it. Much of this is sung without Bowie's usual conviction or passion; some of it is hardly sung at all. 'Station to Station', the song, has more words than *Low*, the album.

More so than any other of his LPs, *Low* is a record of two sides. The first is those five brief songs, bookended by two pacy and driving instrumentals. The second is an even greater departure: four solemn and apparently wordless tracks that seem to represent a wholly other form of art. They can be understood as a way of exiting those rooms, those tight spaces, and opening oneself to a deeper kind of truth.

Eight dolorous monotones spread over 24 seconds introduce 'Warszawa', the first of these tracks. The texture thickens; it is hard to identify individual sounds, which are all played by Eno on a piano and three electronic instruments. Themes rise, fall, rise again, rest, rise again, as if gaining strength, acquiring a slow, graceful momentum. Then, they turn; and after four minutes, there is a human voice. And then more voices: most provide added texture and depth with their long hums and voiced breaths. Over these, a vocal line soon rises, singing mysterious and unintelligible words. These are sung by Bowie, but his voice is soon manipulated to sound like that of a choirboy. Then those earlier themes return. 'Warszawa' ends almost resignedly.

Bowie said the piece is 'about Warsaw and the very bleak atmosphere I got from that city'.[11] Yet what is perhaps most striking about 'Warszawa' after repeated listens is not the subdued stateliness but the sense of humanity that bursts through it. The instruments, mostly electronic, play with great deliberation; but the voices surprise, uttering words never heard before,[12] soaring and swooping in unusual scales, conveying urgency and desperation. Even though the piece ends quite as it began, it sounds different. The voice changes everything.

Eno spoke about this phenomenon in 2022, when talking about the role of vocals on his album from that year:[13] 'I'm a landscape painter in terms of music, I suppose. But this time I wanted to have somebody in the landscape. Putting a human in the picture makes it a quite different kind of picture. I've seen this myself. If you look at a landscape painting, and there's nobody in it, you look at it in a certain way. If you put even the tiniest figure in there, even down in one little corner, a single human figure, your eyes move in an entirely different way. You keep returning to that figure, because what you're then looking at is a human in relation to the world you have created... this person is sort of showing you "here's the world, and here's how I feel about it, here's how I behave within it".'[14]

One way of experiencing 'Warszawa' is to hear in it the sound of the human spirit beautifying the world it inhabits and defying the forces that seek to oppress it. There is a transcendence: it is as if Bowie is singing in tongues. This core belief in what we might call the soul – a belief not only that it exists but that it is a source of transformative power – finds its place at the heart of Bowie's work during this period. When all is stripped away, this is what remains.

The idea illuminates Bowie's musical choices around this time. Years later, he contrasted his approach with that of the German band Kraftwerk: 'We were poles apart. Kraftwerk's percussion sound was produced electronically, rigid in tempo, unmoving. Ours was the mangled treatment of a powerfully emotive drummer, Dennis Davis. The tempo not only "moved" but also was expressed in more than "human" fashion. Kraftwerk supported that unyielding machine-like beat with all synthetic sound generating sources. We used an R&B band.'[15]

The pulse comes not from an electrical current but from a beating heart. This assertion of the human in contrast to the mechanical, of the real in contrast to the synthetic, is an expression of spirituality quite different from those hitherto described. It is less concerned with particular practices or traditions, like Buddhism or Kabbalah, and is more an expression of fundamental belief, or at least hope.

But it has a place within conventional religions, and perhaps found its most influential advocate in the form of Paul Tillich, a German–American philosopher influenced by Søren Kierkegaard, and one of the leading Christian theologians of the twentieth century.

Tillich wrote a book called *The Courage to Be*. It was published in 1952 and was remarkably popular for a work of its kind. It is a hymn to *being*. For Tillich, courage is 'self-affirmation in spite of anxiety over the threat of nonbeing'. There are vast forces that threaten existence: Tillich calls them 'fate and death', 'guilt and condemnation' and 'meaninglessness and emptiness'. Affirming being in spite of all these threats is an act of supreme courage.[16]

There are three more pieces on *Low*. Two of these feature Bowie's voice; on one, he sings again. It is the last track on the album and is called 'Subterraneans'. Bowie said it was about 'the people that got caught in East Berlin after the separation – hence the faint jazz saxophones representing the memory of what it was'.[17] His voice begins in mournful breaths, before he sings a few words that make more sense aesthetically than syntactically: their meaning lies more in their sound. At first, they carry a kind of serene melancholy, before they build into something more impassioned and perhaps anguished. In contrast to 'Warszawa', the words sound like they may be English, but there is no consensus regarding what they are, and they remain impenetrable. The most that can be said is that they twice mention a failing or fading star. To claim this is in any way a joyful piece would be absurd; but the focus again is on the human. Here, the forces of nonbeing comprise a totalitarian regime that has drained colour from life, but cannot destroy it. 'I get a sense of real optimism through the veils of despair from *Low*,' said Bowie.[18]

And there is a word that connects 'Warszawa' and 'Subterraneans'. Bowie asked Eno to begin work on a piece with a 'very emotive, almost religious feel to it'.[19] That piece became 'Warszawa'. A man working for RCA, which was Bowie's record label at the time, also described 'Subterraneans' as 'religious'. Neither mentions God, yet that adjective somehow fits both.

For all its stylistic differences from the past, *Low* was a kind of spiritual and chemical rehab; the best way to make sense of it is to know where it came from. 'Breaking Glass' was one nod to that netherworld. Another was the album's artwork: as with *Station to Station*, the cover was based on a photo by Steve Schapiro of Bowie as Thomas Jerome Newton in *The Man Who Fell to Earth*. This time, Newton looks less imperious, but just as determined.[20]

The most striking difference, though, is in colour and texture. *Station to Station* had a brutal kind of austerity, Newton in clinical shirt and jacket in a monochrome photograph with a pronounced white frame, the only colour coming from the text, which is angular; there are no spaces between the words, giving them an unforgiving and intimidating look. By contrast, the cover of *Low* is amber and persimmon and burnt orange; Newton is pictured close up and stern-faced in imposing profile, but he wears a soft bobbly duffle coat; the lettering is rounded, less formal. It is hardly the cover of a party album, and it remains strange and beguiling and imposing: it looked *new* when it was released in January 1977, and it still somehow looks *new* now. But importantly, the cover tells you of the beating human heart within.

The shift from the terror and tumult of Los Angeles to what is often called the 'Berlin period' seems a change as sudden and dramatic as any in Bowie's career. The paranoid and cocaine-fuelled existence in an LA mansion was replaced by a flatshare in a modest quarter of a modest city. Outfits freakish and fantastical were replaced by flat caps and dad shirts. The swaggering bluesy riffs and rousing choruses were replaced by textures and shapes hitherto unexplored by a mainstream artist. Bowie stopped living like a rock star; he stopped looking like a rock star; he stopped sounding like a rock star.

Once Bowie was in Berlin, Angie noted that 'he didn't seem to be doing as much cocaine as before, if any'.[21] David later said: 'Berlin was the first time in years that I had felt a joy of life and a great feeling of release and healing. It's a city eight times bigger than Paris remember and so easy to "get lost" in and to "find" oneself too.'[22]

The Berlin of the late 1970s fascinated him, and so did the Berlin of the 1930s. He had long been an admirer of the writer Christopher Isherwood, whose 1939 novel-cum-memoir *Goodbye to Berlin* inspired the musical *Cabaret*, the London production of which had left such an impression on Bowie. Isherwood's 1935 novel *Mr Norris Changes Trains*, his other great Berlin story, about a man whose respectable demeanour hides his unconventional character, was included on Bowie's list of a hundred significant books; and when Isherwood went to Bowie's show in Los Angeles in 1976, the 71-year-old was the only one of dozens of stars and celebrities in attendance to be invited into Bowie's dressing room. 'Bowie is awed,' reported Cameron Crowe.[23]

Isherwood captured the city's arty subversion and righteous mischief, and this spirit lived on in Bowie's Berlin; but the enemy was different now. Iggy Pop told him a story about a party he had attended at a punk club to mark the anniversary of the building of the Wall. 'And they'd built an entirely accurate replica of the Berlin Wall,' related Bowie. 'And at the stroke of midnight, fifty savage, demented punks leapt on this wall, and tore it to pieces with their mouths and teeth and fists. But he said it was the aftermath that was the most affecting... There were small groups of them standing around in the corners, pitifully crying, tears streaming down their faces. I thought that was an incredibly moving thing, and a real memory of Berlin, the Berlin that I knew at the time anyway.'[24]

The Wall would be a defining presence on Bowie's next album, '*Heroes*'. The quotation marks are deliberate, because this album is interested not in the heroism of Hollywood blockbusters or ancient legends, but in the heroism of daily life.

'*Heroes*' was released in October 1977, just nine months after *Low*, and is something of a companion piece. Visconti and Eno returned, as did the rest of the band apart from guitarist Ricky Gardiner, who was replaced with Robert Fripp. *'Heroes'* was recorded entirely in Berlin, at Hansa Tonstudio, where *Low* had been completed.

The album sounds different from *Low*. 'It's louder and harder and played with more energy in a way,' said Bowie.[25] The cover suggests as much: it is more urban and glossy, showing a leather-jacketed Bowie in a new monochrome photograph by Masayoshi Sukita that is a study in tension and control, as if Bowie is subjecting his troubles to discipline. His pose is inspired by two paintings by the German artist Erich Heckel, both titled *Roquairol*: Bowie's head mimics one of them,[26] while his arms are positioned unusually, as in the other.[27] Heckel was part of a group of artists called *Die Brücke*, formed in Dresden in 1905; *Die Brücke* means 'the bridge', reflecting their desire to occupy a space between the avant-garde and the older traditions of Romanticism and the Renaissance. This was Bowie's natural habitat too.

But some things remained unchanged from *Low*. The same working practices were employed, with spontaneity and randomness part of the process. The albums also share a general pattern, containing tracks that sound like conventional songs on side one, and more abstract and instrumental pieces on side two.

Two pieces on the second side have a distinct sense of place. The first is called 'Moss Garden'. This is not the intensity and peril of Berlin: this is a Zen Buddhist temple in the city of Kyoto in Japan, where there is a sublime serenity. The principal sound is a koto, a traditional Japanese stringed instrument.

Bowie would use the koto again, in 1999, on an instrumental track called 'Brilliant Adventure'. At that point, he said: 'When I get to write a piece of music that for me is sort of maybe expressing a spiritual life, I tend toward the East, because when I was a kid, the things that fascinated me in terms of spiritual adventures and all that tended to be more Buddhistic in nature – they didn't have much to do with Western religion or Christianity. And so I think I naturally gravitate towards an Eastern form of music when I'm trying to paint a picture of a spiritual existence. That would explain why, often, my instrumental music tends towards the East.'[28]

The second piece is called 'Neuköln'. It is named after Neukölln, a district of Berlin associated again with a dislocated people – in this case, immigrants from Turkey. The track expresses its spirit not with Bowie's voice but with his breath: his saxophone is the only recognizably human element in an oppressively inhuman landscape. Bowie grunts and wails and howls and screeches his way through it, in a performance of vivid expressiveness. It outlives its surroundings, the apparent cause of this anguish, crying out at the end alone; a tale of survival, or defeat.

But elsewhere on the album there is a song that leaves no doubt as to the victor. The duration of this victory is irrelevant: it could be one day, it could be forever. It transcends the temporal, for its truth is eternal. Like the album, it is called 'Heroes'. The song is about two bruised, broken and, by the looks of it, entirely unheroic humans. But in spite of the forces trying to destroy them, they will be transfigured.

It begins with a proclamation: he will be king, she will be queen. Yet the second verse reveals a more squalid reality: the scene is one of shame and degradation, where she can be mean and he drinks all the time. In later performances, this second verse was where Bowie and his band began the song, often low-key and a touch offhandedly.

But there is a metamorphosis, and it is signalled as much by the leap in Bowie's voice as it is by the band's slowly rising intensity. The powers of death, of guilt, of meaninglessness are confronted and defied in a defining and redefining moment: as the guards shoot, the shabby lovers kiss, invincible, regal, heroic. The forces that would destroy are conquered. Love is stronger than death.

Once again, a towering Bowie epic starts on the ground, with the seemingly small and insignificant. As with his previous protagonists, the couple are eyeing the heights. But they get there in a new way: not through technology or fantasy – or, as Bowie might have tried, with elaborate schemes or arcane practices – but through love.

Accentuating the point, Bowie does something new with his vocal melody. He had used it previously to express ascent or escape or transcendence, by leaping an octave from one syllable to the next, most obviously in the choruses of 'Life on Mars?' (from *on* to *Mars*) and 'Starman' (*Star* to *man*), before gravity takes hold, and the tune falls again. 'Heroes' also leaps by an octave, but does so suddenly, shockingly, without warning, accompanied by a fresh energy and larynx-shredding passion; and then it remains in that higher register for the rest of the song. Nothing can drag it down. 'Heroes', exalted on high, for ever and ever.

The song has acquired a remarkable life since it was recorded. It was not a hit when first released; it was perhaps not until Bowie's performance at Live Aid in 1985 that it became the anthem it is now regarded as being. But at heart it remains small and intimate, made majestic less by the seemingly unstoppable force of the band than by the theme of the song and Bowie's total commitment to it. 'They use it for every heroic event, although it's a song about alcoholics,' said Visconti.[29]

'Heroes' is a supreme example of Tillich's 'courage to be'. As he wrote on the power of being: 'One can become aware of it in the anxiety of fate and death… [Courage] returns but not as the faith in universal reason. It returns as the absolute faith which says Yes to being.'[30]

Being. Life itself.[31] It is this absolute faith that powers and radiates from Bowie's greatest work. This belief is as metaphysical as any espoused by conventional religion: it comes from no empirical study and can be shown by no microscope or telescope; rather, it requires a leap. A more rationalist, materialist view may argue for randomness and chance, and for the indifference of the universe; it may see as basically meaningless the phrase *love is stronger than death*, and may place no greater inherent value on being than it does on nonbeing. Yet this is the leap that Bowie has made. The quest for spiritual truth would be ceaseless, but this would lie at its heart, and these albums would be its purest expression. 'If I never made another album it really wouldn't matter now,' Bowie said. 'They are my DNA.'[32]

Big ideas, big words, big faith. One may say this is all very well: we can see what it did for his music, but we might ask what all this meant for Bowie personally. So it is notable that, as he began to heal, his relationship with the world began to change.

There is a common understanding of Bowie that goes something like this: Bowie was an icon of rootlessness who changed how he looked, how he sang, how he wrote, how he spoke, following influences, whims or commercial interests; he seemed untethered from any particular location or tradition or responsibility or even time. He was an icon of individualism, and it was essentially all about himself.

This critique was articulated by the Anglican priest and polemicist the Reverend Giles Fraser in 2016, at a time when hagiographic eulogies to Bowie were ubiquitous. 'Whatever else we mean by society,' Fraser wrote, 'doesn't it have something to do with that very un-Bowie-like idea of an obligation that precedes our responsibility to ourselves and our self-development? When it comes to morality, we precedes I. And this places considerable limits on individual self-creation.'[33]

Bowie happened to have the talent and money and looks to make himself happen; but, Fraser argued, this is no way for the rest of us to live. 'You can't escape the moral demands of a sick mother or a crying child through artistic reinvention. You can't fix the local housing problems or run the local youth club – and I repeat local deliberately – by "floating in a most peculiar way", above the fray, beyond the limitations of the boringly specific.'[34]

This is not to pick on Fraser, for there has long been a fairly widespread suspicion of Bowie when it comes to politics. Some of this is entirely fair. He was certainly no idealist, and his experience of the hippie movement had left him wary, even cynical. There was also, it must be acknowledged, an interest in Nazism; and this interest had been in danger of becoming unhealthy.

Having been intrigued by the Nazis' occultism and Heinrich Himmler's search for the Holy Grail, Bowie seemed to fall more deeply into this grim swamp, and this became evident in interviews, sometimes with cartoonish overtones, sometimes not. 'I think I might have been a bloody good Hitler,' he said in 1975. 'I'd be an excellent dictator. Very eccentric and quite mad.'[35] 'Hitler was the first rock star,' he said the following year.[36] He described his Thin White Duke character as 'a very Aryan, fascist type'.[37] 'You've got to have an extreme right front come up and sweep everything off its feet and tidy everything up. Then you can get a new form of liberalism,' he said in 1976.[38] 'I believe very strongly in fascism. The only way we can speed up the sort of liberalism that's hanging foul in the air at the moment is to speed up the progress of a right-wing, totally dictatorial tyranny and get it over as fast as possible,' he said in, again, 1976.[39] The photographer Andy Kent reportedly took a picture of Bowie giving a Nazi salute on the site of Hitler's bunker in, once again, 1976, and he was apparently detained at the border between Poland and Russia for possessing Nazi-related literature – books about Joseph Goebbels and the architect Albert Speer – in, yet again, 1976.

'That whole Station to Station tour was done under duress,' said Bowie a few years later.[40] 'I was out of my mind totally, completely crazed. Really. But the main thing I was functioning on was – as far as that whole thing about Hitler and rightism was concerned – it was mythology... This whole racist thing which came up, quite inevitably and rightly. But, and I know this sounds terribly naive, but none of that had actually occurred to me, inasmuch as I'd been working and still do work with Black musicians for the past six or seven years. And we'd all talk about it together – about the Arthurian period, about the magical side of the whole Nazi campaign, and about the mythology involved.'

'My interest... was the fact they supposedly came to England before the war to find the Holy Grail at Glastonbury,' said Bowie in 1993.[41] 'The idea that it was about putting Jews in concentration camps and the complete oppression of different races completely evaded my extraordinary fucked-up nature at that particular time.'

'I never felt David was a Nazi sympathiser,' said Andy Kent.[42] 'I'm Jewish, so if anybody would be sensitive to that and have bad feelings... I just think it was what I'd call an adolescent attraction.' Angie Bowie, who has not always been given to charitable interpretations of her ex-husband's behaviour, concurred: his interest in 'the magical side' of Nazism, she said, 'sounds like the David I knew'.[43]

Individualism, cynicism, Nazism: this is not the kind of stuff routinely associated with thoughtful spiritual seekers. But Bowie had shown a feeling for oppressed peoples as a teenager, when he took up the cause of Tibet against China; and there later came to exist in his work a politics of a different kind, more subtly subversive.[44] Alongside this were fears of despots and tyrants, and his warnings of their seductive ways. And as he gained in strength, physically and spiritually, he showed a fresh interest in day-to-day, material, socio-political concerns, expressed in explicit and concrete terms. That is to say, he had opinions about how humans lived, and he began to sing about them in clear language. The early results can be heard on his next album, *Lodger*, released in 1979.

After years of obliqueness, abstraction, ambiguity and collage, the shift is jolting. To draw a comparison with film directors, the sensibility now is more in keeping with Ken Loach than with David Lynch. In one sense, this recalls Bowie's earlier work: the lyrics on his first two albums are often direct and quotidian. But there is something new in their marriage to more forward-thinking music.

The first song, 'Fantastic Voyage', retains a veneer of poetry, a light mist of imagery; but by the time he describes things that can wipe out races, it is clear he is expressing concern about nuclear weapons. On earlier albums, Bowie might have voiced this with visions and sounds of grand apocalyptic horror; here, however, it is the heartfelt gentleness of the song that strikes a note of realism.

Another song on *Lodger* is unlike any he had previously written. It is called 'Repetition', and it is about domestic violence. It is brutal and unsparing. The words are recited bleakly, blankly; the accompaniment pummels relentlessly.

Much of the rest of *Lodger* is an artistic document of Bowie's increasingly extensive travels. The link between physical exploration and spiritual exploration has existed for millennia: journeys and pilgrimages are the very stuff of the practice and mythology of religion. It follows that a man in search of spiritual truth might travel the world to find it; and in this regard, Bowie's job gave him ample opportunity. His 1978 was dominated by his most extensive tour yet, beginning in San Diego in March and ending in Tokyo in December, with a four-month break two-thirds through. For the first time, he performed in Australia and New Zealand. As well as being evidence of his curiosity and global fame, his globetrotting gave him a greater appreciation of global politics. This would now broaden and deepen, and become more explicit in his work. 'I'm starting to get a general picture of what we possibly could be doing to look after ourselves, but I'm not entirely sure,' he told Capital Radio in 1979.[45] 'Still half in dreams, half in reality.'

Most of *Lodger* was recorded in Switzerland, but it is commonly bracketed with *Low* and *'Heroes'* as the final part of the 'Berlin trilogy'. It had the same producer, Tony Visconti, and the same collaborator, Brian Eno, and most of the same musicians. We need not dwell long here, for the songs on *Lodger* are hardly deep spiritual ruminations, and the album is perhaps more of a staging post than a destination in its own right. But below the surface, there were subtle currents that would be ridden by Bowie, taking him to new and unusual places.

In that Capital Radio interview, he was also asked about Buddhism. 'When push came to shove I realized there must be something in the West that I could adhere to, rather than something in the East — surely we must have some kind of spiritual backbone in the West,' he said. 'And I guess everything since has been some kind of search for it.'

So, Bowie was clawing himself out of the abyss, and was in the process of remaking himself. First there was new music, a music reduced to a kind of essential form; to this was added new confidence and exultation and sonic force, with a defining statement of love's victory over all that seeks to destroy it — the rifles and the barbed wire; and then a new way of engaging with the world and its people. All that was left to accomplish was a necessary reckoning with the past, and then he could move on. The 1970s, the 1960s, even the 1950s: hurl the lot into a coffin and bury the dead.

And so he did. The funeral had a catchy hymn: 'Ashes to Ashes', released as a single in August 1980. It tells us that Major Tom — remember him? — is still out there somewhere. That circuit that went dead is now live again. He's back in touch with Ground Control: he says he's happy, but he doesn't sound it. He's become an addict; he wants to come down.

Like 'Space Oddity',[46] it is shallow as a story, but deep as a song. There is a beguiling richness here, born of sublime pathos, words floating above and flowing through and submerged by music of rare subtlety and sophistication, which nevertheless invites a singalong. There are layers of vocals that even now remain a mystery.

And, again like 'Space Oddity', it is open to myriad interpretations. 'Ashes to Ashes' is the death of a dream; it is the Fall of Man; Major Tom drifts ever further into the void, having escaped physical gravity, but he is also The Man Who Fell to Earth, brought low by the vanity of mortals; he is Icarus, he is hubris; he is also literally an outcast, a victim, one to whom terrible things have been done; he is Apollo 12, he is the sequel no one asked for but everyone got anyway; he is what becomes of a forgotten infatuation. The last words he heard on Earth wished him God's love, and that love has turned out to be something worse even than hate: it has turned out to be indifference.

'Ashes to Ashes' makes no mention of God and is not an overtly spiritual work. But it is profoundly existential, and its currency is the folly of humanity. Indeed, the story is given the trappings of religiosity: its name — together with the first line of its chorus — comes from the burial service found in the *Book of Common Prayer*, the cornerstone of Anglican liturgy.

The video for 'Ashes to Ashes' now feels inseparable from the song. Something is being laid to rest. Its video is one of Bowie's most imaginative, a cavalcade of images that instantly imprint themselves on the memory: Bowie as a Pierrot on a beach with pink sea under a black sky; Bowie as himself in a cavernous padded cell; a ballerina and three funereal figures behind a smoking pyre, who are then led in procession by Pierrot, followed by a bulldozer; Bowie in astronaut kit, having apparently ejected from his spacecraft and landed in the 1950s in a domestic kitchen, which then starts to blow up; Pierrot singing in black water; Major Tom, dangling umbilically in some kind of sci-fi womb; finally, Pierrot walking back along the beach while being scolded by a woman, who may be the mother mentioned in the song. Here too is the past: Bowie was a Pierrot, a Commedia dell'arte character, in *Pierrot in Turquoise*, a cabaret piece he devised in 1967; a Pierrot is walking alongside an elderly-looking woman on the back of the eponymous album Bowie released in 1969. And the song stretches even further back: its lyrics seem heavily influenced by 'Peggy Sue Got Married', a song by Buddy Holly, released in 1959. That song, too, is a sequel; 'Ashes to Ashes' quotes some of its lines with only the merest variations.

The song reached number one in the UK in August 1980. Its parent album, *Scary Monsters (and Super Creeps)*, was released the following month. Sparking and sizzling with some of the finest art-rock musicianship of any era, it is the album to which every subsequent Bowie record would be compared. It has a sense of completion, a sense reinforced by its structure: it begins with the sound of recording tape being loaded up and ends with the sound of the tape expiring in a death rattle. Its artwork has the covers of Bowie's three most recent LPs – *Low*, *'Heroes'* and *Lodger* – presented in whitewashed form. It was not obvious at the time, but six of the album's ten songs draw from forgotten earlier works. The record is a royal parade to the reclamation yard.

Bowie had reached the point where his past could be mined, played with, joked about, painted out, recycled for material, deployed as materiel. He was no longer running from it: he had achieved mastery over it. This was neither the end of his troubles nor the end of his search, but he had faced the powers of hell and, so it appears from this vantage point, vanquished them. Like the voices in 'Subterraneans', like the lovers in 'Heroes', he had fulfilled Tillich's maxim, affirming being in spite of nonbeing. Never again would Bowie fall so far; only rarely again would he rise so high.

7

GNOSTIC

In 1945, a young peasant named Muhammad 'Ali al-Samman was digging for fertilizer in a desert in northern Egypt when he struck something unusual. It was a jar, red and ancient. Inside were books of papyrus. On their pages were written stories of angels, gods, miracles, heavenly realms, the saints; there were cryptic phrases and mysterious teachings. What they contained had the potential to spark a revolution.

It transpired that the texts were from the relatively early years of Christianity, when the religion was still inchoate, when it was a dizzying swirl of conflicting accounts and ideas. Most significantly, the texts gave a dramatic new insight into a form of Christianity so unorthodox that it was condemned as heretical. It is known as Gnosticism.

Now *Gnosticism* and *Gnostic* are broad terms which are used to describe a wide range of beliefs and writings and practices. Yet there are certain patterns of thought that are common to many of them. The term *Gnosticism* is derived from the Greek word *gnosis*, meaning 'knowledge'. This knowledge is of a special and secret kind which can be known only by relatively few; it is esoteric. This knowledge can be found by each of us. There is no need for the orthodox Church and its battalions of bishops and priests and deacons. It involves an inner quest, for Gnosticism says that the truth of God can be discovered within oneself. Orthodox Christianity and Judaism place a chasm between God and humankind – Gnosticism denies that chasm. There are similarities with Buddhism, which some scholars believe may have influenced Gnosticism via trade routes and proselytization during those early centuries of the first millennium. There is no great emphasis on sin, no need for confession; there is no established hierarchy of religious authority; there is greater equality between men and women. Gnosticism claims that the entity known by orthodox Christians as God is not the true God, but a malevolent creator, beyond which lies the true God. Gnosticism claims that the words used to describe the orthodox God are deceptive and inaccurate, and that Earth is fundamentally a bad place, a place from which to escape. A typical Gnostic may say that orthodox believers simply accept dogma and teaching as it is presented to them, whereas for the Gnostic, the truth lies in the seeking. Some of the most influential Gnostics held that humanity itself is the essence of the divine.

So, no religion, and no confession. Just God and man. And David Bowie loved it.

Bowie seemed like a new creation in 1983. There was once a David Bowie who was jittery and pale and intense, whose natural constituency was populated by outsiders and misfits, whose art was daring, who lived on the outskirts, who personified the zeitgeist and pointed to the future. Now there was a David Bowie who was healthy and tanned, who was crowned with a blond bouffant, who wanted to entertain the mainstream, whose music filled charts and airwaves and stadiums around the world, who no longer threatened anyone or anything.

He had gone three years without releasing an album, but he had gone nowhere. Since *Scary Monsters (and Super Creeps)* came out in 1980,[1] Bowie had played the title roles in *The Elephant Man* on Broadway and in the BBC's production of the Bertolt Brecht play *Baal*, for which he also recorded an album. He had shot major roles in the films *The Hunger* and *Merry Christmas, Mr. Lawrence*. He had also had a number one single, 'Under Pressure', which he recorded with Queen, and on which more later.

But now there was a change. There had been changes before, of course, yet there was something different this time. Change used to mean risk; now it meant safety. Change used to mean doing what he needed to do in search of fulfilment; now it meant doing what he needed to do in search of money. That was how it appeared, anyway. Look normal, sound normal, write hits.

Bowie has received much criticism for this over the years,[2] but not all of it has been fair. Some is founded in a basic misapprehension about him: a belief that his motives had always been purely artistic. In truth, he had often made compromises with commercial reality: his record company thought the Ziggy Stardust LP lacked a hit single, so he wrote 'Starman'; the Ziggy Stardust LP and *Young Americans* were initially envisaged as rougher and rootsier than the records that emerged; the sound of *Station to Station* was softened late in the production process to broaden its appeal. In addition, Bowie had felt exploited by his managers, and believed he deserved more than he had got. Given all he had achieved, the desire finally to cash in is understandable.

The album he released in 1983 was recorded in New York and was called *Let's Dance*. Its cover had Bowie as a boxer, topless and toned; this was a man who had been pictured on previous albums wearing a dress and resembling an extraterrestrial. He had once sung of being hardly the sort to punch grown men;[3] now, however, he looked like he could give them a decent left hook. The makeover was not all about aesthetics, though: 'David was having Elvis Presley phobia at that time,' said Richard Lord, a boxing trainer in Austin, Texas whom Bowie was seeing to help get him into shape. 'Presley had passed away on tour, and he was thinking if he didn't do some real drastic lifestyle changes, he was not going to be able to survive the rigors of the tour. So he was willing to go all out.' But not everyone was convinced by his new-found machismo: Lord remembers onlookers 'just seeing this skinny old white guy' who looked like he 'couldn't even break an egg'.[4]

The album's personnel constituted a fresh beginning. Its producer was Nile Rodgers, who had produced and played on disco smash after disco smash. But if it was the start of something new, it was also the re-emergence of something old. When Rodgers had asked Bowie how he wanted the album to sound, Bowie responded by showing him a photograph of Little Richard. Having made a series of albums dense with electronic textures, Bowie now wanted to strip it all back and return to the sound he had first fallen in love with: a rock and roll band adorned with a horn section and gallons of panache. Bowie's new lead guitarist was Stevie Ray Vaughan, then in the early stages of a career that would see him lauded as an all-time great; on *Let's Dance*, Vaughan's bluesy playing is the grit in the oyster.

The album opens in exuberant fashion with 'Modern Love'. It is unreservedly, unironically upbeat; it is bright and bold and brisk and bouncy. There is no mystery here, no strangeness, no danger; just a catchy radio-friendly song, the catchiest, radio-friendliest thing he had made. Bowie's first words are not sung but said, in an almost blasé manner, and they advertise his maturity. Then, with the utmost commitment, the singing begins. The song sounds completely different from anything he had ever recorded before, and, well, it seems to be about Gnosticism.

Bowie never explains what 'modern love' actually *is*, only what it *does*. There is the rather attractive possibility that the song might be a sequel of sorts to 'Soul Love',[5] the word *modern* here being used in the sense of something novel, detached from the past, perhaps a corruption of something ancient. The singalong call-and-response chorus, shared with some smiley backing singers, says that modern love walks beside him – remember 'Word on a Wing'? – but just carries on past.[6] Modern love offers no spiritual depth; it is good only for something as trivial as getting people to church.[7] This is terrifying, and the only appropriate response is ecstatic rebellion and the placing of trust only in God and man. He rejects confession, he rejects religion; he does not believe in this modern love.

This interpretation may strike some as a tad far-fetched, an attempt to find weight in a scrap of fluff. But the fact is that Gnosticism was on its way to becoming a major part of Bowie's spirituality. A book called *The Gnostic Gospels*, written by the historian Elaine Pagels,[8] was first published in 1979; it is not known when Bowie read it, but he certainly did, because he later included it on his list of his hundred significant books. He spoke of an abiding interest in early Christianity, before the orthodoxy of the Catholic Church prevailed, and as the years passed he began talking more openly about Gnosticism. 'For someone like myself who comes from... the Judeo-Christian upbringing, something palls with having a god who's a judge and a father and an arbiter of morals,' he said in 1996.[9] 'There's a term that the Gnostics use, which is called the God beyond God. There's a sense that one's trying to find some merit in the chaos that we perceive as our existence... the idea the early Gnostics had that there is in fact the deep, the depth, of the God beyond God, that there's something beyond that that one can't call a singular entity but something that just pervades everything – I think that's one of the major searches that I've probably made in my life.'

Gnosticism maps remarkably well on to what we know of Bowie's beliefs and predilections. The Gnostic concept of the Demiurge – the malevolent creator whom orthodox believers mistakenly call God – has a parallel in Bowie's evil Messiah figures, who purport to be something they are not, who are worshipped as something they are not, and who mask the truth. Gnosticism carries a sense of secret history, the kind of thing Bowie had lapped up since his youth.[10] Gnosticism has aspects of religion but is not itself a religion: like Bowie, it is spiritual, not religious. It is Christianity's enigmatic half-brother: like Bowie, Jesus is in there, but so too is much else. Bowie adored the hidden and the scrappy, the cultish and the eccentric and, here again, Gnosticism surely held much appeal. In interviews, Bowie evidently relished knowing things that others did not – Gnosticism loves a secret. Citing the scholar Professor

Hans Jonas, Pagels describes a 'Gnostic world view' as 'pessimism about the world combined with an attempt at self-transcendence'.[11] There are many possible dictionary definitions of David Bowie, and this could be one of them.

Some Gnostic texts celebrate God as 'Father and Mother', blending the masculine and the feminine; Bowie would doubtless approve. The seminal psychoanalyst Carl Jung thought that Gnosticism expresses 'the spontaneous, unconscious thoughts' that orthodoxy represses;[12] see also Bowie's working methods. 'Realizing the essential Self, the divine within, the gnostic laughed in joy at being released from external constraints to celebrate his identification with the divine being,' writes Pagels.[13] No wonder Bowie sounded so happy.

Pagels also draws a connection between Gnosticism and the existential Christian theology of Paul Tillich, a figure who merits closer examination. If Bowie had had a personal theologian, I think Tillich would have surely been the man. Born in a German village in 1886, he grew up first with a love of the Church – his father was a minister – to which was added a love of freedom, brought about by a move to Berlin. Tillich thought highly of philosophers such as Kierkegaard, who he said 'instigated a philosophy of existence', and Nietzsche, whom he called 'the most impressive and effective representative of what could be called a "philosophy of life"'. Tillich, who later moved to the USA and wrote the bulk of his work from 1936 to 1963, dying in 1965, identified the anxieties that beset humanity, and explored ways in which Christianity might address them.

Among Tillich's works is an essay called 'The Two Types of Philosophy of Religion'. One of these types, according to Tillich, is an idea of God that many hold and that churches sometimes proclaim: 'A man meets a stranger when he meets God. The meeting is accidental. Essentially they do not belong to each other. They may become friends on a tentative and conjectural basis. But there is no certainty about the stranger man has met. He may disappear, and only probable statements can be made about his nature.'

Tillich dislikes this idea. In the other, 'man discovers himself when he discovers God; he discovers something that is identical with himself although it transcends him infinitely, something from which he is estranged, but from which he never has been and never can be separated'. This is Tillich's preference.

Bowie talked of God as 'the deep, the depth'.[14] Tillich also suggested that the word *depth* could be used instead of the word *God*. Bowie talked of God as 'something that just pervades everything'; to Tillich, God is not *a* being, God *is* being, the very *ground of being*. For Tillich, this is not the God of conventional theism, but the God *beyond* that God.

As an undergraduate, Martin Luther King, the great American theologian and activist, studied Tillich closely. In King's dissertation, he derided Tillich's conception of God as 'little more than a sub-personal reservoir of power' and 'a pure absolute devoid of consciousness and life'. But Dr King later wrote, 'When I finally turned to a serious study of the works of Paul Tillich I became convinced that existentialism, in spite of the fact that it had become all too fashionable, had grasped certain basic truths about man and his condition that could not be permanently overlooked.'[15] Tillich held that 'sin is separation', and this inspired Dr King to argue against segregation. In 1965, he wrote of Tillich, 'His Christian existentialism gave us a system of meaning and purpose for our lives in an age when war and doubt seriously threatened all that we had come to hold dear.'[16]

'Modern Love', its chorus deriding religious orthodoxy and expounding Gnostic theology, reached number 2 in the UK charts and was a hit around the world. And it is not the only song on the album to carry a heavy meaning lightly.

The next track is 'China Girl'. Again, it sounds glossy and commercial in a way that was new for Bowie. But in this case, it is not a new song: it had already been around for six years, having originally appeared on *The Idiot*, Iggy Pop's first solo album, written with Bowie. The version on *Let's Dance* is embellished with a generic 'oriental' guitar riff and a singalong hook, but is otherwise essentially the same, albeit smoother and less threatening. What sounds initially like a soft-focus love song reveals itself to be a critique of imperialism: the singer has 'visions of swastikas' and unexplained grand plans. Why? Look at his eyes, and see the whiteness. The menace turns personal: mess with me, and I'll ruin you, little girl.

Bowie later said it was 'sort of about invasion and exploitation'.[17] By the end, that riff returns, as does that vocal hook, and all is disinfected and sanitized and sterilized, and we are back to the daytime radio playlist.

It was another masterpiece of subversion, as was its video. There are scenes of a suave Bowie singing alongside a double-bass player, as if in a cool club; there are playful smiles and larks with the apparent object of his affection, played by Geeling Ng. In a scene that got the video censored in the UK, Bowie and Ng appear to have sex amid surf lapping onto a shore. Amid these are images of barbed wire, a top-hatted imperialist who seems to have shot a young Chinese woman, and Bowie throwing Ng's bowl of rice violently into the air, before she transforms into a kind of fantasy figure and they carry on together in disquieting fashion. It was bright enough for MTV, but a dark heart beat within it.

The third track, 'Let's Dance', brings all of this together. It is a colossal work, and it originally sounded quite different from the song everyone knows. It was at first called 'Last Dance'; and when the shimmering layers of its immaculate production are stripped away, it reveals itself as a sublime affirmation of love's power against the forces of annihilation. That may sound familiar: 'Lyrically, the thing has a lot more to do with "Heroes" than it has to do with a disco lyric song,' said Bowie in 1983.[18] 'There's a desperation behind the lyric.'[19]

After an apparently straightforward and untroubled first verse, we hear of fears of a loss of grace – maybe God's grace, a theme of Hans Christian Andersen's fairytale 'The Red Shoes', to which the song alludes – and of oblivion. A few bars later, there is a vow of devotion – just say the word, and I will run with you, and hide with you. Here is a fierce love: like the lovers by the Berlin Wall, here is a couple defying death through an act of passion.

The notion of love as an almighty force appears by now to have become one of Bowie's core beliefs. It is by nature metaphysical. It would be crass to claim it for a particular religion, but it has a strong tradition at least in Judaism and Christianity: the Song of Songs, a book of the Hebrew Bible and the Christian Old Testament, asserts that 'love is strong as death, passion fierce as the grave';[20] the First Epistle of John, in the Christian New Testament, says 'there is no fear in love, but perfect love casts out fear'.[21]

Another recent song that had shared this theme was 'Under Pressure', released in 1981. It depicts a society placing unbearable strain on its people; the song's claim is that the only way to cope is through love. Love may be an old-fashioned word, so the song says, but it remains an urgent force that challenges us, that dares us to care and to change. This is our last dance.

Loving, kissing, dancing. The video for 'Let's Dance' is again feather-edged and rock-hard: the first minute or so is just fun, people dancing and mooching about in a bar in Australia, before it gives way to a story about Aboriginal Australians, who witness a mushroom cloud erupting over a mountain and then contend with exploitation, humiliation and the deadly treachery of consumerism. After all this, they dance.

Listen closely, and there is even an echo here of Nietzsche, who wrote of an onlooker saying of the prophet Zarathustra: 'Does he not go along like a dancer?' Zarathustra says: 'I should believe only in a God who understood how to dance.'[22] So maybe, after all, Bowie put it simplest and best. Come on. Let's dance.

'Let's Dance' – the album and the song – heralded a new era for Bowie and arguably for pop music itself. The ensuing tour was a breathtaking, record-breaking success, with a show in New Zealand drawing what at the time was the largest crowd by head of population anywhere in the world, and with Madonna and Prince among those who took inspiration from the concerts.

As befitted Bowie's new look and new sound, the new show was warmer and safer than any of his previous major tours. There was colourful lighting, often quite cinematic; the musicians partook of some mild choreography; Bowie would typically wear a pale suit and tie and braces, filling his outfit healthily and looking, really for the first time, like an actual superstar. Only rarely were the band abrasive; they generally sounded pleasing, even twinkly, while the horn section brought a dash of pizzazz. It was top-quality entertainment, courtesy of a showbiz A-lister.

'I was getting really pissed off for being regarded as just a freak,' he said at the time. 'I won't be trying to put on any pose or stance. You won't see Mr Iceman Cometh or weird Ziggy or whatever. I was just gonna be me, having a good time, as best I can.' The idea, as he put it, was to 're-represent' himself.[23]

It went so well that Bowie could afford to take a risk – not artistically, but financially. He extended the tour to Singapore, Bangkok and Hong Kong; he knew he would lose money, but he was desperate to see more of the Far East. For this final leg, he brought a film crew with him; the result, released the following year, was *Ricochet*.

The documentary is ostensibly a fly-on-the-wall travelogue following Bowie through a series of conversations with locals and encounters with native culture, interspersed with scripted scenes telling meagre stories. There is also a dramatic contrivance: Bowie is stalked by a shades-wearing man who looks like the embodiment of cold capitalism, impassive and blankly menacing, and whose presence sets Bowie on edge.

These staged elements could cast doubt over the authenticity of the rest. But there is a genuine sense that Bowie would be speaking to these people and visiting these places even if the cameras weren't rolling. 'He made a point of absorbing culture wherever he went,' wrote Denis O'Regan, the tour's official photographer. 'I've known headline stars who wouldn't drag themselves out of a hotel suite to cross Red Square for a glimpse of Lenin's tomb. Not David. He would put on a baseball cap and off he'd go, blending unnoticed into the crowds, disappearing for hours.'[24]

Bowie's interactions reflect concerns of his that by now will be familiar. In authoritarian Singapore, he asks a journalist if there is 'any kind of rebellion against authority'; Bowie bristles when told it has been 'contained'. He looks aghast as history is demolished to make way for soulless tower blocks. He walks alone, a picture of alienated modern man, around a desolate shopping mall; he is carried by escalators radiating neon blue; he sits disconsolately beside unlit miniature Christmas trees, soundtracked by 'Sense of Doubt', one of the bleaker instrumentals on *'Heroes'*. He seems appalled by Raffles Hotel and its colonial stylings, which is somewhat ironic given that no Englishman has ever looked more colonial than David Bowie in *Ricochet*, white blazer, panama hat and all.

And, naturally, there is evidence aplenty of spiritual curiosity. In Bangkok, he perches in a strip club which seems to have crushed his soul, when he glimpses his nemesis. He flees, eventually arriving at a Buddhist temple, where he undergoes an unexplained ritual. A local man wearing beads sips from a bowl of water, and then spits at Bowie repeatedly. This is intercut with flashes of Bowie's stalker. The implication is that this is a ritual of protection.

After all those years, it is almost heartening to see Bowie once again engaging with Buddhism – albeit in a form that is not widely practised – and he evidently still felt a need for spiritual protection. In his foreword to a book about the tour published in 1984, he wrote: 'Whenever the faces of stewardesses blanche [*sic*] grey-white with fear, and the overhead cupboards open and spill their contents, I hold my little metal Buddha tight and press the crucifix to my chest and tell myself it's just another airplane landing.'[25] It sounds trivial compared with the horrors he experienced in the mid-1970s, but when it came to flying, Bowie's fear was real: he would travel by sea when he could.

The film is named after a song on the *Let's Dance* album. In a further indication of Bowie's burgeoning social conscience, 'Ricochet' paints a somewhat desolate, if oblique, picture of the working man's life – if he can get work at all. This is framed in spiritual terms: holy pictures are turned to the wall, while the Devil breaks parole.

Bowie was also becoming an outspoken opponent of racism. Describing the videos for 'Let's Dance' and 'China Girl', he said: 'The message that they have is very simple – it's wrong to be racist!... I see no reason to fuck about with that message, you see?'[26]

And there was an occasion where he turned the tables on an interviewer for MTV.[27] 'It occurred to me, having watched MTV over the last few months,' said Bowie, 'I'm just floored by the fact that there's so few black artists featured on it. Why is that?' A series of answers came back: 'we're trying to move in that direction'; 'we have to try and do what we think not only New York and Los Angeles will appreciate but also Poughkeepsie or the Midwest', some of whose residents would be 'scared to death by Prince, who we play, or a string of other black faces'; and, black artists like the Isley Brothers and the Spinners 'mean something to me, but what does it mean to a 17-year-old?' Bowie shot back: 'Well I'll tell you what the Isley Brothers or Marvin Gaye mean to a *black* 17-year-old. And surely he's part of America as well?' 'We can't turn around and go "this is the right way" – we can only teach a little bit at a time,' said the interviewer. 'Interesting. OK,' replied a stern-faced Bowie; 'I *understand* your point of view.' Cue awkward laughter.

Challenging authority, asking questions, being suspicious of institutions, bewailing oppressive systems of power, affirming the individual: perhaps Gnosticism is an attitude as much as anything. There is no Gnostic creed as such – apart from one written by Aleister Crowley, of all people – no single holy book, no equivalent of a pope to defer to. Interest in Gnosticism has surged in the twenty-first century, in part because of Dan Brown's 2003 novel *The Da Vinci Code*, the resulting film and the various other works associated with it, which are based on some gnostically tinged intrigue. It is easy to see its appeal more generally in an age of rampant conspiracy theories; Bowie shared something of the conspiracy theorist's mentality.

In light of Muhammad 'Ali al-Samman's discovery, 'we can understand why certain creative persons throughout the ages, from Valentinus and Heracleon to Blake, Rembrandt, Dostoevsky, Tolstoy and Nietzsche, found themselves at the edges of orthodoxy,' Pagels writes in *The Gnostic Gospels*. 'All were fascinated by the figure of Christ – his birth, life, teachings, death, and resurrection; all returned constantly to Christian symbols to express their own experience. And yet they found themselves in revolt against orthodox institutions.'[28] To that list we can now add another name: Bowie.

8

DENIER

And then, the hangover. David Bowie's 1983 had been full of life and colour and adventure and success. But there came a cost. His public wanted more and his record company wanted more. The problem was that he had little left to give. There would soon come an estrangement between Bowie and his music — and it also happened to sound like an estrangement between Bowie and his God.

The period from 1984 to 1987 is widely regarded as Bowie's nadir. Bowie agreed. By the end of it, he felt like giving up. 'I thought "why bother? I've got nothing left,"' he recalled. '"That's it. I've come to the vacuum of my life."'[1]

This collapse in morale was quite sudden. He had looked untouchable in 1983, and was genuinely happy with his work. But he had unwittingly sown the seeds of his artistic destruction by exorcizing his weirdness, for this won him a new audience, and it needed to be placated. He recalled looking out from the stage one night and getting the impression that most in the audience would prefer Phil Collins to the Velvet Underground. He had chased the affection of these people — not bad people by any means, just not quite *his* people — and ended up lost.

It was as if he was looking to the wrong guide, as if his compass had been tricked, because this period also happens to coincide with him distancing himself from matters of the spirit. We can see here how crucial his questing was: when it stopped, so did much of his creativity.

In truth, there had already been signs of a well running dry. Of the eight songs on *Let's Dance*, only four had been original compositions, and only two of those would leave any mark on the world. In the three years since *Scary Monsters (and Super Creeps)* – an album which itself had drawn heavily from older material – that makes two songs of note, plus the Queen collaboration, 'Under Pressure'. In the same length of time a decade earlier, amid a spiritual maelstrom, this same man had written four whole albums, three of them outright classics.

Then there was the fact that Bowie had long struggled to write songs while on tour – and as he entered 1984, he had just spent seven months touring. The conditions for a new album therefore could hardly have been less promising. Nevertheless, product was demanded, so product was supplied. The result was *Tonight*, which was recorded in Quebec, without Nile Rodgers, in the May and June of 1984 and released in September that year.

Its cover speaks of a man who at least retained a taste for interesting art. It is inspired in part by the British art duo Gilbert & George, particularly their 1982 work 'Faith Curse'. One of their series of 'grid' paintings, it resembles a stained-glass window, with blotches of colour bursting around the head of a Christ-like statue or sculpture. On the album cover, this head is Bowie's, and it is painted blue, in an ode to Vladimir Tretchikoff's 1951 work *The Chinese Girl*, known as *The Green Lady*. The cover was designed by Mick Haggerty in consultation with Bowie, and has promise.

It transpired however that *Tonight* was, by most critical measures, his worst album yet. Bowie had an inkling of this himself: 'I feel on the whole fairly happy about my state of mind and my physical being and I guess I wanted to put my musical being in a similar staid and healthy area,' he said. 'But I'm not sure that that was a very wise thing to do.'[2]

He had written only two new songs of worth. One was 'Blue Jean', which had some verve and was likeable, if insubstantial; its long-form video, essentially an extended comic skit about himself, was one of his best efforts that decade. The other song was 'Loving the Alien', an attempt to recapture the grandeur of yore and to say something meaningful. It was at least ambitious, and it was the last conventional Bowie song of the twentieth century explicitly to examine and critique religion.

There is a degree of playfulness about the title. Even though it was 11 years since Ziggy Stardust was killed off and eight years since Bowie had played the lead in *The Man Who Fell to Earth*, there remained in the public imagination a link between Bowie and extra-terrestrial life. But the alien on this occasion was not an inhabitant of a distant planet; rather, it was a distant inhabitant of the same planet, or perhaps even a distant inhabitant of the same mind. There is a further implication that 'the alien' should be read as something like 'whatever is alien'; think of phrases like 'the lost' or 'the lonely'.

The music tries hard to establish an expansive and vaguely exotic landscape: a refrain is played on a marimba and there are thin strings. Its lyrics begin with an impressionistic account of the Crusades, medieval wars of religion instigated by Christians and supported by the Roman Catholic Church. Their aim was to 'save' Jerusalem and its surrounding area from the Muslims who had conquered it. The song's early words allude to the most famous warriors of the Crusades, the Knights Templar; the knights bear the cross of Richard the Lionheart, or *Coeur de Lion*, King Richard I of England and Duke of Normandy, who was a commander in the conflict.

One of the song's more powerful lines speaks of 'salvation for the mirror blind'. Mirror blindness is a psychological phenomenon: humans can struggle to recognize images that have been flipped horizontally, as in a mirror. And then we hear what sounds like a mocking repudiation of prayer and confession before we reach the chorus, which continues the theme. Here, prayer is shield and sword: it conceals malign intent and slashes the heavens, dividing the divine.

The second verse draws parallels between the ancient and the recent. There is Palestine — still a problem, he sings — and terror.

There is a potent image of believer and unbeliever alike hanging on the cross. The message seems to be one of bitter frustration: go on, you fools, just carry on praying and carry on in your delusions.

'Loving the Alien' is perhaps best understood as misbegotten. This does not make it bad – it's brave, the songwriting is sophisticated and the chorus sticks. But there are things about it that suggest insecure foundations and incompleteness. It seems unsure of what it is.

This much is clear from Bowie's own relationship to it. He was always unhappy with the rather damp, puffy production, which was handled by Derek Bramble and Hugh Padgham, both newcomers to the Bowie fold. 'You should hear "Loving the Alien" on demo,' Bowie said in 1989.[3] 'It's wonderful on demo. I promise you! But on the album, it's… not as wonderful.' Bowie had a chance to capture the spirit of the demo when he played the song live in 1987; however, it is fair to say it was not much more wonderful then, either.

Bowie revisited the song in 2003, for a benefit concert for Tibet House in New York. Gone were the strings, the marimba, the general indistinct sprawl of the thing; it was now just Bowie with an acoustic guitarist and a loop pedal. Bowie liked the arrangement and repeated it in subsequent concerts; he said this was 'the way it should maybe always have been done'.[4] It was arguably the most effective version, and yet something remained awry, the evident attempt at intimacy undone by the song's ungainliness.

Then there is the matter of what Bowie said about its subject. If the song failed to work out what it was, so, clearly, did the man who wrote it. 'That one was me in there dwelling on the idea of the awful shit that we've had to put up with because of the Church,' he said of the song in 1984 in an interview with Charles Shaar Murray of the *New Musical Express*. 'That's how it started out: for some reason I was very angry.'

That interview[5] is most revealing, for it shows a man seemingly keen to deny he was ever into that spiritual stuff: 'I know…

'Eyes of infinite curiosity': David Bowie aged about seven, adopting a pose that would serve him well through the decades.

The grand East Window above the altar at St Mary's Church, Bromley.

Floral tributes placed outside 4 Plaistow Grove, Bromley, Bowie's childhood home.

Bowie with his first wife Angie in 1973.

The Berlin Wall, pictured in October 1976. Bowie sang about it in 'Heroes' and Where Are We Now.

The European canon: Bowie on the Isolar tour at the Vorst Nationaal in Brussels in 1976.

Bowie on the Isolar II tour, his biggest to that point, at NHK Hall, Tokyo, in 1978.

David Bowie as Thomas Jerome Newton, stumbling through the hymn Jerusalem in *The Man Who Fell to Earth*, with Candy Clark as Mary-Lou. Jerusalem was a favourite from his days as a choirboy.

David Bowie as Pontius Pilate in the Martin Scorsese film *The Last Temptation of Christ*, 1988. Bowie invented a biography for Pilate in preparation for the role.

Above: David Bowie on the Glass Spider Tour at Festivalground, Werchter, Belgium, in 1987. Bowie later claimed to have taken the spider to a field and set it on fire.

Below: A highlight of the shows on the Glass Spider Tour was his performance of the song 'Time', which began with him high on a gantry, winged like an angel.

David Bowie and Moby on stage performing during the Tibet House Benefit Concert at Carnegie Hall in New York, 2001.

David Bowie performing at Live Aid, Wembley Stadium, 13 July 1985. Bowie dropped a song from his set in order to play a short film that was later described as 'the turn-around moment in the entire event' by its main organizer, Bob Geldof.

'Like a man of gold': David Bowie performing at the Glastonbury Festival in 2000.

'It was a magical thing': the night David Bowie prayed the Lord's Prayer at the Freddie Mercury Tribute Concert for AIDS Awareness, Wembley Stadium, April 1992.

'He said "Ivo, let's do the next one"': David Bowie's final public appearance, at the opening night of *Lazarus* at New York Theatre Workshop on 7 December 2015, with Ivo van Hove and Cristin Miloti.

'My attraction to her was immediate and all-encompassing': Bowie and his wife Iman attend the amfAR Benefit Honors Gala in February 2003 in New York City.

this [fingers the crucifix around his neck] is strictly symbolic of a terrible nagging superstition that if I didn't have it on I'd have bad luck. It isn't even religious to me – I've hardly even thought of it as a crucifix, anyway, probably because it's so little.' This may well have come as a surprise to the Bowie of 1975.

Bowie goes on to tell Murray about a book called *The Jesus Scroll*. It was written by Donovan Joyce and published in 1972, and Bowie read it in the mid-1970s. 'The conclusion of that book,' says Bowie, 'is that Jesus died at the age of 70 at Masada and wrote a scroll himself, which is currently in the hands of the Russians, who are holding it over the Catholic Church... it really stayed with me.' And then: '"Alien" came about because of the feeling that so much history is wrong... It's extraordinary considering all the mistranslations in the Bible that our lives are being navigated by this misinformation, and that so many people have died because of it, and all the power factions involved.'

The Jesus Scroll is a very different kind of book from Pagels' *The Gnostic Gospels*, which is a work of reputable scholarship (it will probably come as no surprise that *The Jesus Scroll* is not). Yet Bowie seemed at this point to treat them as equally authoritative. Since childhood, Bowie had been attracted to the fringe story and the unofficial account, to what we might now call conspiracy theories. This attraction evidently remained undimmed.

'Loving the Alien', then, is an angry song, hostile to religion and the lies it tells and the conflict it foments. At least, that was the case in 1984. By 1993, however, the song had been recast: 'What I was trying to do was set up some line of thought that surrounded the possibility of harmony between Islam and Christian peoples,' said Bowie. 'Little did I know that one day I would marry a Muslim. This must have been prophetic!'[6]

The Muslim in question was Iman Abdulmajid. A supermodel known to the world by her first name, she described the song as 'one I'm particularly fond of. It seemed to anticipate our meeting'.[7] The couple married in 1992. Iman published her autobiography in

2001, and early copies came with a CD. One of its five songs was 'Loving the Alien'. The song had been on quite a journey.[8]

Anyone seeking clarity about the meaning or intent of the song will not be helped by its video. After the rather more linear promos for 'Let's Dance' and 'China Girl', it represents a return to the style of the celebrated video for 'Ashes to Ashes': a series of apparently disparate scenes placed together in a kind of collage. But whereas 'Ashes to Ashes' still feels coherent, 'Loving the Alien' seems a jumble of tones and textures and moods. Such an approach would work were the scenes to play off each other in interesting ways, as Bowie's lyrics often did; but the result is not so much beguiling as bewildering.

We have a blue-faced Bowie in a prayerful pose jerking about in apparent anguish; we have him ostensibly performing the song in an affectedly hammy manner; we have musicians bedecked surreally; we have some postmodern exposing of artifice; we have a set constructed of stereotypically Middle Eastern architecture; we have a woman wearing a niqab forcing Bowie to behold his troubling reflection; we have a dungeon or temple, in which a deliberately smarmy Bowie plays an organ, as if entertaining the audience of an end-of-the-pier horror show; we have an industrial wasteland in which Bowie is a distracted bridegroom marrying a Muslim woman whose traditional dress is plastered with what look like dollar bills; we have Bowie gliding on his knees on the surface of water upon which petals have been scattered; we have Bowie as a Crusader; we have the Muslim bride throwing the cash at her bridegroom with contempt; we have Bowie getting a nosebleed;[9] and, as a sort of coda, we have Bowie on what looks like a sickbed, listening to the song on his headphones and being comforted by a woman who may well be the same woman seen earlier in the niqab, but now wearing modern Western clothes, before their near-kiss propels Bowie into another, terrifying dimension.

Striking as some of those images are in themselves, they all add up to remarkably little. Where all was once surefootedness and conviction even in ambiguity, now there is uncertainty, and of the least interesting kind. Above all, there is a sense of something having gone wrong.

Yet the song and video retain an odd sort of appeal. There is something in their reaching for that which they fail to grasp. There is something in their pathos, which is unintentional: the pathos of fading greatness. There is something in their straining to impress.

So maybe 'Loving the Alien' is less important than it thinks it is, but more important than it seems. Something like a coherent belief system is developing here, perhaps as follows: there is some sort of universal God that transcends the word *god*; various religions have insights into it, and can lead followers part of the way to it; but the structures of those religions are corrupting, and not of God. Remember 'mirror blindness': believers of different faiths are blinded to their fundamental similarity by their supposedly radical difference. This is how 'Loving the Alien' is both a song of anger and a song that, in Iman at least, evokes tenderness.

There is scope here for a comparison to be made between religion and the music industry, both of which left Bowie with a sense of unease. Bowie knew what music could do: he had felt its force. He had seen it fill lives and places with colour; he had used it to convey emotions that lay far beyond the province of language. He understood music as a thing of beauty and wonder and love and fearsome power. But he had also seen it debased by a priesthood of label bosses and managers and their hunger for power and wealth. His record company had been unhappy with *Low* and wanted him to make another *Young Americans*; he resolved in the late 1970s never to have another manager. To Bowie, the industry was to music what religion was to God.

Up to this point, Bowie's art had pretty much survived the rapacity of the money men. But that was now starting to change. You could say they led him into temptation: bigger crowds, bigger sales, bigger money. He followed this path, arguably to his eventual artistic ruin – though this becomes even more persuasive when one considers what happened when he made forays in other directions. It is revealing that Bowie's best work of this time came at the behest of other artists. Left to his own instincts and desires, he drifted; but when others gave him a sense of purpose, the Bowie of old sometimes shone through.

He was asked on various occasions in the 1980s to write songs for films, and he faced the task with a commitment and conviction that was often absent from his albums of that era. A year before 'Let's Dance' (the album and the single), there was 'Cat People (Putting Out Fire)', a song of suitably feline menace written with the visionary producer Giorgio Moroder as the title track of the erotic horror film *Cat People*. Bowie's first record after the generally insipid *Tonight* was 'This Is Not America', from the soundtrack to *The Falcon and the Snowman*, an American spy thriller. The track was recorded with the Pat Metheny Group, a jazz fusion band, and its lyrics had a weight and depth and delicacy that Bowie had failed to muster for his latest LP. He hit number one in September 1985 with a cover of the Motown classic 'Dancing in the Street'. Recorded with Mick Jagger to raise funds for Live Aid, it was enjoyably carefree and wildly daft.

But Bowie's next single, 'Absolute Beginners', was as good as just about anything he released that decade. The song, written for the 1986 film of the same name, channels some of the more powerful motifs and imagery from Bowie's strongest work. There are similarities with 'Heroes': musically it is vast and sweeping, but lyrically it is intimate, with an uplifting and commercially appealing chorus. There is also the now familiar idea of a couple's love transcending the world. And the chorus speaks of mountains and oceans, epic topography that recalls 'Station to Station' and 'It Ain't Easy'. The music itself is full of hope – as with 'Heroes', the short vocal lines relative to the musical phrasing give a sense of space and momentum, running here towards a golden horizon. 'Absolute Beginners' was also a bigger hit than 'Heroes' ever was, reaching number two in March 1986.

The next single was 'Underground', written for the fantasy film *Labyrinth*, in which Bowie played the alluring antagonist Jareth the Goblin King. 'Underground' is a somewhat shallower listen than one might expect, given its themes and personnel: it concerns mythologies which hold that underground is where hell is; the song's cry of 'Daddy, Daddy, get me out of here' could, in other contexts, sound chilling; the closing refrain suggests that hell might actually be preferable to an alternative; and the chorus has a gospel choir that includes Chaka Khan and Luther Vandross. But despite its lack of depth, it does its job.

'As the World Falls Down', another song from *Labyrinth*, is also worth mentioning. As a love song it sounds conventional, even cloying. But again there is the idea of love enduring and defying all, even as the world falls down.

Then came 'When the Wind Blows'. It was the title song for the animated film of the same name, based on the graphic novel by Raymond Briggs; his previous film was *The Snowman*, which was released in 1982, and for which Bowie had provided a charming spoken introduction. *When the Wind Blows* is a distressing portrayal of an elderly couple's response to the detonation of an atomic bomb and the ensuing radioactive fallout. There had long been an apocalyptic dimension to Bowie's work, and his 1979 song 'Fantastic Voyage' and the video for 'Let's Dance' were explicit in their concern about nuclear weapons. Moreover, two of his greatest songs, 'Let's Dance' and 'Heroes', had at their heart a couple who confront annihilation with love, so Bowie's involvement in *When the Wind Blows* made sense.

In 1986 he produced an Iggy Pop LP, *Blah-Blah-Blah*, the first album-length collaboration between the two since *The Idiot* and *Lust for Life* in 1977. Among the tracks on *Blah-Blah-Blah* were 'Shades', soon regarded as one of Pop's best efforts of the 1980s, and 'Real Wild Child', which became his first top ten hit in the UK.[10]

Bowie played various roles on film in the 1980s, but one feels especially relevant. He was cast as the Roman governor Pontius

Pilate in *The Last Temptation of Christ*, directed by Martin Scorsese, shot in 1987 and released in 1988. It was one of the more controversial films of the decade. Press coverage focused on a scene in which Jesus, while being crucified, briefly imagines having sex with Mary Magdalene, as part of a sequence in which he sees himself marrying her and raising a family with her.

Pilate is a key figure in Christianity, responsible for the trial of Jesus and ultimately sentencing him to death. The four Gospel writers each depict Pilate in subtly different ways, but it is John whose writings have most come to define Pilate in the popular imagination. John gives the impression that Pilate found Jesus especially compelling, asking searching question after searching question, apparently keen for Jesus to be set free, with his sense of justice ultimately being fatally compromised by ambition and fear. John has Pilate at one point asking: 'What is truth?' It is hard to think of a line more suited to Bowie.

Bowie does not say this, however, because the film differs significantly from the biblical narratives. What we have instead is a Pilate created for the film by Scorsese, by the screenwriter Paul Schrader, and by Bowie himself, who prepared for the role by making copious notes about Pilate's life.

'He mismanaged two campaigns in his rule,' Bowie scrawled. 'His father was a divorce attorney who paid little attention to him.' Pilate's need to impress his parents through his work was, Bowie wrote, 'essential'. He 'misread the Hebrew situation time and time again. At one time he brought pagan statues into Jerusalem and started a riot. He backed off.' He also, according to Bowie's notes, had a bad relationship with his wife, used Roman soldiers to suppress a revolt, had problems with deafness in his right ear caused by a molar tooth problem and heard voices in his head as he aged.[11]

All this was doubtless helpful in informing Bowie's performance. But it was also all made up. Very little is known about Pilate's life, so Bowie went to the effort of concocting a biography, which shows how seriously he took the role.

Uneven as they may be, these assorted works show a Bowie who sounded as though he was at least on speaking terms with his core creative impulses, a Bowie whose work could still be fired by his interest in the world and the spirit. The inspiration of other figures and the desire to repay their faith brought out something good in him. The problem was that his next album would be written by David Bowie for David Bowie; and David Bowie was lost.

The record came out in 1987 and was called *Never Let Me Down*. He had already committed himself to a major world tour, and made the record with that in mind, writing songs he thought would sound good when played live by a small band. In an interview for *i-D* magazine headlined 'Is The Lad Too Sane For His Own Good?' the journalist Tricia Jones asked him about his apparent desire to embrace the mainstream. He replied: 'I don't think that I've actually strayed any closer to the mainstream, I just think that nowadays my music is the mainstream; it has become the mainstream... The stuff that I'm doing on the new album isn't so very different melodically or musically inherently from *Aladdin Sane* or the harder rocking stuff on the *"Heroes"* album or *Scary Monsters*... I don't think this one was intended to be inherently commercial. Otherwise I'd have been doing another *Let's Dance*.'

It seemed like he was already trying to distance himself from the artist he had become and remind the world of the artist he once was. In the same interview, he said the album he most regretted was *Tonight*. Indeed, the songwriting credits for *Never Let Me Down* suggested some creative rejuvenation: of its 11 tracks, only one was a cover, and nine were written by Bowie alone, more than he had mustered for *Let's Dance* and *Tonight* combined. The signs were promising.

There is more verve in the first 30 seconds of *Never Let Me Down* than in 30 minutes of *Tonight*; the rest of that opening song, 'Day-In Day-Out', passes by generally without embarrassment. The second song, 'Time Will Crawl', is robust and thoughtful and urgent, catchy hooks framing disturbing scenes articulating Bowie's fears of nuclear calamity; in an oblique tirade against authority, he sings: 'I could not take on the church.' For much of the remainder, however, one is left wondering quite what has happened to David Bowie, whether it is even the same David Bowie who made all those albums in the 1970s. His personal life certainly looked like someone else's by then: he was living in Switzerland and spent much of his spare time skiing.

Now, it is a while since God has been mentioned. It is not as if Bowie's lyrics or music had become entirely meaningless: indeed, *Never Let Me Down* is concerned with social issues to an extent hitherto unknown on a Bowie album. But there is little of any spiritual weight or heft: bar a few minutes here and there, it is dreadfully thin.

The song 'Glass Spider' is the closest the record comes to mystery. The desperate seriousness of its spoken introduction is hard to listen to with a straight face, but the rest of the song carries tension and drama, and not only through references to heaven and hell. There is a refrain of anguish, a cry to a mother who has long gone. Yet such moments are rare – the general impression is that God has scarpered, and taken the old David Bowie with him.

Matters are not helped by the album cover. Bowie had a gift for devising artwork that reflected the music contained within: sadly, on this occasion, it was all too accurate. Bowie is there, but only just, a weirdly small figure trying to attract attention by leaping towards the viewer: the camera catches him mid-jump, but there is no real sense of movement, more a kind of animated inertia, a suspension. His hair is all wrong, distracting from his face. The image is cluttered with props that refer thunkingly to some of the album's lyrics: one of the songs mentions clouds that are like candyfloss, and lo, there is a cloud of candyfloss. It looks like a scene from a small and bad circus.

Never Let Me Down had an accompanying tour, and it is difficult and arguably misleading to treat the two as discrete artefacts, for the one would not exist without the other. The tour was named after the song 'Glass Spider'; like the album, it was conceived as a break from his recent commercial past and a return to what had inspired him at his artistic peak.

Bowie had long wanted to stage a musical, and this was as close as he had yet come. His band were joined by a troupe of urban dancers, who attempted to convey some of that stylized outlaw menace with which Bowie was besotted. There were snatches of elliptical dialogue. It was a multimedia spectacle of the kind Bowie envisaged for some of his Ziggy shows and the Diamond Dogs tour. It was his first overtly theatrical performance since the 1970s, with a scale and ambition and bravery that had been absent for a decade.

It is now remembered as the lowest point of Bowie's career as a live performer. Some of the criticism it has received is doubtless unfair, and it inspired future large-scale shows by other artists, most obviously U2. But, reflecting on it in 1997, Bowie said: 'Individually there were some incredibly good ideas on that stage. And in a small environment, it really worked well – when your nose is pressed against it all, it's like a wonderworld. But when you're a thousand rows back, it just becomes this huge mass of confusion. None of it makes any sense. And that was a really bad mistake. I was designing on an intimate level. I was too thick to realize that it wouldn't translate. I soon found out.'[12]

The show had its merits. Tellingly, its most effective moment came when it embraced the spiritual and arcane: in his performance of the 1973 song 'Time', Bowie began on high, as a louche angel, before he plummeted earthwards, whereupon he adopted the pose of The Hanged Man figure from tarot. But this showed only what was absent elsewhere. There lacked a core, a fundamental purpose, anything that might hold it together. It was spinning apart, and Bowie was miserable. The set was dominated by an enormous structure shaped like a spider; Bowie later claimed to have taken the spider to a field and set it on fire.

And then some strange things happened to *Never Let Me Down*, which Bowie came to regard as his worst album. The first was that he deleted one of its songs, 'Too Dizzy', from future reissues; it remains unavailable through official Bowie channels. It is the only solo song of his to have suffered such a fate, and the reason has never been made clear. It may be connected to the lyric, written from the perspective of a violently jealous lover; or to its co-writer Erdal Kızılçay, with whom Bowie appears to have had a complicated relationship, Kızılçay later becoming one of vanishingly few collaborators to criticize him; or to misgivings over the song's quality.

The second odd thing was that Bowie asked for the album to be re-recorded. He had at times spoken of his enduring belief in the songs themselves, regretting more their arrangement and production. But he would not live to see his wish fulfilled: the album was re-recorded only after his death, by some of his most trusted musicians, and still using Bowie's voice. The result was released in 2018, and while it is a significant improvement on the original, it remains rather jumbled and confused, incoherent and incohesive, suggesting that something is awry at the level of the soul. The void remains unfilled.

And another curious thing: Bowie later named it alongside *Station to Station* as one of his 'drug albums'.[13] What he meant by this is unclear, and it certainly contrasts with his public image at the time. He was, however, drinking to an extent that was evidently troubling him. Before long, he swore off alcohol.

Drugs or no drugs, there is no doubt that he was in the midst of a crisis. Discussing this period in 1997, he said: 'I felt I was destroying everything that I thought worthwhile in my work and I felt really disappointed in myself. I thought I was letting myself down and letting my work down. I would have quit. I would have gone back to just immersing myself in the visual arts. It seemed at one time a real easy decision. Here I was making lots of money, performing to these huge audiences, and thoroughly uncomfortable and unhappy with life.'[14]

There is a sin called *selling out*. The phrase suggests an unholy transaction – relinquishing one's artistic soul in return for commercial riches. Bowie stood accused of this in the 1980s. But this is not entirely fair.

Consider Live Aid in 1985. Queen's performance has become the stuff of rock legend, but Bowie's was significant in its own way. He was due to play five songs; he played only four. He dropped the fifth because he wanted a short film to be shown instead. The film had moved him profoundly when he had seen it the previous day. It showed scenes of the immense suffering in Ethiopia; the soundtrack was 'Drive', by The Cars. 'Let us not forget why we are here,' Bowie told the crowd. 'People are still starving.'

'That tape was the turn-around moment in the entire event,' said its organizer, Bob Geldof. Immediately after the film was broadcast, Live Aid received a surge in donations.

But a short film of his own made a different kind of impression when it was released. The song 'Day-In Day-Out' has a kind of feelgood eighties zappiness to the sound, but the subject matter is altogether more weighty, telling of a poverty-stricken woman who falls into sex work and drug addiction. The video is perhaps Bowie's most effective foray into social commentary. It depicts the woman's plight unsparingly, and drew most of its extras from a charity supporting homeless people. It was all too much for various broadcasters around the world, including the BBC, which refused to broadcast even a diluted version.

So there remained a heart there, a desire to make a difference, to use the fame he had acquired for the good of the wider world. Yet, however noble all this was, this was not the kind of art that had made Bowie famous. There was the sense even in 1987 that Bowie knew he was straying into territory that he would never make his own. 'I'm not consciously prolific in terms of didactic statements,' he said. 'I would leave that very much to the Clash kind of band, or Dylan, or the way that Lennon would work with his songs. My things tend far more towards an impressionistic, almost surrealistic approach to a statement.' He later expressed this more succinctly: 'It wasn't so much about how I felt about things, but rather how things around me felt.'[15]

There is a quiet tragedy to Bowie's interviews in 1987, a keenness to remind the world of his old great daring adventures, making out that he was setting forth on another, because this time would be different from the last time, and different from the time before that. But he was kidding everyone – maybe even, on occasion, himself.

Denial can take many forms. 'I tried hard to feel OK with it all but it was obvious to me that it was all going incredibly wrong,' he said later.[16] The denial here was that it was possible to feel OK with it. Only when he stopped trying to feel OK with it did his recovery begin.

Bowie's sole public performance of 1988 took place at the Dominion Theatre in London at a benefit concert for the Institute of Contemporary Arts (ICA). It was a relatively low-profile affair and the best thing he had done for years: a sharp, theatrical performance with blazing music and explosive dance. Artistically, he seemed to know this is where he should be, but as had so often been the case, he was helped there by others.

One of those who helped him was an American, Reeves Gabrels. Bowie met him via the Glass Spider tour; Gabrels's then-wife Sara Terry had been its publicist. Gabrels would play a key role in Bowie's creative revival: first personally, by talking him out of his dejection through directness and humour; and then musically, by being the guitarist of Bowie's dreams, summoning chaos, squall and even, when the occasion demanded it, melody.

At the ICA benefit concert, Gabrels played guitar, and Bowie danced on stage with Louise Lecavalier and Édouard Lock from La La La Human Steps, an avant-garde Canadian company with a taste for blending elegance with aggression. Together, they mesmerized and thrilled. There is a dimension in which this is the Bowie who saw out the eighties and saw in the nineties: sharp, sleek, edgy, contemporary, daring, genuinely cool, arguably for the first time since 1980.

But that is not the dimension in which we find ourselves, because Bowie and Gabrels ended up forming a band, Tin Machine. Their drummer was Hunt Sales and their bassist was his brother, Tony Fox Sales; they had played with Bowie on the Iggy Pop album *Lust for Life* and its ensuing tour in 1977. The pair were no-nonsense, old-school, bluesy rockers, brash and crude, and in theory the ideal foil for the more cerebral and artsy Bowie and Gabrels.

Tin Machine tend these days to be written out of the official Bowie story.[17] Bowie was at pains to assert they were a proper, bona fide band, rather than the latest method by which he could project his vanity. Whenever he was interviewed and photographed, he would be with his bandmates, and when not engaging in laddy banter they would all speak unceasingly of their collaborative and democratic approach to making music. The extent to which Tin Machine reflected Bowie's own artistic impulses is therefore debatable, but their role in his rehabilitation is unquestionable.

Tin Machine, the band and the project more widely, gave Bowie permission not merely to peer into the abyss but to jump right in. Unconcerned with keeping stadiums full and record labels happy, he had a new kind of freedom. There had been something lacking from Bowie for years; now, he was confronting that lack.

Sometimes, the result would be fury, as heard on the song 'Tin Machine', from the band's self-titled debut album, released in 1989. In a full-on gruff south London accent not heard for years, to a rowdy and booming backing, he reels off a litany of his hates: alcohol, wife-beaters, preachers, Tories. This leads to a crushing admission of artistic struggle: he once sang of quietly sitting and waiting for sound and vision, but here he is enraged, 'burning in my room,' berating himself. There was a time when inspiration came as a gift; now it taunts him, and he sweats and strains for it, growling and grimacing.

And a few tracks later, there comes a breakthrough. The song, 'I Can't Read', is a portrait of spiritual and creative impotence. In the verses, backed by a musical thoughtfulness that was unusual for Tin Machine, Bowie sings blankly of money, bodies, hell, aimless television-watching. In the chorus, the singer is in a place of emptiness and desperation, sitting back, ignoring, failing. The lyrics are 'I can't read shit anymore', but they sound like 'I can't reach it anymore.' Reaching, striving, grasping, touching: this has been the stuff of his quest. This man knows he has become pitifully detached.

And as is so often true with Bowie, the lyrics tell only part of the story. So much of the song's meaning is in the music. Its verses are in the chilly key of E minor, the tune spanning only four semitones. Yet its chorus breaks into a battered but expansive and welcoming C major: the second time he sings it he sounds elated, liberated. The moment the depths are plumbed, the heights are scaled. In defeat, victory. The song rattles and wails out, back to E minor, and Bowie howls in catharsis. 'I Can't Read' was by some distance Bowie's favourite Tin Machine song, and no wonder: it is the point where his story turns.

There is a truth here known to Buddhism and Christianity: that enlightenment – or salvation – requires an unsparing honesty about ourselves and our failings. Living in denial is spiritual death. Bowie had tried to tell himself he was happy and tried to tell others that he was happy; he had claimed that his crucifix had meant nothing to him; having once sung his own prayer, he now sang *against* prayer. He was in denial about his music and evidently in denial about the vital importance of spirituality to his creativity, which is why he was led astray by false gods.

Finally, the denier finds the wisdom to cease this denial. Now is the time for acceptance. Bashed and bruised, he acknowledges he can no longer reach it. And at that moment, he does.

9

HOLY MAN/SHAMAN

The comeback was swift and momentous. God's comeback, that is. He returned in a big way to David Bowie's life and work in the 1990s, coinciding with a period of creative invention and exploration for Bowie that had far more in keeping with the 1970s than it did with the 1980s. And just like the old days, there was a careering around, all ricochets and slingshots, from the conventional to the unconventional. He went from something that looked like Christianity to adventures in paganism via a dash of Buddhism before landing pretty much back where he had started. 'I'm not sure if I'm a closet shaman or a closet holy man,' he said, as he hurtled through the decade.[1]

What changed? one may ask. Well, everything. In 1990, Bowie was lonely; his hairdresser noticed, and invited him to a party. His hairdresser also invited Iman, and this is where they met for the first time. 'My attraction to her was immediate and all-encompassing,' Bowie said.[2] 'That she would be my wife, in my head, was a done deal. I'd never gone after anything in my life with such passion... I just knew she was the one.'

Related to this, at some point in the early 1990s, Bowie stopped drinking. He later gave an insight into the ruinous effects of his alcoholism; when asked in 1999 if he might drink as little as a glass of wine, Bowie replied: 'No. It would kill me. I'm an alcoholic, so it would be the kiss of death for me to start drinking again. My relationships with my friends, my family, everybody around me are so good and have been for so many years now, I wouldn't do anything to destroy that again. It's very hard to have relationships when you're doing drugs and drinking. For me, personally, anyway. You become closed off, unreceptive, insensitive... and I was very lucky that I found my way out of that.'[3]

Bowie had attended Alcoholics Anonymous, whose meetings typically end with the 'Serenity Prayer', the origins of which date back to the 1930s, and which is credited to the Protestant theologian Reinhold Niebuhr.[4] It reads, 'God, grant me the serenity to accept the things I cannot change, the courage to change the things I can, and the wisdom to know the difference.' Bowie had a Japanese variation of this prayer tattooed on his left calf in 1991, along with an image of a dolphin, a reference to one of his favourite books, *A Grave for a Dolphin*, written by Alberto Denti di Pirajno and published in 1956. Bowie summed it up: 'A young European traveller finds himself stranded in an African village situated near the sea. By day he befriends a dolphin, and at night falls in love with a beautiful but elusive girl who, he presumes, comes from the village. In short, the girl disappears one night and the next morning he finds the dolphin has dragged itself across the sand and up to his hut to peacefully die.' The mention of a dolphin in 'Heroes' is inspired by the story. Bowie said the tattoo was a confirmation of his love for Iman and his 'knowledge of the power of life itself'.[5]

Amid all of this, Bowie the artist was showing signs of life, albeit unsteadily. In 1990, he went on a solo world tour. The premise was that he would sing all his famous songs, but for the last time. The public helped choose the setlist by voting via telephone.

The resulting tour, named Sound+Vision, succeeded only partially. It looked good, a world away from the clutter of the Glass Spider shows: along with concerts years earlier by Kate Bush, it pioneered the use of large-scale projection, a seemingly ubiquitous feature of performance today; and there was a return to stark lighting, with Bowie looking like a slightly more flamboyant version of the Thin White Duke. But it often sounded weak, Bowie's small band at times underpowered. Bowie's mood worsened, too; he grew chippy in interviews and his voice struggled, leading to at least one uncharacteristic display of frustration as he flung his guitar off the stage.

Bowie was also still a quarter of Tin Machine. Their second album, *Tin Machine II*, came out in 1991, to little acclaim; their second tour ran from October 1991 to February 1992 and was troubled in its own way. The band were by then well aware of their detractors, and affected to face the opprobrium with defiance: the tour was called the It's My Life tour and the band wore T-shirts bearing the words 'Fuck you, I'm in Tin Machine.' If Bowie had been in danger of becoming another stadium-filling crowd-pleaser a few years earlier, now he and his band seemed intent on repelling, displaying antagonism and confrontation as they played intense gigs in tight and sweaty rooms. The outcome was understandably divisive, doubtless to the relish of the band members, but it was the release of a live album in July 1992 that would finish them. It laboured under the name *Oy Vey, Baby* – an attempted play on *Achtung Baby*, the title of U2's album from 1991 – and failed even to chart, a fate that had never befallen any Bowie album. *Melody Maker* said of Bowie in relation to his part in it: 'This is the moment where finally, categorically and, let's face it, lumpily, he ceases to exist as an artist of any worth whatsoever.' There were strong rumours of hard drug use by Hunt Sales, too: speaking years later, Bowie said only that 'personal problems within the band became the reason for its demise. It's not for me to talk about them, but it became physically impossible for us to carry on.'[6]

So although the last Tin Machine record came out that summer, Bowie was in truth a solo act once again by that spring. His first performance in this new era was at The Freddie Mercury Tribute Concert for AIDS Awareness, held at Wembley Stadium on 20 April. Mercury, with whom Bowie had duetted on 'Under Pressure' in 1981, had died in November 1991 from an AIDS-related illness.

Bowie's set was going well. It was his first show on that scale since 1987, but he looked comfortable, a radiant and triumphant figure in a lime suit, in front of 72,000 in the stadium and hundreds of millions watching on television. He sang with bravura a version of 'Under Pressure' with Annie Lennox; he had brought Mick Ronson on stage to join him for only the second time since that last Ziggy show; he had roused the crowd with a skyscraping 'Heroes'.

Seven years earlier at Live Aid, Bowie had broken the celebratory atmosphere to play a film showing distressing scenes from the Ethiopian famine. Now, coming out of 'Heroes', Bowie again returned to the purpose of the concert, paying tribute to those 'that have been toppled by this relentless disease'. Looking straight at the camera, he continued: 'I'd particularly like to extend my wishes to friend Craig – I know you're watching, Craig – and I'd like to offer something in a very simple fashion that's the most direct way that I can think of doing it.'

Then Bowie did something outrageous. He fell to his knees; and then he said the Lord's Prayer.

'I had no idea whether I was going to carry it out or not until that break at the end of the song, then whoosh... I was down,' said Bowie years later. 'I felt as if I were being transported by the situation and that I no longer had any control. In hindsight, it was so alien a gesture within the context of rock, it remains a favourite personal rock "moment" for me. It was astounding to find I could complete the prayer in front of so many thousands of people without hearing a pin drop. It was a magical thing. I was so scared as I was doing it, I could feel the jaw-dropping quotient fill the stadium.'[7]

The prayer dominated media coverage of the concert. The response was predominantly one of surprise: 'It was one of the most unexpected gestures of the evening,' began a piece by a press agency that was published in newspapers across the UK. Elsewhere, there were cringes: 'By common consent at least in the *Whitstable Times* office the most embarrassing moment in the otherwise magnificent televised concert tribute to Freddie Mercury on Monday was when David Bowie got down on hands and knees to say the Lord's Prayer.' The *Daily Mirror* ran an opinion piece headlined 'The danger in Bowie's prayer', arguing that the 'cosy, glossy, star-filled hype of the concert' obscured the harrowing reality of AIDS.

Readers had their say, too. The Irish newspaper *The Sunday World* published a letter from a Mr P. Ryan of Dublin, who wrote: 'I felt absolutely embarrassed when I beheld David Bowie dropping to his knees at the Wembley AIDS gig and reciting the Lord's Prayer. Why do these stars have to use religion as part of their act? When was David Bowie last inside a church?' The curious truth – and Mr Ryan could be forgiven for not knowing this – was that David Bowie was getting just about as holy as a British rock star ever would.

Two days after the Wembley concert, Bowie married Iman in a private civil affair in Switzerland. They held a more godly wedding a few weeks later in Florence, at St James Episcopal Church. Bowie contrasted the two ceremonies: 'We did all the bureaucracy and all the paper signing but we didn't really feel married. I know the forms were signed, but at the back of our minds our real marriage, sanctified by God, had to happen in a church in Florence.'[8]

There is an American branch of Anglicanism called the Episcopal Church. It is this to which St James in Florence belongs. Its forms of worship would be recognizable to anyone familiar with fairly traditional Church of England services: orderly, dignified, robed clergy, robed choir, organ, hymns, a friendly formality. Bowie wrote the music for the wedding himself.

'I knew he would get married in a church because he told me all about this beautiful church in Florence he liked,' remembers George Underwood. St James Episcopal was designed by an English architect, was completed around 1908 and has an interior that resembles, of all places, St Mary's Church in Bromley.

Bowie asked Geoff MacCormack, his lifelong friend, sometime musical collaborator and fellow former St Mary's choirboy, to give a reading at the wedding. He read Psalm 121:

I will lift up mine eyes unto the hills; from whence cometh my help?
My help cometh from the Lord, which made heaven and earth.

*He will not suffer thy foot to be moved: he that keepeth thee will
not slumber.
Behold, he that keepeth Israel shall neither slumber nor sleep.
The Lord is thy keeper: the Lord is thy shade upon thy right hand.
The sun shall not smite thee by day, nor the moon by night.
The Lord shall preserve thee from all evil: he shall preserve thy soul.
The Lord shall preserve thy going out and thy coming in from this time
forth, and even for evermore.*[9]

The reason for this choice of psalm has never been disclosed. But it gives a promise of protection, which brings to mind all those torments and balms of times past.

The wedding was plainly an occasion of seismic importance in the life and work of David Bowie. From then on, he gave the appearance of living not for his career, or for his art, or even for his own survival, but for his family. In 1995, the journalist Simon Witter asked him what event or achievement convinced Bowie that he had made it. 'Marrying my wife,' replied Bowie. But as a musician? 'Nothing else counts.'[10]

His love for Iman was palpable. And Bowie was becoming ever more vocal about his faith, too. 'God plays a very important part in my life. I look to him a lot and he is the cornerstone of my existence – even more as I get older,' said Bowie the day after his Florence wedding. He added, in terms familiar from 'Modern Love': 'But it is a one-to-one relationship with God. I believe man develops a relationship with his own God.'[11]

He told *Rolling Stone*: 'I've never bought in to any organised religion. But now I have an unshakeable belief in God. I put my life into his hands every single day. I pray every morning.' He saw the Lord's Prayer as a 'universal prayer': 'It's a prayer about our Father, not so much about Christ.'[12]

In an interview with Tony Parsons for the magazine *Arena*,[13] Bowie said: 'In rock music, especially in the performance arena, there is no room for prayer, but I think that so many of the songs people write are prayers. A lot of my songs seem to be prayers for unity within myself. On a personal level, I have an undying belief in God's existence. For me it is unquestionable... Looking at what I have done in my life, in retrospect so much of what I thought was adventurism was searching for my tenuous connection with God.'

He was also open with Parsons about what he believed were the spiritual forces at work during those dark days: 'I was always investigating, always looking into why religions worked and what it was people found in them. And I was always fluctuating from one set of beliefs to another until a very low point in the mid-seventies where I developed a fascination with black magic. And although I'm sure there was a satanic lead pulling me towards it, it wasn't a search for evil. It was in the hope that the signs might lead me somewhere. There seemed to be a path inherent in Kabbalistic religion. There seemed to be a path that one could follow. And of course it helped greatly that it was all so drug-induced. That really helped to blur the sense of reality of what I was getting involved in.

'I felt totally, absolutely alone. And I probably was alone because I pretty much had abandoned God.' He seemed determined never to repeat that mistake.

Having kicked booze, kicked Tin Machine, found Iman and rediscovered God, it was time for Bowie the artist to remake himself, again. And just as he had a decade ago, he turned to Nile Rodgers. There was a certain irony here: Rodgers was instrumental in creating the mainstream superstar version of Bowie that Tin Machine had set out to destroy. The first result of the reunion was relatively low-key: the snappy but inessential title song 'Real Cool World' from the film *Cool World*. But Bowie and Rodgers continued working, and the result was Bowie's comeback album, *Black Tie White Noise*.

In 1993, the tides of culture were turning, in the UK at least. And something unexpected happened: Bowie became cool again, cited as an inspiration by a new generation of British bands. Foremost among them were Suede. They were proclaimed widely as saviours of British guitar music, and barely a paragraph could be written about them without referring to their love of Bowie. It forced something of a rehabilitation for the long-derided fortysomething Bowie: the *NME*, which had been among his more biting critics, now put him on the front cover with Suede's frontman, Brett Anderson. Bowie later likened it to 'passing on the baton'.

In *Rolling Stone*, David Sinclair wrote: 'The joke in London media circles is that Suede is really just an invention of Bowie's record company, the band's mission to pave the way for Bowie to make a suitably spectacular comeback.'[14] Suede's self-titled debut album was released on 29 March 1993 and went straight to number one. It was dislodged the following week by *Black Tie White Noise*.

The name reflected an abiding desire of Bowie's to combine, to merge, to synthesize: to fuse disparate elements and thus create something new. Now he was applying this practice to his life. 'The underlying thread of *Black Tie White Noise* tried to unify a sort of passion and the spiritual font from which it flowed: the wedding thing,' said Bowie in 1994.[15]

The album involves wedding after wedding. The first track is called 'The Wedding': it begins with a peal of wedding bells in traditional fashion, to which are soon wedded sounds from other times and places – synths, beats and Bowie's saxophone breaking the constraints of conventional melody with Arabian-tinged blasts of expressive energy. Many songs on the record involve similar clashes of cultures: an infectious pop track, 'Miracle Goodnight', is intruded upon by a burst of Bach-like organ; that saxophone is deployed here and there to season pretty rudimentary fare with surprising flavours.

The most explicit case of this marriage of ideas is the title track. A week after their official marriage, Bowie and Iman flew to Los Angeles, and that night, riots erupted. The spark was the acquittal of four white police officers who had been accused of brutally beating a black man. 'The one thing that sprang into our minds was that it felt more like a prison riot than anything else,' said Bowie, who duets on the song with the R&B singer Al B. Sure! 'It felt as if innocent inmates of some vast prison were trying to break out, break free from their bonds.'[16]

Black Tie White Noise was the first true Bowie album of the CD age, and it feels like it. The format meant albums could be longer and less disciplined, but two standout tracks show Bowie at his focused best.

One is 'Jump They Say', a jerky, nervy, yet brilliantly polished hit single, aided by one of his strongest videos. It is inspired in part by Bowie's beloved half-brother, Terry Burns, who had taken his own life in 1985. But there is a spiritual element too. Bowie said it is 'connected to my feeling that sometimes I've jumped metaphysically into the unknown and wondering whether I really believed there was something out there to support me, whatever you wanna call it; a God or a life-force?'[17]

And there may be a further influence. Since the mid-1970s, Bowie had hoped to make a film based on a novel called *Miraclejack*, by Michael Baldwin. It was published in 1963, and tells of a Christian preacher known as the Miraclejack who scales immense buildings to demonstrate and manifest his faith. The book quotes a passage from the gospels in which the Devil takes Jesus up to the pinnacle of a temple, and dares him to jump off. The novel is narrated by a drink-sodden news reporter, a cynic who nevertheless finds the Miraclejack captivating, whose thoughts are suffused with biblical references, who draws parallels between climbing towards the sky and reaching up to heaven. There is a third major character, the crowd, a mass of indistinct humanity that gathers to witness and remark upon the feats of the Miraclejack – a man who, like the protagonist of 'Jump They Say', is said at one point to have no mouth. A story of faith, doubt, individual heroism, media manipulation, transcendence and the tension between commercial pressures and personal integrity – Bowie never made the film, but you can see why he wanted to.

The other is 'Pallas Athena'. The Bowie of the 1970s had sought to bring a conventionally European melodic sensibility to R&B; the Bowie of the 1990s sought to do the same with house music, and the result was one of his most effective tracks of the decade.

The music starts off sleek and crisp, becoming hypnotic and mysterious and maybe even menacing: relentless beats, minor-key synths, smoky trumpets, eerily-layered vocals. The lyrics are few but weighty. Bowie, sounding like a Pentecostal preacher, places God above everything, or in control of everything, on top. He is later joined by massed voices chanting beneath him, over and over again; piece it together, and it transpires they are all praying. The song takes its name from the Greek goddess of wisdom and warfare; it is not a gushing profession of faith, and the God in question sounds as much an object of fear as one of love or hope.

The album ends with 'The Wedding Song', which revisits the opening track and gives it words. These depict the unifying of the divine and the human in love: all is heaven and saints and angels, and a woman dressed for marriage. It is hardly original to describe one's love in angelic terms – Bowie himself had been doing so for decades – but it does at least reinforce a major theme of the album. Then, once again, the wedding bells ring.

The album's cover is similarly direct. On *Never Let Me Down*, Bowie's image was lost in a garish jumble. This time, you couldn't miss him: the cover was his face. No illustration, no gesture, no evocative or abstruse references – just a photograph of his face, the colour cooled to bring out the blue of his eyes. He had learned a flattering pose when very young: a little turn of the head to the right, down and tilted slightly, so the left eye is higher than the right. He adopted this in various pictures taken from the late 1950s to the early 1960s. He's doing that again here, as downright confident as he had ever looked, curiosity burning in that gaze as beguilingly as it had done long before. The message is: I'm back.

One overcast autumn day in 1993 David Bowie found himself in the middle of St Matthew's Drive, Bromley. He was wandering about alongside its bungalows and ornamental birdbaths and modest attempts at topiary. A year earlier, his wedding had been the subject of a 23-page feature in *Hello!* magazine, and at that time he was glossy, aglow, a full-blown A-list celebrity product: even his teeth, once endearingly tarred and misaligned, looked properly Hollywood. Now, the rock god swanned about these little rockeries.

Bowie had been a cosmopolitan man of the world for the best part of two decades. There had been LA and Berlin; from the late seventies onwards he flitted around various locales, including New York and the Caribbean island of Mustique, with Switzerland being the closest he had to a settled home. Any connection with Bromley felt long forgotten, but now Bowie the artist had returned — and here he was, returning.

Bromley has other famous sons and daughters besides Bowie, many with a similarly subversive spirit. One of them is the visionary science-fiction writer H. G. Wells,[18] among whose works are *The War of the Worlds* and *The Time Machine*. Others with connections to Bromley include various musicians who emerged during the late 1970s: Steven Severin of Siouxsie and the Banshees, Poly Styrene of X-Ray Spex and Billy Idol of Generation X formed part of what *Melody Maker* called the Bromley Contingent, who helped popularize punk music and fashion.

The writer Hanif Kureishi is also from Bromley. He interviewed Bowie for a magazine article in February 1993. It so happened that the BBC was at the time working on an adaptation of Kureishi's greatly acclaimed novel *The Buddha of Suburbia*. Kureishi took the opportunity to seek permission to use Bowie's songs from the seventies, in keeping with the setting of the series. 'I thought you were never going to ask,' said Bowie. But Bowie misinterpreted the request, and thought he was being asked to write a new soundtrack. So he did.

The Buddha of Suburbia, loosely autobiographical, has certain parallels with Bowie's own life. The story is set in south London, and follows a teenager through mysticism, music and sex. Its title alone mentions two formative influences on Bowie. He wrote varied instrumental pieces for the production and also composed the title track, his most confident and accomplished exercise in traditional songwriting and performance since 'Absolute Beginners'. Unusually for him, it made direct lyrical and music references to his past – the first words are 'Living in lies by the railway line', an apparent nod to Plaistow Grove – and his stroll down St Matthew's Drive was captured for its video. Bowie's work for the series was nominated for a BAFTA Award.

But then Bowie did something of pleasing artistic adventurism and charming commercial naivety. He went back into the studio with the multi-instrumentalist Erdal Kızılçay and producer David Richards and completely reworked the music. Employing experimental methods he had used with Brian Eno in the 1970s, he made an entirely new album: what started as slight instrumentals became substantial pieces.

The resulting record was released in November 1993. It was called *The Buddha of Suburbia* and was labelled as a soundtrack, despite not being a soundtrack and despite having only a tangential relationship to Kureishi's *The Buddha of Suburbia*. Bowie's name appeared on the cover, but was barely noticeable, while his face appeared only on the back.[19] It was a great lost Bowie album from the moment it was released.

To this day, *The Buddha of Suburbia* remains something of a forgotten gem. It is rarely discussed; it is often overlooked. It has never had the audience it deserves, and many who would enjoy it have not heard it. Years later, Bowie rated it among his best albums. He was dismayed by its shambolic marketing, but perhaps it belongs in the shadows; perhaps it would be damaged by exposure to sunlight.

It is notable also for its liner notes, which are written by Bowie and form a kind of essay. He uses them in part to explain his working methods, which included compiling a list of 'residue' from his past: there are bands (Roxy Music, T. Rex, Neu!, Kraftwerk), there are people (Brian Eno, the experimental composer Harry Partch), there are places (Croydon and, of course, Bromley). Elsewhere, it reads as a grand lament ('we have been parading a numbed, self-degrading affair over this last decade') and as something of a rallying cry for British artists; he sees 'our inherent love of the narrative form' and an inability to 'follow through in pure hard sell' as grave limitations.

This frustrates him, especially as 'No other country, least of all the States, has been able to smoothly incorporate unpatronizingly so many diverse cultural elements into a cohesive and socially stable music form as we have on this isle.' Given that he had not lived in Britain for nearly 20 years, it is quite something to see him identify so strongly with his old home; indeed, the album is in part the sound of a man returning to his roots, musically, creatively and geographically.

This entailed spiritual rumination. A particular tension had long been threatening to erupt, and it finally does so here in one of Bowie's odder compositions, 'Sex and the Church'. In truth, the issue wasn't just the Church: he had to work things through with Gnosticism, too, and maybe even a bit of Buddhism.

Many forms of Gnosticism and Buddhism value asceticism, the denial of worldly pleasures in pursuit of spiritual truth. Underlying this is an understanding of the world, the material realm, as something essentially bad, destructive or misleading. In Gnosticism, this world is the creation of the malevolent Demiurge, obscuring the nature of the true God. But, of course, Bowie loved this world, as well as a fair amount of its pleasures.

Christianity has a complex relationship with all this. In simplistic terms, the Old Testament portrays the world as basically good: God rewards the faithful with material blessings, be they livestock, land or riches. But the New Testament portrays the world as corrupted: Jesus calls Satan 'the ruler of this world';[20] the apostle Paul calls Satan 'the god of this world'.[21] God loves the world, and it will be redeemed, and maybe is being redeemed – but we live at a time when evil holds sway. There is a fundamental conflict between the flesh and the spirit: 'For what the flesh desires is opposed to the Spirit, and what the Spirit desires is opposed to the flesh,' wrote Paul.[22] But this stuff is complicated: after all, Jesus turned water into wine, not the other way round.

Bowie evidently felt a need to address these matters; maybe they had been nagging at him. He does so baldly: nothing is hidden and there is nothing to interpret. The song is just Bowie talking at length about sex, and the Church. He expresses puzzlement at the notion, which derives from the New Testament, of Jesus as a bridegroom and the Christian as his bride. He appears to contrast Christianity with what he calls mystic religions: when it comes to notions of sex, he favours the latter over the former. Then he presents a brief manifesto of sorts, a belief in a union between the flesh and the spirit, concluding: 'Give me the freedom of spirit and the joys of the flesh.'

One of Eno's Oblique Strategies, quoting the artist Dieter Rot, read: 'When faced with a choice, do both.' Flesh or spirit? Yes please. 'I'm a born librarian with a sex drive,' said Bowie.[23]

A crude and sorry mannequin stands in an artist's studio. Other battered human forms appear; some unknown violence has been done to them. There are jars of organic matter. A scrawny little Minotaur staggers and then leaps, as if it has just been born. And there, with a lean and aggressive insouciance, is David Bowie, in gothic mascara, moving wildly and gracefully, affecting a kind of menacing comedy.

Near him is a gang of savage young artists, pierced liberally, who treat bodies as frames or canvases. A fleshy forehead is stuffed with nails in a pattern evoking an industrialized crown of thorns; there are rituals, the cutting and hanging and beheading of things shaped like people. And finally it seems their work is complete: they have crafted their own Minotaur, around which they perform some sort of rite, before partaking in their own gluttonous Last Supper. It's a wild, disquieting and somehow seductive scene; quite a statement, given it was the video for the first single from the new album. And in it, the 48-year-old veteran rocker looks like a creature in its natural habitat.

It was 1995, and the holy man had made way for the shaman. The decade was splintering: the dreaded certainties of the Cold War had dissolved, the impending new millennium was spreading hopes and fears, and there were the first stirrings of a new disruptive entity, the internet.

'We live in fragmentation, we live in chaos, and I think there's more of an acceptance of that,' said Bowie. 'But my take is that you can either take a positive or negative attitude to it. A negative attitude is to believe that we're just ripping apart our civilization. But I think the positive take is that the chaos and fragmentation that we do find are the bricks and mortar of a future society.'[24]

Crucial to this was a reformed spirituality. 'This is the chance to rebuild everything – rebuild our beliefs, and our social systems. I think it's almost like the old adage of having to destroy God to reinvent him. Not in one's image, don't think I'm saying that, but to take the idea of a spiritual life out of the enclave of a medieval and feudal way of thinking, and restructure it for the way that things really are now.'[25]

The video was for 'The Hearts Filthy Lesson'. It came from an album called *1. Outside*, a rambling and sometimes bizarre record that veers from industrial rock to brooding balladry to funk-pop to electronica to light drum and bass, via spoken-word interludes in which Bowie's voice is manipulated to make it sound younger or older or female. Despite its disparate nature, the album is lent a kind of coherence and purpose by a tale straight from Bowie's imagination: the death of a 14-year-old girl, Baby Grace Blue, killed in a ritualistic 'art murder'.

We have grown used to Bowie's album artwork telling stories. This time it literally did. The CD booklet – and this is a CD album *par excellence* – included a piece of fiction written by Bowie called 'The Diary of Nathan Adler'. Adler is an old-school gumshoe investigating Baby Grace Blue's murder in an alternative near-future. But this is no straightforward work of crime writing. 'The narrative and the stories are not the content,' said Bowie. 'The content is the spaces between the linear bits. The queasy, strange textures.'[26] Some of those textures were on the cover, which was a self-portrait in unnatural colours, skewed and smeared and smudged.

The booklet also shows Bowie morphed by computer into the guises of the various characters who populate the album. The most pertinent here is The Artist, shown with various piercings beside a disembowelled corpse. Behind his head is the word 'Burden', referring to Chris Burden, a performance artist who crucified himself on a Volkswagen Beetle in 1974.[27] Next to him is the word 'Nitsch', referring to another performance artist, Hermann Nitsch, whose work was often ritualistic and sometimes involved animal carcasses and entrails, along with Christian iconography.

The album reflected what Bowie called 'the ritualisation of life at the moment': 'I think the taking away, the foundation or reliance upon or belief in an organised established religion, the need for ritual is still very much with man, and he has to ritualise to some extent. It's a series of gestures and movements and words and phrases and chants that he believes evolves his spiritual life. But if you haven't got the church and you haven't really got a replacement for it, you develop your own very human kind of ritualisations. And that's what's led to the preoccupation with body art in the visual arts, with the general referring of everything to the human body, because the human symbolically becomes the religion and the organisation and the church, and so you start destroying that and taking it apart.'[28]

In another interview, he said the culture of the time was 'pulling together all the real myths and all the synthetic myths of the late part of the 20th century. It works on the assumption that we're all undergoing the revival of some kind of paganism, and in that act there's some way that we have to appease gods to get through to the 21st century.'[29]

In addition to ritualism and body art, Bowie was becoming ever more enthralled by another aspect of paganism, Greek mythology. The clearest example was the figure of the Minotaur, the part-bull, part-man who lived in the centre of the Labyrinth. The Minotaur plays a shadowy role in what passes for the narrative of *1. Outside*: his image is imprinted on the CD itself, and he seems to be an alter-ego of The Artist, who killed Baby Grace Blue. Three songs are sung from his perspective: 'The Voyeur of Utter Destruction (As Beauty)', 'Wishful Beginnings' – one of the most chilling things Bowie recorded – and 'I'm Deranged'. The Minotaur also appeared frequently in Bowie's paintings in the mid-nineties. He contributed a series of them to a charity exhibition in 1994; they were imaginary memorabilia of an imaginary play called *We Saw a Minotaur*, written by a Joni Ve Sadd. Bowie did like an anagram.

Another figure, the Centaur, was also in Bowie's thoughts around this time. He got his bassist Gail Ann Dorsey to dress in a tail and hooves, along with devil horns, for one of his videos[30] and a performance on *Top of the Pops*; Bowie had made a sketch of a similar outfit in 1971. Consider the half-dog, half-man on the cover of *Diamond Dogs*, and it all begins to look like another manifestation of a core Bowie theme: the tension between humankind's contrasting natures, the animalistic and the civilized. This shows up all the time, not least in his fascination with the droogs from *A Clockwork Orange* and in his love of music that blended the savage with the cerebral. It is no surprise to see this re-emerge in a neo-pagan form: humanity was becoming simultaneously more technologically advanced and more spiritually primitive.

Bowie wanted *1. Outside* not only to reflect this neo-paganism, but to be part of it. He envisaged it as the first of five albums leading up to the year 2000: 'I see it as a symbolic sacrificial rite. I see it as a deviance, a pagan wish to appease gods, so we can move on. There's a real spiritual starvation out there being filled by these mutations of what are barely remembered rites and rituals.'[31]

As it happened, *1. Outside* stood alone. It came out in September that year and was notable for being Bowie's first collaboration with Brian Eno since the 1979 album *Lodger*, which Eno had found artistically unsatisfying, the paths of the two men then diverging until they were reunited at Bowie's wedding.[32] *1. Outside* also includes contributions by players from a deeper past, such as the pianist Mike Garson and the guitarist Carlos Alomar, as well as those by more recent acquaintances, including his creative saviour, Reeves Gabrels.

Bowie also staged his first art exhibition in 1995. A melange of styles, media and subjects, it was held at The Gallery in Cork Street,

London, and was called 'New Afro-Pagan and Work 1975–1995'. 'I'm anti-consistency in style, much as I am in music,' he told ITN.[33] 'I'm very certain in my work. I don't feel as though I'm open to anybody or anything. I know its worth.' Among the works on display was an image of crucifixes lit in different colours, a mushroom cloud bursting behind a distorted head, various depictions of the Minotaur, a child's coffin and a number of gloopy acrylic abstracts.

The tour that followed the album shared the record's aesthetic. The stage was dressed like an artist's studio, with billowing drapes, a bare wooden table and chair, a few prominent stage lights and little else. The music seemed at times deliberately antagonistic: the setlists were light on crowd-pleasers and heavy on Bowie's more challenging work, the seven-piece band sounding at times unbearably intense, almost punishing. Bowie's persona was hardly that of a bantering entertainer either, appearing more aloof than he had since the mid-1970s. His choice of attire, meanwhile, hinted at a more turbid spirituality: that white-striped outfit from his Kabbalah days returned in distressed form. He had worn a version for parts of the Glass Spider shows in 1987, but now it looked like it fully belonged.

Then, as had happened during his 1974 tour, it began to go somewhere different. After a four-month break in early 1996, Bowie cut the band down in size. Where there had been seven musicians, there were now four: Gabrels, Garson, Dorsey and the drummer Zack Alford. The result sounded more raw and primal and supple. They played more festivals, and musical influences that had shown themselves subtly on *1. Outside* became more prominent. The stage set, which was hardly elaborate to begin with, was stripped back too, while there was a shift in Bowie's persona. Something appeared that was more feral, more manic; the clothes were more showy, Alexander McQueen's distressed dandiness to the fore; the hair went Ziggy-ish orange. Where there had been a certain hauteur, now there was a kind of brashness. Fans have taken to calling this particular incarnation his 'Rave Uncle' phase.

Bowie often shared the bill that summer with acts who were taking dance music towards the realm of rock, acts such as The Prodigy and the Chemical Brothers. Ever a fan of the hybrid and the chimerical, Bowie was heading to the same destination but from the other direction, attempting to take rock towards the realm of dance music. He was especially interested in the emerging sounds of drum and bass and jungle, and the hard-hitting frenetic aggression of The Prodigy. Enraptured by the potency of his band, he recorded his next album, *Earthling*, that year in New York; the record was released in 1997, shortly after his 50th birthday.

There is a recurrent sense of questing and seeking. One song has Bowie 'Looking for Satellites', and questions abound: Where are we going? Who can we look to? But maybe he wasn't really after an answer anyway; maybe he was after something deeper. 'What men really want is not knowledge but certainty,' said Bertrand Russell; it is a sentiment Bowie quotes on the album's closing track, 'Law (Earthlings on Fire)'.

In the midst of this is a return to an old love: Tibetan Buddhism. 'Watching over the past couple of years how vocal and articulate the Dalai Lama has been, informing and educating people about what's been happening in Tibet, and what's at stake, has prompted my guilt – I had such a strong interest in Tibet when I was young and it seems to have dissipated or been relinquished somehow over the years,' said Bowie.[34] It prompted him to write a song named after that book that had been so formative for him, *Seven Years in Tibet*. The lyrics give an impressionistic account of the violence visited upon Chime Youngdong Rinpoche and his fellow Buddhists as they fled Tibet. The verses slink; the choruses crush. Around this time, Bowie described himself as a 'mid-art populist and postmodernist Buddhist surfing his way through the chaos of the late 20th century'.[35]

The length of the tour, and the level of curiosity surrounding Bowie's durability, meant he was interviewed frequently and in some depth. And it is striking just how often talk would turn to matters of the spirit. 'There's one line of continuity throughout my work, ever since I began – some kind of spiritual search,' he told Israeli musician, critic and broadcaster Sharon Moldavi in 1996. 'I resign myself to the fact that what I really was in need of all my life is some spiritual base, which I know is not a terribly popular thing these days to want to have as a centre to revolve around but I find – I don't know, there's something about the established church for instance that had absolutely no appeal to me. I'm terribly suspicious of established religion.'

It was at this time that he was quoted on Finnish television as saying that he thought there was a God, but not the one with a white beard on a cloud. 'I believe in a God beyond God, or a heaven beyond heaven,' he said.[36]

He added: 'I have very strong needs to have an identity within the universe. I don't think religion is for me – I have great distrust of the constructs of the Church, both with Protestantism and Catholicism. But I have an abiding fascination with the beginnings of the Church. But as important to me is a sense of the unfathomable reason why we have faith, and why we're cowards, and why we're heroes, and what brings these things about, and if shades of one thing influence another – does one have to be a coward to be a hero? The juxtapositions of all the facets of our personalities, I find interesting, and how we relate this to a God beyond God.'

Bowie's Gnostic streak, by now familiar, shines through these answers. And Bowie believed this to be the direction spirituality would take. He elaborated on all this in January 1997 in an interview with the Canadian journalist Kim Hughes: 'If we do move away from organised religion, we'll develop what's called the American Gnosticism, I think. There's a writer called Harold Bloom that wrote a great book last year called *The American Religion*. I was sent a copy not too long ago because somebody spotted that he says the same line that I said in one of the songs on the new album – I just happened to throw out that "God is an American" on one song.[37] And Harold Bloom actually almost says the same thing. He says the

Americans believe that Jesus is an American. But what I think he's really saying – he's not being hostile at all to that idea. He himself is a Jewish Gnostic. But I think he's saying that the idea of Gnosticism, or one's own one-to-one relationship with God, without the interfacing device of a church or a priest or somebody who can give you permission to talk to God, is very much what our needs are becoming.'

But this could not be vague, watery stuff. 'We're finding the materials of a new religion, but I think we have to find a new discipline. I think there is no real sense of purpose without a shaping of fragments. I think we have the fragments and the pieces of a new way, but I think we have to construct a path out of those pieces – the bits of concrete are merely crazy paving at the moment, but we have to develop a form.'[38]

His hair looked like the result of a botched electrocution, shocked into orange. His gown was the sort of thing a Mughal emperor might find a little excessive. The setting was a triumphant concert at Madison Square Garden, where he had just celebrated his 50th birthday by performing a predominantly pounding and screeching set with Lou Reed, Sonic Youth, the Foo Fighters, Robert Smith of The Cure and Frank Black, the former and future frontman of the Pixies.[39]

So when David Bowie said, near the show's end, 'I don't know where I'm going from here but I promise I won't bore you,' there was every reason to believe him. But what no one saw coming was a return to convention, musically and spiritually.

The year 1998 was as quiet as any of Bowie's adulthood, at least in conventional terms. He recorded barely a handful of songs, all of which were one-offs that would forever remain obscure;[40] he played one gig, at a birthday party for the DJ Howard Stern; he acted in three films that few would ever watch.

Yet conventional terms are not always the best way to judge Bowie's work. He was embarking on a project that would elicit sighs and scepticism but prove prescient. It was called BowieNet, and if you were in America you could surf your way to it on Netscape Navigator or Internet Explorer from 1 September 1998, and from other countries in the following months. Bowie had built much of his career on mystique and distance; now he was extremely available, popping into chatrooms, subjecting himself to matey online Q&As, posting diary entries online, sharing his art and his enthusiasms directly, unmediated.

It is hard these days to convey, or perhaps recall, the sense of excitement that existed around the internet, and Bowie was among its most ardent evangelists. It is also worth mentioning that this excitement was far from universally felt. There was in various quarters a good deal of eye-rolling about it all. But to be fair to Bowie, this was not a case of him spotting the next cool thing, commandeering it and proclaiming himself some sort of pioneer – he had used email as early as 1983, and he had ruminated on the 'World Wide Internet' while recording *1. Outside* in 1994.[41] His interest was true, deep and informed. And in a curious way, it helps us piece together what we might see as his belief system. Bowie was suspicious of intermediaries, middlemen, gatekeepers; the internet felt like it might be their comeuppance.

This is evidently where Bowie's excitement was directed, because suddenly the music shifted down a gear or two. The crackpot experimentation, the playing with form, the subversion of the medium, the wilful antagonism: these would all be left behind, as would the outlandish clobber and hair. Songs with tunes and recognizable words and structures, songs that sounded like they were played by a man or a band, recorded in a normal way: these were the future, and would remain so until the end neared.

Bowie's more conservative sound and appearance could be seen as the inevitable next step in a career that rebounded all over the place; as the product of a man who grew bored quickly with everything, even with pushing boundaries; as a daring turn to stability and order at a time of chaos. It could be seen as a continuation of the subtle shift from the improvisational nature of much of *1. Outside* to the tighter *Earthling*; indeed, as Bowie continued to tour, he and Gabrels developed a greater interest in performing songs in stripped-back form on acoustic guitars. Less charitably, it could be seen as the result of Bowie seeking greater commercial success, as part of an effort to keep the Bowie brand at least in some tenuous contact with what passed for the mainstream.

And perhaps there is another reason. Bob Dylan had released a new album, and its effect on Bowie was soon apparent. The relationship between the two men had long been curious and complex: both had peddled a kind of mystique, but Dylan's was always that bit more rooted and grounded, Bowie's more alien. Dylan was plainly an influence on the folky Bowie of the late 1960s, but seemed to exist in a different universe from, say, the second side of *Low*. The Bowie track 'Song for Bob Dylan', from the 1971 album *Hunky Dory*, is a barbed tribute. After Bowie broke up the Spiders from Mars, Mick Ronson's next major assignment was as Dylan's guitarist. Dylan disliked *Young Americans* but liked *'Heroes'*. 'I'm not a great Dylan fan. I think he's a prick,' said Bowie in 1976.[42] Bowie covered Dylan's song 'Maggie's Farm' with Tin Machine and 'Like a Rolling Stone' with Bryan Adams's band. A curious and complex relationship, like two street cats stalking each other.

Five months after Bowie released *Earthling*, Dylan released *Time Out of Mind*. 'When I first put his new album on I thought I should just give up,' said Bowie in 1998.[43] Next to *Time Out of Mind*, much of *Earthling* sounded ephemeral, even juvenile. For all its charms, Bowie's album was a skittish affair, a bright thing caught on the breeze; Dylan's was weighty as a tombstone. Dylan was only six years older than Bowie but sounded as though he was inhabited by the centuries, casting his gaze backwards over cities and ruins, drinking with ghosts, interrogating Death, desperate for a glimpse behind the curtain. Bowie was trying to get all the names of the Seven Dwarfs into a song that sounded a bit like something by The Prodigy.[44]

So pretty much the first song that Bowie recorded in 1998 was 'Tryin' to Get to Heaven', from *Time Out of Mind*. The contrast with the sound of *Earthling* could hardly have been more marked: where so much was once frenetic and processed, now there was something stately and sedate to the point of soporific. The weight of the song seems uncomfortable for Bowie, and he sounds unsure how to carry it. But it can be considered a session in the gym, the sound of Bowie exercising muscles he would need so he could swim in deeper waters.

Bowie was stirred by something of the old in Dylan; but now he was given fresh motivation elsewhere by something of the new. He was asked to write music for a video game. Bowie had always been good at seeing what was not there: he could see the place where melody could go in R&B; he could see the space for humanity in robotic German music. So he knew what he wanted to contribute to the dry world of gaming: genuine emotion.

The game, in which the player could explore a city, was called *The Nomad Soul*.[45] It was hugely ambitious for the time, stretching the existing technology to its limits.[46] In the game, Bowie was a character called Boz, and one of his bands was called The Awakened. He contributed ten original songs to the game, and wrote them with Reeves Gabrels.

Many of these songs, albeit in different forms, made their way onto Bowie's next album, called '*hours...*'[47] The only thing radical about it is its difference from *Earthling*: the change of direction is more whiplash-inducing than any before, which is perhaps its most notable achievement.

'*hours...*' is an album by a middle-aged man inhabiting the character of a middle-aged man. At least now, no one could accuse him of trying too hard. In most of these songs, this character is quietly rueful, in low mood, made low by his life, by the fact it has proved disappointingly colourless and pedestrian, flames snuffed out, passions dulled. There are flashes of hope, but maybe these only add to the hushed tragedy. Bowie was keen to stress that this character was not him.

If *'hours...'* had a place anywhere, it was in a broader current of British guitar music, which had typically been bright and bold from 1994 to 1997, before losing its energy and turning inwards, as if hungover, as shadows lengthened on the decade. Yet *'hours...'* is no write-off, partly because there are good songs yearning for escape, and partly because there is something important stirring here, among the drift and listlessness. As Bowie reaches for a new way of being Bowie, he reaches too for God. It is there on the front of the album, on the back of the album, within the album.

The cover of *'hours...'* is inspired by the Pietà, which has been a motif in Christian art from the Renaissance onwards. The classical image depicts the Virgin Mary cradling the body of Christ after the crucifixion. Bowie's version depicts Bowie cradling the body of Bowie – the former being a fresh-looking, angelic Bowie sporting Bowie's new haircut; the latter being an approximation of the *Earthling*-era Bowie. Something is being laid to rest.

The lyrics of the album are leavened with Christian terminology: there are hymns, gods, the eternal, the damned. Most intriguing of all, there are 'angels of promise', a term used for the spiritual beings that convey God's promises to humans; the best-known is Gabriel, who told Mary that she was pregnant with the son of God. Bowie owned an altarpiece painted by the Venetian Renaissance artist Tintoretto, depicting an angel warning St Catherine of Alexandria of her impending martyrdom; she was killed early in the fourth century, aged about 18, on the order of the Roman emperor Maxentius, for refusing to renounce her Christian faith. In the 1990s, Bowie named his music publishing company Tintoretto.

The song 'Seven' is spiritual in a broader sense: Bowie described it as a song of 'nowness'. Introducing it on *VH1 Storytellers* in 1999, the year the album was released, he recalled the 'revolutionary hippie' Abbie Hoffman telling him over a drink: 'Tomorrow isn't promised.' In an interview with Chris Roberts, also in 1999,[48] Bowie said: 'My real ambition is to feel that I don't waste my day. I feel a bit guilty if I feel like I've wasted the day. I kind of go "there's another one that's gone down the drain"... One's personal day to day existence I think is the achievement.' Such ideas are customarily associated with Buddhism, but they are present in Christianity too, both in the teachings of Jesus[49] and in disciplines such as the Examen, in which one looks back systematically over one's day.

On the back of the album are a trio of Bowies and a snake. The image evokes classical depictions of the Fall of Man: there is Adam on one side, Eve on the other, one of them in distress; and there is God, and there is the Devil, in the form of a serpent. Bowie chose the album title for its multiplicity of meanings reflecting its myriad themes – most obviously 'hours' and 'ours', though it also suggests the 'books of hours' popular among Christians in the Middle Ages, marking and hallowing the passage of time with prayer.

And there was a further development, which was quite unexpected, but which seems to be of a piece with all this: Bowie incorporated into his live sets a song he had not sung since 1976. It was 'Word on a Wing'.

10

DOUBTER

'We may be a little wary or jittery about what's around the corner,' said an upbeat David Bowie in 1999, 'but there's no feeling of everything's going to end in the year 2000. Instead, there's almost a celebratory feeling of "right, at least we can get cracking and really pull it all together."'[1] Before long, that optimism collapsed into despondency and desperation. 'I had personally really quite high expectations about the future,' he said in 2002.[2] 'I had no idea it would sort of capitulate into this awful mess.' It left him weeping, wailing, raging. And the target of his fury, the recipient of his spittle and tears, was God.

Bowie was entering a season of profound doubt. He doubted God's nature and even God's existence. In the Bible, another David had sung: 'How long, O Lord? Will you forget me for ever? How long will you hide your face from me?'[3] Now, Bowie lent his voice to that same cry.

The light of the new millennium was kind to him at first. In musical terms, he did only one thing of note in 2000, but it would resound for decades: he headlined on the final night of the Glastonbury Festival. This Bowie was a new creation, a Bowie who was as comfortable with crowd-pleasers as he was with obscurities. He was like a man of gold that night, his hair shoulder-length and wavy and fair as it was in 1971, the last time he'd played at Glastonbury, his attire initially flouncy and flamboyant before a change into a cooler and sleeker look that still denoted a sense of occasion. He felt no shame in conducting a singalong, no embarrassment in giving people what they wanted. This is for them, not us, he had told his band, and the response from the 250,000 in attendance was duly ecstatic.

The performance seemed to engender a fresh affection towards him: his body of work, presented in this way, with such power and warmth and vulnerability, was unanswerable. There was perhaps a relief in some quarters that this had not been a three-hour drum and bass set or a reunion of Tin Machine, but anyone who had been paying attention for the past couple of years would have detected that something had changed. That the show still had room for songs from *1. Outside* and *Earthling*, and finished with a pulverizing 'I'm Afraid of Americans', was testament to his mastery. At last, everything fitted together; at last, there was a sense of completion. The alienatingly abrasive shows of 1995 felt a lifetime ago, but the artistic integrity remained. After antithesis, synthesis.

Something else happened that summer, too, something occupying a different dimension of significance. Bowie and Iman welcomed into the world their daughter, Alexandria Zahra Jones, known as Lexi. 'My soul feels complete,' Iman told *Hello!* magazine. 'Well, I can't better that,' said Bowie. 'That seems about perfect really. It is amazing how a new child can refocus one's direction seconds after its birth. Everything falls into a feeling of "rightness".'[4]

There were further signs that the plates were shifting. A figure from Bowie's past, Tony Visconti, had come back into his life. He had been Bowie's first great collaborator, had produced some of his earliest songs and had gone on to produce some of his finest records. The two had not worked together since 1981, but they had reconvened in 1998 to record a cover of 'Mother' by John Lennon and a song for, of all things, *The Rugrats Movie*.[5]

They talked at that time about doing a whole album together, but Bowie was unsure: 'I really didn't want to tarnish the work that we'd done before, because it was so good and people have such a great feeling about the work that we've done before. So it was really waiting until I found songs that were the right weight for the two of us to do together, that didn't require engineering the past or mining it for particular kinds of sounds.' He noticed something change in January 2001: 'I started writing a weight of song that I really felt happy with. And I thought this is the kind of thing I could do with Tony.'[6]

Then came more emotional upheaval. News emerged in April that David's mother, Peggy, had died, aged 87, at a nursing home in Hertfordshire; David attended the funeral, and his conduct was described as 'absolutely wonderful'.[7] Bowie's friend Freddie Burretti, who had helped to sculpt the image of Ziggy Stardust, died the following month, aged 49.

Bowie found himself wanting to write 'narrative, crafted' songs, and to create what he called a 'personal, cultural restoration'. On the recommendation of one of his guitarists, he investigated a recording studio that was quite different from any in which he had previously worked, about 2,000 feet above sea level in the Catskill Mountains, approximately 120 miles north of New York City.

The place affected him deeply, as he told *Interview* magazine: 'It was almost an epiphany I had. Walking through the door, everything that my album should be about was galvanised for me into one focal point. Even though I couldn't express it in words that second, I knew what the lyrics were already. They were all suddenly accumulated in my mind. It was an on-the-road-to-Damascus type of experience, you know? It was almost like my feet were lifted off the ground.'

There were many newcomers to his band. This was to be bold, big, meaningful; it would inaugurate a new phase of Bowie's career, but it would also reach back, well before his own work, before even his own life, into the art and philosophy that coursed around Europe a century earlier. Friedrich Nietzsche returned to Bowie's thinking, while his affinity with Richard Strauss deepened: in the mountains, Bowie listened earnestly and recurrently to what have become known as Strauss's Four Last Songs, which Bowie called 'probably the most beautiful songs ever written'.[8] He spoke of wanting to emulate the composer's creative longevity, keeping on 'like Strauss at 84'.[9] In tone and mood, Bowie was resembling ever more closely the figure in Caspar David Friedrich's *Wanderer above the Sea of Fog*, an icon of German Romanticism painted in 1818:[10] dignified, serious, enigmatic; masterful, vulnerable, alone.

If you want to meet God, get climbing. That's what the Bible suggests: Mount Sinai is where God gave Moses the Ten Commandments; Mount Carmel is where the power of God was shown, defeating the prophets of Baal; the Mount of Olives is where Jesus often taught his disciples, and from where Jesus ascended into heaven; there is also the mountain where Jesus preached his sermon; and there is the mountain upon which Jesus was transfigured. The air is thin up there.

Bowie had always suspected this. He had met so many mountains before in his work, but they had existed in the realm of spiritual symbol: the mountains of Lhasa, the mountain in 'It Ain't Easy', the mountains of 'The Supermen', the mountains on mountains in 'Station to Station', the mountain that manifested 'incomprehensible forces'.[11] Now he was up there, and it changed him. He was in a new place: the surroundings were stark, and there were wild pigs and deer and bears. 'This is not cute, on top of this mountain,' he said.[12]

Bowie had nearly finished recording the album when horror unfolded in the city he had made his home. So clear was the air in the Catskills that he could see with the aid of binoculars the embers of the World Trade Center. 'And I look at my daughter and sometimes the first few days after 9/11 I looked at her and couldn't feel happy. Which is a terrible thing to feel. I looked at her and just felt fearful.'[13]

The album, when it arrived in June the following year, was called *Heathen*. 'Heathen felt right inasmuch as it was about the unilluminated mind,' he explained. 'It was an idea, a feeling, a sense of what 21st-century man might become if he's not already. Somebody who's lowered his standards, spiritually, intellectually, morally, whatever. There's a kind of a – someone who's not even bothered searching for a spiritual life any more, and is completely existing on a materialistic plane.'[14]

Before you hear the album, you feel it. The look and texture of the thing is superior in every way to any record of his since 1980; it has an unnerving presence.[15] The imagery is portentous, sometimes eerily serene, sometimes searingly violent. Bowie cuts a vaguely chilling figure on the cover, his face restored to its old prominence, still with that tilt to the right – he is in monochrome, and there is something of the early twentieth-century philosopher-scientist about him. This time, he looks upwards, and there is a subtle message in his eyes. They are intended to resemble the eyes of a fish; Christians used a symbol of a fish as a secret way to identify themselves while they were persecuted in pagan times.[16]

Unfold the cover and there are details from classical works of art slashed, defaced, desecrated. Each has a biblical theme: *Massacre of the Innocents* (1611) by Guido Reni, *Madonna and Child with Six Angels* (1300–05) by Duccio di Buoninsegna, *The Magdalene* (1660–70) by Carlo Dolci, and *Christ and St. John with Angels* by Peter Paul Rubens (c.1615; Rubens lived from 1577 to 1640). Some versions of the packaging had a further image, *Saint Sebastian* (1501–02) by Raffaello Sanzio. 'I wanted to illustrate the subtext of the word "Heathen" being barbarian or philistine,' said Bowie, 'and an unacceptance of culture or high culture, a wish to destroy everything that we have created to express ourselves.'[17] This involved 'the destruction of religious things'.[18]

Remove the booklet containing lyrics, struck through and obscured, and there is image showing early editions of three weighty books: *The General Theory of Relativity* by Albert Einstein; *The Interpretation of Dreams* by Sigmund Freud; and *Die fröhliche Wissenschaft*, here translated as *The Gay Science*, by Friedrich Nietzsche.

As Bowie explained: 'From the late half of the 19th century, the accumulation of material of scientific progress caused people to believe that they had more control over their lives and their environment, and then it was something of a catastrophe at the time when Nietzsche suggested God was dead. And then around the same time, and later, Einstein changed our concept of time and space, and Freud changed the idea of how we felt inside. So by the time we were into the 20th century, everything that we knew was wrong. It was a brand new understanding that we in fact were there to fill the void that was taken by God. And filling that void, the only thing we were able to do was create the bomb. That was our greatest piece of creativity in the role of God.'[19]

A sense of having been cut adrift infuses the album. The question is: who has done the cutting – God or humanity? 'This was the culmination of all our knowledge, to create something which was utterly, thoroughly destructive,' continued Bowie. 'And I think that act threw us into chaos, and I don't think we've ever recovered. I think we've lost our ability to connect with any kind of spiritual life, and I think we've lost a sense of purpose, and we're not absolutely convinced that there's some kind of plan.'[20]

The packaging acts rather like the title sequence of a film, preparing the listener for a certain state of unsteady contemplation. When it comes to the point of pressing the play button, there is immediately a sonic depth that had long been absent; welcome back, Tony Visconti. After five seconds of synthesized choral 'ahhs' and glitchy guitar come Bowie's first two words: 'Nothing remains.' The phrase evokes one of the great reflections on the hubris of mankind, the poem 'Ozymandias', by the English Romantic poet Percy Bysshe Shelley.[21]

The song is called 'Sunday'. The word does not appear in the lyrics, so its significance is for the listener to discern. 'Sunday' is ambitious, not merely in terms of structure and music, but in what it is trying to do and where it is trying to reach. It depicts a landscape that is barren and hostile, but colours and shapes come forth gradually, from the music as much as anywhere; then an explosion, as if we had been listening to a fuse, and then a fade into nothingness.

One section of the song has voices chanting in a quasi-Gregorian style: 'In your fear, seek only love.' The words bring to mind 'On Love', by the mystic poet Kahlil Gibran, who was named in a song by Bowie 32 years earlier.[22] Bowie, stentorian, sings over them in monotone a series of phrases evoking these lines from 'On Love': 'When love beckons to you, follow him / Though his ways are hard and steep. / And when his wings enfold you yield to him.' Bowie's last words in the song concern his trials, and sound like they are sung to God.

'I would get up very early in the morning, about six, and work in the studio before anybody else got there,' recalled Bowie. 'And often the lyrics would come as I was sort of putting the music together... the words to "Sunday" were tumbling out... there was something so still and primal about what I was looking at outside that there were tears just running down my face as I was writing this thing. It was just extraordinary.'[23]

'David was very jovial,' said Visconti. 'But he would go somewhere in the mornings when he was writing these songs. You could see he was really struggling with questions. After a few weeks I said: "It seems like you're addressing God himself."'[24]

It is fair to say, however, that the album is not all like this. There are 12 songs on *Heathen*, and only four of them have quite this weight, the other three being 'I Would Be Your Slave', '5:15 The Angels Have Gone', and 'Heathen (The Rays)'. Another song, 'A Better Future', is deceptively light.

Bowie described 'I Would Be Your Slave' as 'an entreaty to the highest being to show himself in a way that could be understood'; he said it was 'too disturbing'.[25] Having once praised God as the cornerstone of his existence, he now questioned God's silence, and suspected or feared God's mockery. In 1976, he sang to his God that he would walk alongside him, all his days; he sang this again in 1999. Now it feels pointless, and there are 'no footprints in the sand.'

There is an allegorical Christian poem called 'Footprints'. It ends with God whispering: 'My precious child, I love you and will never leave you / Never, ever, during your trials and testings. / When you saw only one set of footprints, / It was then that I carried you.' But Bowie repeats himself, embittered and abandoned, singing loudly, rebukingly, beratingly. God is offered a way back, but on Bowie's terms: I would be your slave, he sings, if you would only show yourself to me.

The instrumental backing is strange: there is the repeated sound of breathing, but it is mechanical, and its rhythms are not those of the song; music is played by a string quartet, but for the most part it is hesitant, making apparently confident beginnings before turning back on itself, allowing moments of stability, rising into hope, before returning to uncertainty and doubt and despair. A man trying, believing, reaching, failing, again and again.

As Bowie put it in an interview with John Wilson for BBC Radio 4 in June 2002: 'I'm a very spiritual person inasmuch as I've had this awful bloody journey searching for a spiritual life that... firstly actually meets my expectations of what a spiritual life should be, and what kind of part it should play in my life. Maybe I asked too much. But I keep coming to a dead end, but as I get older my questions are fewer. But I ask them – I bark them more than ask them, actually.'

'5:15 The Angels Have Gone' is one of many Bowie songs in which angels skulk and come and go. There is one in which the angel is perfect – 'The Wedding Song' – and there is the lovable if endangered angel in 'Golden Years'. But Bowie's angels are usually unimpressive: in 'Look Back in Anger', from *Lodger*, the angel coughs, has crumpled wings, yawns with sleep in his eyes, and goes unnoticed; in 'New Angels of Promise', from '*hours...*', the angels are despairing scapegoats, silent admin officers; there is an early Bowie song from 1968 called 'Angel, Angel, Grubby Face'. In '5:15 The Angels Have Gone', they are gangly and ungainly, and they are either departed or invisible.

'A man who could once see his angels – hopes and aspirations, maybe? – can't see them anymore,' Bowie said of '5:15 The Angels Have Gone'. 'And he blames the crushing dumbness of life for it.'[26]

There is a lot going on and it is hard to see any of it clearly. In the chorus, he bellows with a kind of fury to an unnamed lover and object of adoration; the two no longer speak. The narrator is left waiting in the rain at a cold and desolate station.

The song has celestial synths and heavenly voices, wrenched and rent by merciless, clattering drums and a piano dancing in the chaos. There is a chugging shuffle recalling the locomotive sounds from 'Station to Station'. It all sounds blue-black, like a bruise. But somehow, at the end of it all, there is a kind of peace.

'A Better Future' is the penultimate track on *Heathen*. The lyrics are plain, Bowie once again setting out his demands to his deity: end suffering, keep us and the world alive, make my children happy, or I'll turn from you. It is as if Bowie could no longer be bothered with the poetic and the abstract. He's tried everything, so he might as well just spit it out. 'They're naive declarations – "if you're not going to do anything about our world, you're not going to have any support for your plans in the future, God!",' Bowie said. 'That kind of bald-faced idiot statement. But it's the frustrations of day-to-day life.'[27]

'Heathen (The Rays)' is where the album ends. There are haunting guitar chimes and faintly oppressive synths, and then Bowie sings what sounds like a poetic description of a city of skyscrapers, symbols of an empire which will pass, as all empires do. There is something here again of 'Ozymandias', and a disquieting prefiguring of the events of 9/11, rhyming 'sky made of glass' with 'all things must pass': Bowie maintained that the words were written before the attacks. He is waiting, looking, questioning the existence of any purpose.

Then, quite devastatingly, he disgorges an almost infant howl at the prospect of abandonment.

And over a weird squall of synths and guitars, over drums that sound like a sinister false smile, over chords that seem to be heading towards an epiphany but soon stumble – finally the day dies, and something else with it. Then, wordless cries.

Watching Bowie sing this song in concert can feel like intruding on private grief; he sometimes seems in genuine torment. Performances of 'Heathen (The Rays)' tended to end in solemn theatre, Bowie covering his eyes as he was guided off stage, blind and hobbled. He described the song as 'a dialogue between a man and life itself, rather than a man and his god', adding: 'It has kind of a pagan feel to it – it's a man confronting and resigning himself to the fact that life is gradually saying goodbye to him.'[28]

'Heathen (The Rays)' is the most explicit evidence of Strauss's influence. The last of his Four Last Songs is called *Im Abendrot*, of which there is no consistent rendering into English; the great critic William Mann, whose translation is printed with the Deutsche Grammophon recording, has it as 'At Gloaming'. Literally, *abendrot* means 'evening red', you could call it 'At Sunset', as Wikipedia does, but that feels insufficiently specific. Nothing in English is quite equivalent, but we know it when we see it. 'The idea of fear is very strong within the album,' Bowie told John Wilson in the 2002 Radio 4 interview. 'I think one of the major fears that underlines it all for me personally is the fear that there is no spiritual life.'

Bowie explored the potential consequences of a godless universe in conversation with George Stroumboulopoulos of the Canadian 'MuchMusic' TV channel: 'Is the reality that there is no morality? Which is kind of scary, because that means there's no reason for life, in which case why do we bother? I hate that. I don't want to go there. But you do. You keep confronting that all the time. I do anyway. We all feel very alone, don't we, often.'

Bowie told NPR: 'I realised the resonance of the word "Heathen" is quite applicable to the way we conduct ourselves, and always have – that we're really morally and spiritually in the same endless decline that we always have been... I don't think evolution has much place in our vocabulary at all – I don't think we evolve at all. I think we're quite as awful as we were 20,000 years ago.'[29]

But maybe there was a kind of hope, somewhere, on the other side. 'There's quasi new religions, but there is no direct sense of what our purpose is any more,' he said. 'Now that may be a good thing, because it may show itself to be that we don't have a purpose. Are we big enough and mature enough to exist like that? Are we mature enough to accept that there's no plan, there's no going somewhere, there's no gift of immortality at the end of this – if we evolve far enough we may never have to die! I mean, that seems to be the reach from the past. Or maybe we can't live like that. Maybe we have to exist and live on the idea that we have one day at a time. Can we do that? Because if we could do that, we may be serving some really great thing.'[30]

'I'm not quite an atheist and it worries me,' said David Bowie in 2003. 'There's that little bit that holds on: "Well, I'm almost an atheist. Give me a couple of months."'[31]

He had railed at God, despaired at God, tried to bargain with God. He had obeyed, rebelled, strayed, drawn close. The desire for spiritual truth had driven him and dragged him through decades of creativity. It had inspired him, comforted him, tormented him. He seemed perennially dissatisfied with what he found. But for some reason, David Bowie kept going. He seemed unable, or perhaps unwilling, to tolerate fully the idea that he was looking for something that was not there.

Indeed, atheism seemed hardly to have occurred to him. He scarcely mentioned it: he spoke in 1997 of 'a need to vacillate between atheism and a kind of Gnosticism', but that was pretty much that. The early years of the twenty-first century were fertile ground for what was known as 'New Atheism', a wholesale and forceful rejection of religion on the basis of reason. Its leading proponents were the biologist Richard Dawkins, the writer Christopher Hitchens, the cognitive scientist Daniel Dennett and the neuroscientist Sam Harris. One might have thought such thinkers would have influenced Bowie at this time. After all, the artists and scientists of the nineteenth century had enthralled him, and Hitchens's book *The Trial of Henry Kissinger* was one of

Bowie's favourites. But no, the New Atheists could not count Bowie among their converts. Not quite.

'Do you believe in a creator, a higher power?' asked the BBC Radio 2 presenter Johnnie Walker. 'No, I don't think I do... But it's something that I vacillate on tremendously. I don't think I'm a committed atheist, as much as I'd like to be. I still keep seeing a silver lining every now and again, that has got a magical glow around it.'[32]

Still, Bowie's next album was to be called *Reality*. The name suggested that, having emerged from the spiritual trials of *Heathen*, he was now devoted to the material and the concrete. The music would be more direct ('thrusty' was how he put it),[33] played by his live band, recorded not in the strange air of the mountains, but on the streets of New York. Less of the greyscale subtlety: this would be daubed in primary colours, built to fill arenas on a huge world tour. And that is what he gave us. Although, being Bowie, only up to a point.

There is an immediacy to *Reality*. Bowie described its creation as 'very simple'. *Heathen* had been 'very different' and 'written as a deeply questioning album'. For *Reality*, however, 'I'd just written some songs, and I amalgamated them with a couple of covers I'd wanted to do. I didn't approach this with any kind of through line involved. It wasn't a conceptualised piece at all.'[34]

On the surface, *Reality* is Bowie's '9/11' album. The World Trade Center had been attacked during the recording of *Heathen*, but only when that album was nearly finished. *Reality* was made in its aftermath, in New York City in the first few months of 2003, by which time America and the UK had become embroiled in wars of supposed retaliation in the Middle East. The attack and its consequences, military, political and psychological, are addressed by various songs on the album. The record as a whole has a nervy, jittery air.

Yet there is another theme, of which all this is perhaps a part. It is to do with ageing, mortality, and reflecting on how a life has been lived. Two songs appear to be non-identical twins in this respect, although they are really part of a brood of triplets. One, 'Never Get Old', is a generally ironic, wry and absurdist take on the subject. The sound here is huge and quite empty; the verses are more neurotic and wiry, the melody descending in steps to the depths, apparently assured but bedevilled by weird harmonies. 'There is the image of a petulant rock singer sitting in a half-darkened room saying, "I'm not gonna get old,"' Bowie said of the song. 'I thought it was a funny image and I had to write it before someone else my age did.'

Its partner on this album is the title track. There is no wishful thinking here, just a man wondering where he has been and fearing where he is going. The music is energetic and full-bodied and careers about the place. The time for delusion is over.[35]

Another song, 'Days', develops a theme that began on *'hours...'* with 'Seven' and to some extent 'Thursday's Child', which runs through days of the week. Bowie had evidently become focused on living one day at a time, and 'Days' is a song of gratitude to an unnamed companion for 'all the days I owe you'.

The album's final song inhabits a different place again: different from *Heathen*, different from the rest of *Reality*. It is different in tone and mood and sound. It is a remarkable work called 'Bring Me the Disco King' and it involves Mike Garson's jazz-tinged piano, a simple drum loop, and Bowie, joined occasionally by other Bowies. Images float by like vapours. There is a repeated refrain of suspicion. As a song, it stands alone. It is hard to think of much else like it, besides perhaps 'The Bewlay Brothers', which closes Bowie's 1971 album *Hunky Dory* in a similar tense, with a flow of reminiscences, fluttering between the real and the imagined. And still, no God.

Along the way, however, is 'Looking for Water', a deceptive song that demands reflection. In formal musical terms, it is slight: it is mostly a couple of chords, drums crashing the same relentless beat, a vocal melody that sounds underworked, a vocal hook that uses only two notes. But guitars spin off in strange directions,

Bowie sounds like an anguished man, and the song is part of a story that runs deep.

First, there is the War on Terror. 'When I wrote ['Looking for Water'], I just had this image of somebody crawling through the desert looking for the water, which is the most clichéd image that you can come up with,' said Bowie. 'But then that made me think, well, the only thing he would be looking at would be the oil pumps. And the oil pumps seem to be working, but there is no water.'[36]

This could go down different paths. 'This must be about a military, industrial situation – a complex of some kind,' offered Bowie. 'It must be about an administration that has a manifesto that was probably written in the late nineties that's being carried through now. That's kind of what was on my mind.'

But there is another path, and it takes us back, all the way to Thomas Jerome Newton and *The Man Who Fell to Earth*. Newton comes to Earth looking for water, but finds poison, and it ruins him. In 1987 with 'Glass Spider', too, there was a repeated refrain, again against drums clattering the same relentless beat, wailing over the disappearance of water. There is a repeated search here for the substance and source and sustainer of life, only to find it corrupted or evaporated, which invites comparison to Bowie's search for spiritual truth.

Reality, the album, faces two ways. It is sonically bright but, at least sometimes, thematically bleak. The cover shows a cartoonified, Manga-esque Bowie surrounded by abstract blobs, washes, lines and sprays; there is none of *Heathen*'s considered seriousness here, but that does not mean it is joyful. If *Reality* captures a new tendency towards godlessness, Bowie doesn't seem especially happy about it.

Asked by *Soma* magazine[37] whether he felt a sense of futility spreading across society, he said: 'If you accept that we live in absolute chaos, it doesn't look like futility anymore. It only looks like futility if you believe in this bang up structure we've created called "God", and all. It's like, don't tell me that the whole system is crumbling; there's nothing there to crumble. All these structures were self-created, just to survive, that's all. We only have a moral code, because overall, it helps us survive. It wasn't handed down to us from anywhere.' But, he also added, 'I'm not going to tell my daughter that.'

Since the arrival of Lexi, there was a new need for hope. 'I'm going to tell her that she's going to have a great life, and it's a terrific world, and that she should embrace all experiences... carefully. You see, I have to do that. It's really important for me to work hard on developing a positive attitude.'[38]

His own childhood had been emotionally tough, and he didn't want Lexi to suffer in the same way. 'Images which spring to mind when I think of my youth,' he said in 2003, 'is that my father used to work at the east end of London and we'd go up occasional Saturday mornings – he'd take me to the office because he used to work also on Saturdays – and it was passing block after block after block of destroyed houses. It was extraordinary. I mean, it was really, literally, a wasteland... So you really kinda had a sense of destruction and a sense of sad poignant images about the walls of one building being taken down and you still see the staircase running up and the shape of where paintings and pictures and photographs used to hang and all the floors were still intact... And you could just imagine the families being in there. It was such an impressionable image for a nine- or ten-year-old kid.'[39]

David Bowie had been very busy. After *Heathen* was released in June 2002, earning his best reviews for decades, a nomination for the Mercury Music Prize, a chart placing of number three and his first gold disc since *Black Tie White Noise*, he set out on what began as a small live tour. There was no stage set to speak of. Bowie's attire may have been formal – suits, ties, sometimes untied, waistcoats – but his manner was usually relaxed. The arrangements of his songs tended to stay close to the originals. He spoke of being an interpreter of his own material, a kind of postmodern Sinatra.

The tour began in medium-sized venues, before rolling into a round of festivals across Europe and North America. Dates kept being added, returning to more intimate settings in the autumn. Some of the concerts were epic in duration: Bowie surprised his audience in Berlin by telling them he was going to play the whole of *Low* live later that evening, a promise he fulfilled. He promoted the shows via countless interviews on television and radio. The tour ended on 23 October; a little more than two months later, he was back in the studio, recording *Reality*. There followed more intensive media work and the longest tour of Bowie's career; it was called A Reality Tour. Note the 'A'.

Now in artfully distressed casual clothes, playing in large arenas and with his most elaborate staging since the 1980s – a huge LED screen and raised platforms, the edges of the stage softened by feathery white twigs that dangled with pretty menace – Bowie performed night after night after night with apparently unbounded energy and commitment and enthusiasm. He expertly blended material old and new, flipping from chatty repartee to sombre intensity as the moment demanded. Around the world it went; Scandinavia, Europe, North America, New Zealand, Australia, Japan. The shows typically ran for more than two hours. Most reviews were rapturous. How is he doing this? asked critics in awe. His attitude to touring had previously been ambivalent, even hostile, but now he spoke of enjoying himself more than ever, delighting in his band and in his relationship with the crowds. He turned 57 in January 2004, and there was still two-thirds of the tour to go. It ran for nine months, 110 shows. But the end came prematurely.

Nine songs into a show in Prague on 23 June 2004, Bowie left the stage. He felt agonizing pain in his chest; the cause was thought to be a trapped nerve in his shoulder. The band played two songs without him. He returned to perform but soon had to step away again. The concert finished early.

He was back on stage two days later, playing at the Hurricane Festival in Scheeßel in Germany. He seemed happy and well and he moved freely; but there was one apparent moment of discomfort, and he clutched his arm. The air fell cold that evening, so during the concert he put on a sweatshirt; he looked as casual, normal, everyday as he ever had on stage. There is always a risk that events are misinterpreted via knowledge gleaned subsequently, but there is something different about the performance of 'Heroes' that night. Even more so than usual, it explodes with life; it was as if Bowie and his band believed they were playing it for the last time.

Bowie closed the concert as planned, with Ziggy Stardust; he walked off with his band, and collapsed. He was flown to hospital in Hamburg, where he underwent emergency heart surgery. It had not in fact been a trapped nerve, but a blocked artery, widely interpreted as a heart attack.

'I'm so pissed off because the last ten months of this tour have been so fucking fantastic,' said Bowie in a statement. 'Can't wait to be fully recovered and get back to work again. I tell you what, though, I won't be writing a song about this one.'

David Bowie never gave another concert. The lights came down. Nothing would be quite the same again. It may be tempting to view this episode as a kind of supernova, the point where Bowie gave all he could, gave more than he could, leaving incandescently. But this would be to imbue it all with a crass romanticism. There are videos of this concert, and they are awful to watch. They don't show *a* reality. They just show reality.

This was not the end, but it was an ending. In a broad sense, it was the end of Bowie as he had been understood since the 1960s, as a singer who would record albums as a matter of routine and who would then promote them with a slew of media appearances and a live tour. But in a narrow sense, it curtailed this promising little phase, where matters of God's presence and absence permeated his work and his words more explicitly than ever, and lent his music a unique character.

Bowie's albums from this time highlight the distinction between denial and doubt. Denial, the path Bowie walked for a while in the

1980s, is essentially a dead end. It could also be seen as a thing that represses, even crushes. But doubt is dynamic: it wrestles and it questions. It is open to possibility. It is no surprise, therefore, that this phase of Bowie's work was so fruitful.

Moreover, many believers see doubt as a healthy part of their faith. 'A faith without doubts cannot advance,' said Pope Francis in 2021; 'the thought of being abandoned by God is an experience of faith which many saints have experienced'.[40] Doubt 'helps us understand that God is always greater than we imagine him to be,' he said the following year; 'his works are surprising compared to our calculations; his actions are different, always, they exceed our needs and expectations'.[41]

'That's the shock: All clichés are true,' said Bowie in 2003.[42] 'The years really do speed by. Life really is as short as they tell you it is. And there really is a God – so do I buy that one? If all the other clichés are true… Hell, don't pose me that one.'

11

LOVER

God is love. So says the New Testament. It's there in the first epistle of John, chapter four, verse 16. The actual words John wrote were Greek: Ὁ θεὸς ἀγάπη ἐστίν. Greek has words for different kinds of love, and here it is ἀγάπη, '*agape*', typically understood as unconditional love, the highest form of love. Its power is transformative, eternal, unbounded. This love is not sentimental, but elemental.

This is the kind of love with which David Bowie was becoming preoccupied. He had made no music for a decade, but when he returned, it was with a song of this love. The song was followed by an album that examined this love, but as an absence, as if thrown into relief. Bowie was a master of contrast: it turns out that you can sometimes see love more clearly when it isn't there.

In 2013, Bowie came back by going back – back to Berlin and all it meant. Tears and the Wall, and time and love, and ruins and light: from these, Bowie made something great. The song, rooted and rootless, new and old, was called 'Where Are We Now?' It materialized seemingly from nowhere one Tuesday morning, 8 January 2013. Everyone thought Bowie had gone, so his return was greeted like the benign ghost of a lost loved one.

It was some trick though, a reappearance without a disappearance. Yes, things had changed since his heart attack in 2004, but Bowie had done things in public pretty much every year since. In September 2005, he sang 'Life on Mars?' at the fundraising event Fashion Rocks. It was a compelling performance; he was made up to look like he had donned his suit just after rising from his hospital bed. He sang two songs with Arcade Fire, whom he adored. That year, he was interviewed by the musician and broadcaster Courtney Pine for his BBC Radio 2 show *Jazz Crusade*; Bowie sounded different somehow, sweet and thin-voiced, exceptionally Bromley.

In March 2006, filming began on the film *The Prestige*. It was directed by Christopher Nolan and was about feuding Victorian magicians; Bowie played the visionary engineer Nikola Tesla. Two months later, Bowie sang the Pink Floyd songs 'Arnold Layne' and 'Comfortably Numb' alongside David Gilmour at the Royal Albert Hall. In June, Bowie recorded his appearance in the Ricky Gervais sitcom *Extras*; it was broadcast three months later and included what may well qualify as a new Bowie song, 'Pug Nosed Face', a slight work of comic mockery. In October, he voiced the character Lord Royal Highness in the Spongebob Squarepants extended episode 'Atlantis SquarePantis'. Then in November he sang 'Wild is the Wind', 'Fantastic Voyage' and 'Changes' at the Black Ball charity gala in New York; it would be his final official concert performance. That year, he also appeared in a very short film, or long advertisement, about record stores. Bowie began: 'I've made a journey out of my life; I've been trying to find what is the essence of it.'

In May 2007, Bowie curated a festival in New York; one of the acts was Ricky Gervais. To welcome him on stage, Bowie sang 'Pug Nosed Face'. He would never again sing before a live audience. Ten months later, Bowie filmed a cameo appearance for the 2009 film *Bandslam*; the plot had him discovering a new act on MySpace. In June 2008, he chose songs and wrote some revealing notes for a new compilation called *iSelect*; it came free with, of all things, the *Mail on Sunday*, exposing its millions of readers, not typically known for their sense of artistic adventure, to various obscurities and curios like the melody-free *Lodger* track 'Repetition' and the *Low*-era offcut 'Some Are'.

Only then was there something closer to radio silence, but Bowie would still pop up here and there. He had told the *Observer* newspaper in January 2010 what he had been listening to on his iPod:

tracks included 'For With God No Thing Shall Be Impossible' by John Adams (in Bowie's words: 'The emotional in search of the divine'). And around that time, unknown to the world, he began making tentative steps towards rekindling his own creativity.

There were two projects. One, according to the Pulitzer Prize-winning author and screenwriter Michael Cunningham, was a new musical. Cunningham, whose books include *The Hours* and *By Nightfall*, wrote a piece for the magazine *GQ* in 2017 telling how Bowie had asked him to write a script for a daring work of theatre.[1] According to Cunningham, it was to be 'a musical about an alien, a dead Bob Dylan, and the work of Emma Lazarus'. The alien was inspired in some way by Thomas Jerome Newton from *The Man Who Fell to Earth*; Dylan was dead in the musical but the story involved the discovery of a cache of unheard Dylan songs, which Bowie would write; and Emma Lazarus is the poet who wrote 'The New Colossus', on which the Statue of Liberty stands, with the lines 'Give me your tired, your poor / Your huddled masses yearning to breathe free'. But Bowie's heart problems returned at some point during their collaboration, wrote Cunningham, requiring emergency surgery. Given other details in the article, this must have been around 2011. They never worked together again.

The other project was an album. Bowie called some of his collaborators from over the decades; they signed non-disclosure agreements, forbidding talk of their new work with him. There had long been privacy; now, there was secrecy. Out in the world, this led to a growing sense that Bowie had sung his last. Then two odd things started happening.

First, there were strong rumours among well-placed figures in the media and the music industry that Bowie was gravely ill. The Flaming Lips recorded a song called 'Is David Bowie Dying?'; it ends with a line about the sun, suggesting they had been paying attention to 'Heathen (The Rays)'.

Second, Bowie was somehow becoming *Bowier*. His time away from the stage and the cameras had restored to him a certain mystique. In the late 1990s, he had pioneered a strategy that other artists would soon follow, a process of demystification – predominantly by communicating directly with fans online. But by the early 2010s, Bowie once again carried a sense of quietly beguiling enigma and unquestionable artistic credibility. This was demonstrated to spectacular effect at the opening ceremony of the 2012 Olympics: the proceedings were directed by Bowie devotee Danny Boyle, who had the British team enter the arena to a particularly immense 'Heroes'. Writing in the *Guardian* at the time, Robin Turner said it 'resonated like a national anthem beamed from an alternate universe'. The organizers asked Bowie to perform (of course they did), but he turned them down (of course he did). After all, David Bowie was gone.

And then his return was small and monumental. It relied on technology that had not existed at the time of his previous record: swift video streaming to enable 'Where Are We Now?' to be published unannounced, and social media to spread the word. That morning, 8 January 2013, which happened to be Bowie's 66th birthday, the story of the new song was picked up by *Today*, BBC radio's flagship current affairs programme. It appeared in news bulletins around the world throughout the day. British newspapers on Wednesday 9 January were packed with response, analysis and photos. A little drop had generated a tsunami.

But in order not to be overwhelmed by the simple fact of Bowie's return, the song itself had to be strong. It was. What also helped was that Bowie seemed to be embracing his age: his voice was markedly older, brittle in places, befitting the man in the song, looking back and wondering what had happened. In composition and execution, it was rich, elegant, graceful and affecting; there was no attempt to sound young or to fit in with current trends.

But there is something else going on with 'Where Are We Now?', a certain magical quality; and here we return to the story of Bowie and spirituality, of the deepest kind. He once spoke about singing 'Heroes' in Berlin when the song sounded 'almost like a prayer'.

The show was in 1987. 'I'll never forget that,' he said. 'It was one of the most emotional performances I've ever done. I was in tears.' That night, his backdrop was the Wall. He could hear thousands of East Berliners on the other side, cheering and singing. 'God, even now I get choked up. It was breaking my heart. I'd never done anything like that in my life, and I guess I never will again.'[2]

The opening lines of 'Where Are We Now?' are sung to a companion by a man remembering. There was a time when he caught a train from Potsdamer Platz, to the surprise of his listener. That single memory exists on the fringe of life, like a faltering resurrection. As the singer puts it, he's 'walking the dead'. Other places are briefly called back into being: the Dschungel nightclub, the KaDeWe department store, at least as it once was. The winding chords map out the streets; the melody ambles along them, and is sometimes reflective and sometimes puzzled.

The second verse contains a direct historical reference, hitherto rare for Bowie. It recounts events from 1989, as the border between East Berlin and West Berlin was opened, as the Wall fell down. But where is this place, really? 'The past doesn't really exist,' Bowie once said.[3]

Then the song builds into something deeply moving and stirring, made all the more so by its being so delicate and humble. The chords find a new stability; they are resolute, assured. From these firm foundations emerges a guitar part of beautiful simplicity, vulnerable and defiant, courageous. There is a gathering of strength from the drums. As long as we have what we need to live, he sings: sun, and rain, and fire, and me, and you – the meaning is too much for words, so the sentence is finished by music.

In the video, the song is sung by the particularly craggy face of Bowie projected onto a curious two-headed puppet; on the other head is projected the face of a woman. Later, a man stands at a distance from them, looking at them. The man is David Bowie. The video has images of Bowie's old address in Berlin, apparently filmed by himself when he lived there. But maybe this couple have spoken to us before; maybe they were standing by the Wall all those years ago. Love and being. All else falls away. That moment, the song says, you *know*.

'Where Are We Now?' is a colour print. There followed the strip of negatives. Two months after the comeback song came the comeback album, *The Next Day*. Its cover celebrates the past and rejects it: it is the cover of *'Heroes'*, only with the brightness dialled down a little and a big white square slapped on the front and back, giving space for the new album title and track listing. The original title is crossed out rudimentarily.

The effect is bracing, an act of auto-iconoclasm in which the outline of the icon survives. But a whole load of other associations spin off it too, such as the white paint daubed over classical art in the packaging for *Heathen*, which also has words struck through, and the manner in which the covers of *Low*, *'Heroes'* and *Lodger* are depicted on the sleeve artwork for *Scary Monsters (and Super Creeps)*. *'Heroes'* was promoted with the slogans 'Tomorrow belongs to those who can hear it coming' and 'There's old wave, there's new wave, and there's David Bowie'. These were revived for *The Next Day*. There are layers to this thing, as reflected in the actual packaging: the first layer is the cover, which opens to a second layer, a new photograph of Bowie with that same white square over his face, and then there is a third layer, that same photograph now unobscured. He is lean and confrontational, wearing a what-are-you-looking-at scowl, eyes narrowed, lips clenched, in chilly monochrome.

And yet again, the artwork describes its contents, because *The Next Day* typically does about a dozen things at once, hurtling in all directions, spraying out constellations of references. A song might begin with an allusion to one point in Bowie's career and end with a quote from another. But it does all this while appearing to function as a very straightforward record: 14 songs, most of them fairly conventional art-rock, most of them lasting between three and four minutes. Those trusted musicians – including Earl Slick from the seventies, the saxophonist Steve Elson from the eighties, Gail Ann Dorsey, Sterling Campbell and Zack Alford from the nineties and the guitarist Gerry Leonard from the early 2000s – make familiar sounds. It was all recorded in Bowie's adopted home city of New York City and produced by Tony Visconti. Indeed, part of what makes *The Next Day* such an effective work of subterfuge is that it all seems, by Bowie's standards, quite conservative.

The first song, the album's title track, is a fine example. It is linear and rocking and all over in less than three and a half minutes. But to seasoned Bowie listeners, it immediately recalls 'Repetition' – the same chords, the same monotonal vocal line – then Bowie sings *listen* like he did on 'Breaking Glass'; then it all gets crankily intense like something from the *Scary Monsters* album; then he sings about corrupt priests, resurrecting his old antipathy towards organized religion; then he sings about not dying, which sounds like it might be responding to that Flaming Lips song; then for a second he sounds just like Lou Reed.

It continues in this vein, each reference in turn bringing its own colour and texture and reference points. Just look at the first: 'Repetition' and 'The Next Day' share a violent pounding relentlessness, one claustrophobically domestic, the other frigidly wild; the effect of both is like a boot stamping on a human face – forever, as George Orwell wrote in *Nineteen Eighty-Four*, which inspired Bowie to write a musical which became the album *Diamond Dogs*, and hang on, the video for 'Where Are We Now?' features a diamond and a dog. The rabbit holes are endless; the footnotes have footnotes.

And lest the listener gets lost in it all, Bowie provided a sort of map, or at least a torch. He had long stopped giving interviews, but he did send a list of 42 words about the album to the novelist Rick Moody, who wrote *The Ice Storm*, which became a film to which Bowie contributed a song.[4]

It soon became apparent that each track on the album was represented in sequence by three words on the list. The three words for the song 'The Next Day' are *Effigies, Indulgences, Anarchist*. The first seemingly refers to the figures being made of the 'whores' in the song. The second refers to a Catholic concept by which the punishment for sins can be reduced if the sinner performs certain acts, such as prayer or pilgrimage; the medieval Church grew notorious for selling these indulgences. The third may describe the man in the song who is punished by having his body dumped in a tree. But there could be more to it than that.

Then there are songs on the album that refer to other songs on the album. Then there are songs on the album that refer to songs that were seemingly recorded for the album but do not appear on the album. Then there are songs on the album that refer directly not only to songs by Bowie but to songs by other artists. Then there is Emma Lazarus and her poem inscribed on the pedestal of the Statue of Liberty and the musical Bowie wanted to write. Tony Visconti described the songs on *The Next Day* as 'engraved'; they go deep, sure enough. And there, in the substance chiselled from the stone: the sacred.

The album was going to be called *Love Is Lost*. As a title, it is perhaps less helpful commercially than *The Next Day*, which suggests a fresh start, a new chapter. But *Love Is Lost* is a far more satisfying title artistically, for the album depicts time and again the horrors that ensue from love's absence. It therefore stands as Bowie's great celebration of love, oblique as it may be.

The exception that proves the rule is 'Where Are We Now?', which is unique in that it shows us love unabashed, transcendent and glorious. But that song, simple as it sounds, is again replete with ghosts and echoes and foreshadowings. *Where are we now?* happen to be the first words that appear on the screen in the film *Moon*, which was released in 2009 and is a work of existential science fiction, set in space, exploring ideas of identity and doppelgangers; it is directed by Bowie's son. The video for 'Where Are We Now?' has Bowie wearing a T-shirt emblazoned with the phrase *Song of Norway*, long associated in Bowie's mind with his heartbreak at being left by his first real love, Hermione Farthingale.[5]

And there is something particularly telling in the music itself. It evokes Robert Wyatt's version of the Elvis Costello song 'Shipbuilding'; even Bowie's vocal, uncharacteristically fragile, sounds like Wyatt's. In 1997, Bowie was asked what song he wished he had written. '"Shipbuilding",' he said. 'I think it's one of the most beautiful songs... Makes me cry, just the opening bars. Specifically the Robert Wyatt version – I think it's just the most tragically beautiful song.'[6] 'Shipbuilding'[7] concerns the Falklands War and its effect on life in Britain's decaying shipyard communities. The war brings work, but it also brings fear as young men are sent to the frontlines. Here we have the beauty and joy and hope of youth, destroyed: not diving for pearls, but diving for life.

Which takes us to another song on the album, 'I'd Rather Be High', about a young soldier who would rather be doing anything other than aiming his weapons at other men. This in turn brings to mind Bowie's various songs about reluctant servicemen whose penchant for independent thinking puts them at odds with their superiors, songs like 'Bombers', recorded in 1971, and 'Running Gun Blues', a perky-sounding number from 1970 depicting the brutalizing effect of a violent culture upon a young man.

This then takes us back a couple of songs on *The Next Day*, to the jaunty 'Valentine's Day' (Bowie's three words: *Isolation*, *Revenge*, *Osmosis*), about a boy who embarks on a shooting spree. But the music here is a clear reference to The Kinks song 'Waterloo Sunset', which Bowie once covered. 'Waterloo Sunset' tells of innocent love between a Terry and a Julie; 'Valentine's Day' has a Teddy and a Judy, slain.

Back to 'I'd Rather Be High'. We can explore its numerous literary references, including a likely allusion, via Lady Manners, to Evelyn Waugh,[8] whose novel *Vile Bodies* influenced *Aladdin Sane* and sets youthful love and spiritedness against the brutality of war, culminating in a party in a limousine on a battlefield. We can jump forward a few songs to 'How Does the Grass Grow?', where war once again obliterates hope in a macabre rhyme from the military camps.⁹ Somewhere here may be the story of Bowie's grandfather, Robert Haywood Jones, a private who was killed on the last day of the Battle of the Somme. The song repeatedly quotes 'Apache', a galloping instrumental by the Shadows, inspired by a Western. It ends with a lengthy musical quote from one of Bowie's own songs, 'Boys Keep Swinging', a tongue-in-cheek celebration of youthful masculine vitality.

Youthful masculine vitality – a flashback to earlier in the album, and to a more shadowy song, 'Dirty Boys'. It reflects Bowie's enduring fascination with stylized, stylish gang violence: by all means smash windows with a stolen cricket bat, the lyrics suggest, but please make sure you sport some natty headwear while doing so.

And so from the twisted familial embrace of the gang to the pain of utter isolation in 'You Feel So Lonely You Could Die'. Despite the title, this is not a song of sympathy; on the contrary, such a horrifying fate is one the narrator craves for his subject. Again, the song points beyond itself, this time to Elvis Presley and 'Heartbreak Hotel', whose every subsequent verse ends with a variation of Bowie's words. At its heart is the idea that a life without love is the worst end imaginable.

These enraged songs speak of the annihilation that comes upon a man when love is lost. But when the victim is a woman – well, that may be even worse.

Some of the songs on *The Next Day* seem a little aimless, even a bit off. This is where Bowie's list of 42 words becomes invaluable: with its help, they suddenly start to make a kind of sense. A picture emerges of woman after woman being patronized, denigrated, manipulated, trafficked, exploited, terrorized by men who claim to care for them, who deploy love as a weapon. These women exist in a climate of fear. They are promised a new life, but it is a living death.

Take, for example, 'Boss of Me'. Heard on its own terms, it could be the worst song Bowie recorded this century. Its chorus is singularly unprepossessing, voicing incredulity that power might be wielded over him by a humble girl; we might hope that Bowie would be above this kind of casually belittling sexism. He sings it over and over again, every *me* sounding uglier than the last. There is some weird line about flying in the night, and her crying. But it is crowded out by all this *Boss of MeEEEeegh* stuff.

Still, we all know Bowie could be bad, and the album has been good so far, so we can let him off this one. But if we linger a moment over Bowie's three words for this (*Displaced, Flight, Resettlement*), suddenly the real story materializes. Bowie is playing a character here, a man who is taking a woman against her will to a foreign country.

The original version of *The Next Day* came with an extra track called 'I'll Take You There'. It has another uninspired chorus, a dialogue in which one character asks what their new name will be in the USA, and who they will become there, while the other fails to answer, merely asking for trust that they will get them there. Bowie did not provide three words for this, as it did not officially form part of the album, but it is surely part of the same story as 'Boss of Me'.

And there is another song that did not make the album but which was released initially as a bonus track in Japan, and later, on an expanded version of *The Next Day*. It is a decidedly catchy and upbeat number called 'God Bless the Girl'. We are told of a woman, Jacqui, who loves her work, who believes her job has been given her by God. But then it transpires she is afraid, cannot leave, is effectively enslaved. Maybe Jacqui's work is not love, at least not in a healthy, life-giving sense. Maybe one of the voices here is indifferent to her suffering, the one who says: 'I just wanna have some fun.' Maybe something is very wrong.[10]

Which brings us to what should rightfully have been the album's title track, 'Love Is Lost'. Bowie's three words for it are *Hostage, Transference, Identity*. *Hostage* describes the situation of the subject, a young woman. *Identity* is a constant theme: her voice is new, her accent is new, even her eyes are new. *Transference*, however, refers to where the emotional devastation has been wrought. It is a term from Freudian psychoanalysis, describing the phenomenon whereby someone effectively superimposes a memory of a particular person onto a different person. It is more profound and potentially dangerous than someone merely reminding you of someone else; it is more like a form of mistaken identity.

The lyrics suggest a deep tragedy, and an abominable betrayal of the woman. The music is harsh, ruthless, unyielding. And the man from 'God Bless the Girl' returns, singing a melody that promises freedom but brings horrific incarceration: 'Say hello, you're a beautiful girl.' Terrifying voices, from the outside, from the inside, blame her for all this. Love has been twisted into a weapon; love has become a means of cruelty; love has been desecrated. This is what happens when love is lost.

This album being what it is, 'Love Is Lost' again directs the listener here and there. Perhaps its most distinctive sonic element is the effect applied to a drum, a sound pioneered on *Low*. The first side of *Low* has three songs where there are women and confined spaces: the woman in whose room the singer has been breaking glass; the woman who is so deep in her room, who never leaves her room; and the woman in the car 'peeping' as the driver puts his foot down on a manic drive round and round a car park. The first line of 'Love Is Lost' may put one in mind of Bowie at the age of 22, disconsolate at the loss of his love with Hermione. And there is another connection – to the warm and gentle John Lennon song 'Love', whose pattern of mirrored lyrics is here echoed and emptied of all love.

'Love Is Lost', together with the songs to which it is surely related on this album and on its fringes, resurrects one of Bowie's more disturbing themes: the suffering of women and girls at the hands of men. It goes back all the way to his first album and one of his strangest songs, 'Please Mr. Gravedigger', telling of a ten-year-old named Mary-Ann, whom the narrator has killed. There is the woman abused by her partner in 'Repetition'; there is the woman colonized by her lover in 'China Girl'; in a song from 1987 there is Julie, whom it seems has been shot by a man out of jealousy; there is the woman accused of provoking her partner into violence in 'Too Dizzy', a song Bowie all but disowned; there is Baby Grace Blue, the teenage girl drugged and killed on *1. Outside*.

Male violence against women and girls, often in the context of purported love, is a frequent source of horror in Bowie's writing. But it feels different on *The Next Day*. There had been times when it had been employed to construct a story, to conjure a mood, made into an instrument in order to achieve a particular artistic end. Here, the point is the act itself. It is the difference between a woman being killed in order to start a story, and a story about a woman in which the woman is killed.

Finally, we are back to 'You Feel So Lonely You Could Die'. Bowie's three words: *Traitor, Urban, Comeuppance*. What if the subject here is the trafficker, the abuser, the exploiter whom we have previously encountered? What if this is the man upon whom Bowie wishes a grisly and dismal end?[11] There are musical clues too: 'You Feel So Lonely You Could Die' refers to Bowie's own 'Rock 'n' Roll Suicide', whose distinctive guitar line the song quotes, and also to his 'Five Years', whose distinctive drum beat is repeated at the song's end. The songs were respectively the last and the first tracks on *The Rise and Fall of Ziggy Stardust and the Spiders from Mars*. 'You Feel So Lonely You Could Die' is not the last song on the album, but it represents the end of a cycle.

And resettlement, identity, the alien, Emma Lazarus, whose words have welcomed generations of the hopeful to the USA: all themes of Bowie's putative musical, which no one knew anything about, and all of which run through and around *The Next Day*. Fourteen songs, 53 minutes, as simple as love, as complex as love.

All this, and we have not really mentioned God. At least, not by that name. There are, however, songs on *The Next Day* that deal explicitly with religion and spirituality. The title track depicts a debased godliness; its video is a parade of Catholic and broader Christian imagery presented in a satirical manner.[12] And for all its riotous and cinematic savagery, the story starts with a small scene of great tenderness: lovers look into each other's eyes as they part; she begs him not to cry; he leaves to meet his fate, and she is left with thoughts of his love. Then he falls victim to violence unleashed by religion: another love is lost.

A further track, 'If You Can See Me', is a return to one of Bowie's oldest fears, that of the tyrannical Messiah. The song is unstable and unpleasant. Bowie's three words for it are *Crusade, Tyrant, Domination*. 'The Stars (Are Out Tonight)', the second single from the album, uses the gods of antiquity and the spirits of folklore to explore the phenomenon of celebrity; Bowie's three words are *Vampyric, Pantheon, Succubus*.

But we have seen throughout this book that Bowie's work can be intensely spiritual without talking directly of God. This album may be the most potent example. There is something of the divine in Bowie's conception of love: in its presence, there is redemption and peace; in its absence or corruption, there is brutality and degradation. *The Next Day* is the fullest examination of a kind of love Bowie had been singing about for decades: the pure ideal of love wrenched into hate in 'Cygnet Committee'; the love of 'Soul Love', a transformational force that has its own mind; the love of 'Under Pressure', that dares us to care and to change. This love is disembodied, in that it exists as an abstract entity, but it desires to be embodied, to live through us.

Saying that God is love, as John does in the New Testament, is not necessarily the same as saying that love is God. Many believers would see a great danger in equating the two, but one Christian mystic did precisely that. She was called Marguerite Porete, and she was burned at the stake in Paris in 1310. She wrote *The Mirror of Simple Souls*, a poetic treatise on *agape* which fell foul of Church authorities, in part for its supposed heresies. It includes these words: 'I am God, says Love, for Love is God and God is Love.'

It would be a surprise if Bowie had been unaware of Porete and her work, as she is precisely the kind of figure who would have enthralled him.

Christian mysticism is pertinent to *The Next Day* in another sense too. The mystical tradition has long cherished what is known as apophatic theology, which is based on the idea that God defies human description, because God is essentially unknowable and unnameable. It tells what God is only by telling what God is not. So rather than saying 'God is kind', one might say 'God is not unkind.' The former restricts God to human ideas of kindness; the latter liberates God from our limited understanding. This could be viewed as another way of approaching the 'God beyond God'. Apophatic theology is not unique to Christian mysticism, but has a close relationship to it: it was advocated by the great German mystic Meister Eckhart, who lived around the same time as Porete, and who would pray: 'God, rid me of God.'

This all sounds quite Bowie-ish in general, but there is something particularly apophatic about *The Next Day*. It is above all a work about love, only shown in reverse, extolled by depicting what it is not, again and again and again. The screaming hordes in 'The Next Day' are certain that God exists. Why? 'The Devil told them so.' The sacrilegious presupposes the sacred.

As Bowie albums go, *The Next Day* is especially studied and intentional. It took longer to make than any other Bowie album: sessions began in May 2011 and finished in October 2012.[13] It is not one of those records of his that harnesses chaos, or results from a bunch of experiments, or creates new musical worlds. Nor is it in any sense a pandering record, a crowd-pleaser. Rather, it might be as close as Bowie came to recording what went on in his head. It is an album on which Bowie is the paint and the brush, the marble and the chisel. There is vastly more to it than there initially seems, and this is almost tangible: it is hard on the ears, and pretty much everything is loud, as if the music is being forced at you through something that is too small for it.

To promote the record, the photographer Jimmy King took a number of pictures of Bowie, and even these seem quite uncomplicated: one shows a white-shirted and healthy-looking Bowie smiling in the studio; another is a simple picture of him in a flat cap and casual sweater; another finds him in a moment of reflection with his back to his keyboard; in another he's looking out over Manhattan from the roof of his apartment. But examine them more closely and they become a little unnerving, and not only because they are airbrushed heavily. In the first, there is a skeleton figure behind him; the second and third have weirdly pronounced shadows; the fourth is clearly a homage to the cover of *Earthling*, right down to the shape of his hands and direction of his feet, even the length of his coat, which in turn evokes Caspar David Friedrich's *Wanderer above the Sea of Fog*.

So, pay attention. Don't just see – look. And don't just hear – *listen*, as Bowie commands in the last word of the song 'The Next Day'. The album's final track is an aching thing called 'Heat', another study in contrast. The narrator can love someone only by hating someone else. Love is juxtaposed with war, 'the theft of love'.

Weighty stuff, so much so that we might forget what this love actually is. For a time, the artist and critic Matthew Collings was frequently in contact with Bowie. 'During our last encounter, we didn't talk about art: David instead spent a lot of time raving about his daughter,' wrote Collings.[14] 'If you could invent a drug', Collings asked him, 'what effect would it have?'

'A shot of hug,' Bowie replied. 'Preferably from a three-year-old like my daughter, that age, that brief window of time when a child hugs you with all its might and conviction and pure, undiluted love, without it expecting a reward. The kind of gift that a great painting gives you: it's just there for you to marvel at, it lifts your spirits, instils you with hope and beauty, but it doesn't expect anything in return.'[15] *Agape*: for Bowie, there was nothing so divine.

12

MAGICIAN

There are three kinds of magician. There is the conventional conjuror, who practises an honest kind of deception: they trick you, but they do not claim for themselves any genuine supernatural power. You are willing to be deceived, and they are just fulfilling their part of the deal. Think of Paul Daniels or the illusionists Siegfried & Roy. Someone else who fitted the description was David Bowie, master of undisguised artifice. 'Part of my entertainment factor is – lying to you,' he said.[1]

Then there are the more ambiguous kinds, whose personas convey mystery, who appear part of this world and part of another: these are not cheeky patter-merchants or tanned Las Vegas entertainers, but slightly offbeat characters who leave open the possibility that they just may have access to a hidden dimension. David Blaine could be one, and so again could David Bowie. 'He's from his own universe,' says a fan in *Cracked Actor*, the 1975 BBC documentary. What universe? 'Bowie universe.'

And then there are those who say they work genuine miracles, or who purport to consort with the world of spirits or cast real spells. David Bowie surely qualifies here as well: he exorcized his swimming pool, he was more than familiar with the work of Aleister Crowley, he sang his own song of 'sex magick'[2] and he had absorbed tales and practices from the 'Risks Incidental to Ceremonial Magic' chapter in Dion Fortune's *Psychic Self-Defence*, which rather suggests he had indulged in occult rituals.

As Bowie moved through the late nineties and early 2000s, he became more of that first kind of magician, the human entertainer. The other two kinds, the somewhat otherworldly figure and the full-on man of magick, were long buried. Buried, but not dead, for they all returned in his final years, at least as art or performance. And this playing with fact and fantasy, this magical movement between realms, is an essential reason his last works carry such power. That old conflict between the flesh and spirit became inescapable.

Life can only be understood backwards, but it must be lived forwards. So said Søren Kierkegaard. But one problem with understanding Bowie's life backwards is that all is shaped by what we know today. We know he died in January 2016, and we know he had been ill with cancer for some time. The natural assumption, then, is that his final works are about dying or death; moreover, that they were part of a plan, that he knew he would make nothing else, and that these were crafted in that knowledge. But the truth may be a little more complex.

Bowie received his diagnosis sometime around summer 2014. However, he did not learn until around November the following year that it would be terminal. By then, he had at last finished his final theatre piece, as well as an album. He was working up a new musical in 2015; it was to tell colourful tales of 18th-century London, complete with public hangings, lovable thieves and that enduring Bowie fascination, stylish hoodlums. And besides, Bowie had sung about death for decades: it is a morbid thought, but 'Bring Me the Disco King' might have been a fitting final song, as might 'Heathen (The Rays)'. There was little that made his last works exceptional in that regard.

Perhaps, though, this misses the point. He may not have known that these were his last works, but he made them as if they were. Being Bowie, this did not mean that they were moribund; rather, it meant they were urgent and vital – these pieces of art emerge in an eruption of creativity and imagination and inspiration. They are not the works of a man who was slowly dying, but the works of a man who was ferociously living.

They are discrete works but created in parallel. What unites them are two words that have by now become familiar, the two words remaining when all else has been stripped away. One of these words is *life*; the other, *love*.

There had been for some time a sense of taking stock. *The Next Day* was an archive in song; its release in 2013 preceded by three weeks the start of another trawl through the vaults, a monumental exhibition called *David Bowie Is*.

Bowie's people had contacted the Victoria & Albert Museum in London in 2010, suggesting it may want to display items from his archive; it numbered nearly 75,000 pieces and formed an astonishingly exhaustive record. The museum was given total access, and Bowie gave the V&A the freedom to present the resulting exhibition as it wished. It is fair to say the museum was not banking on it being a hit. 'No other museum had booked it for the tour,' said its co-creator Victoria Broackes, 'and we'd published 10,000 copies of the catalogue. There wasn't a lot of optimism that it was going to be a rip-roaring success.'[3]

As it turned out, it became the most popular exhibition in the history of the museum and proved successful everywhere it went for the next five years: London, São Paulo, Berlin, Paris, Melbourne, Barcelona, New York – a series of Bowie residencies in prestigious venues, a world tour for which Bowie had to do nothing.

Before long, there was a compilation album. There had been many in the past, their titles often alluding to Bowie's mercurial nature: there was *Changesonebowie* in 1976, *Changestwobowie* in 1981 and *Changesbowie* in 1990. This new one, released in 2014, took a different approach, emphasizing continuity: it was called *Nothing has changed*.[4] Unlike the others, it spanned his whole career, reaching back to 'Liza Jane' in 1964. It was released in various forms, each with a different cover showing Bowie at different ages looking in a mirror; but the full three-CD version was unusual too for its sequencing, opening in the present day and leading the listener backwards through time.

Its first track, 'Sue (Or in a Season of Crime)', was something new. If the end had a beginning, it was here.

The song marked a return to sonic adventure. Moving away from the rock bands who had backed him for so long, Bowie was instead in the quivering grip of an avant-garde jazz orchestra, led by Maria Schneider, a pioneering composer. They made a sound that was roiling and unstable, sometimes akin to a dozen competing tunes blaring out at once. Bowie ducked and swerved around it, sometimes rode on it, sometimes burst through it, narrating a first-person account of a man who, so it seems, kills his wife on account of a supposed betrayal. The style evokes the work of Robert Browning, the nineteenth-century English poet; it also echoes 'Please Mr. Gravedigger', that macabre monologue from Bowie's first album. Again, the music gives up relics: at one point, the woodwinds quote from the *Low* track 'Warszawa'; there are elements of drum and bass in the rhythms, recalling *Earthling*. It lasts for seven minutes, and has a strange tune and no chorus.

The recording soon passed into obscurity, but its signal was clear: David Bowie was doing something different. *The Next Day* had been considered, pored over, shaped and honed over years; this new thing was bold and spontaneous, carried by the spark of the moment. Geoff MacCormack wrote to Bowie about it: 'It reminds me of the psalms we sang in St. Mary's choir together when we were kids.'[5]

With spontaneity came simultaneity. Bowie began working on a new album, while working on his play. There were also two music videos. Richard Strauss had those Four Last Songs, and here was Bowie's equivalent.

The first of these to be released was a new video and song, 'Blackstar', styled officially as ★. It was premiered on television by the broadcaster Sky on 19 November 2015, and there was a lot to take in: it is ten minutes long, with at least four songs' worth of ideas, wild improvisation, Middle Eastern tones, sinister soul moves, treacherous jazz flair, baroque terrors... And that was just the music.

★ was the first Bowie work for decades that seemed to have been transmitted from a different plane of existence, yet it remained rooted and grounded by the tactility of its sound. Bowie was back again (again), and this time he had brought it all with him: magic, occultism, spirituality, religion, truth, deceit, stardom, war and even beauty.

There are two things that the song communicates immediately. The first is that we are in an unusual place, the scales and tones alien to standard rock and pop. The second is that there is something eerie and unknowable afoot: the words tell of a candle standing in the Villa of Ormen. There is no such place in the material world, and no explanation is offered. An early draft of the lyrics calls it the Villa of Allmen.

Already, there are associations and echoes that ring out beyond ★. The very notion of a ten-minute Bowie song will, to numerous fans, bring to mind 'Station to Station', Bowie's ten-minute magickal treatise. Both songs have sections that are incantatory, with vocals multi-tracked, low and high. Of all Bowie's songs, 'Station to Station' is also arguably the closest relative to ★ in terms of structure, drawing together multiple sections and styles into a coherent whole. In those incantatory lines from 'Station to Station' there is a reference to *White Stains*, a work by Aleister Crowley; a repeated line in ★ is reminiscent of 'The Centre of All', a line from *The Star Sapphire*, a ritual created by Crowley.

The lyrics then tell of executions, before ★ enters a time of wordlessness, the instruments tracing the melodies and harmonies with a sense of unease; then the words we have already heard are repeated before the music carries the listener through extraordinary colours to another place, somewhere we may think we know. Here are conventional chord sequences and something as old-fashioned as a tune; these words are not chanted but sung; the air is suddenly clear and sunlit. Then, in multi-tracked vocals, in the vague distance, a man claims that he is a blackstar. There is talk of an angel falling; there is talk of sacred ground. And we find ourselves at the centre of a clash of cultures which Bowie had sung about before, in 'Loving the Alien'.

Bowie apparently told his new saxophonist Donny McCaslin that the song was in some way about ISIS,[6] a group of murderous Islamic extremists also called ISIL and Islamic State. ISIS became known in the 2010s for a campaign of torture, 'execution' and suicide bombing in the cause of establishing an Islamic caliphate. We have only McCaslin's word for it, and Bowie's people denied it, but it seems a very odd thing for a man so seemingly honest as McCaslin to have invented. There may have been an understandable fear that the song would be diminished by narrowing the range of possible meanings; but the lyrics and style of ★ support McCaslin's claim.

★ can be interpreted as a representation of the perverse kind of stardom sought by Islamic State militants. One destroys himself and gives way to another. Bowie sings of passports and sedatives: some ISIS supporters burned their passports;[7] others made their own Islamic State passports;[8] suicide bombers have been known to take sedatives.[9] A blackstar finds the fame he craves, and when he dies somebody else takes his place. The narrator does not know why, but he can tell us *how*, which is by some fundamental disorientation, by being 'born upside-down'. This sense of profound inversion is magnified by a series of apophatic declarations, the blackstar defining himself by what he is not – for example, a popstar, or a pornstar. Whatever I may be, he seems to be saying, I am not a Western star.

An earlier draft of Bowie's lyrics lends weight to this reading. In these, the blackstar is not a 'Christstar' or a 'Jewstar'. But in this earlier draft, he declares he is also not a Sunni or a Shia – that is, he is not a member of either of the two largest denominations of Islam. ISIS officially associates itself with Sunni Islam, but rejects many Sunni traditions. Understood this way, ★ fits smoothly into the broader context of Bowie's work, especially its examination of the political consequences of religious belief, and the ensuing conflicts between cultures and civilizations.

After this passage, the song darkens again; we are back where we were, but the place has changed. The words are fewer, the repetitions deleted. Where the instrumentation was skittish and excitable, it is now heavy and doleful. The otherworldly harmonies remain, but there is a sense of exhaustion. Drums stumble; synths bump along aimlessly in search of rest; flutes flicker, burn out.

That is ★ the song. Then there is ★ the video, and yet more portals open here. The first thing we see is the suit of an astronaut: we are being reminded of Major Tom, with the suggestion that this is where he has finally ended up. We are also being pointed towards another work of existentialist science fiction: the suit bears the image of GERTY, the computer on the spacecraft in the film *Moon*, made by Duncan Jones, Bowie's son.

It becomes clear after a few seconds that the astronaut is a stranger in a strange land, lost and dead. The place has a generically Middle Eastern appearance. A woman finds the suit and lifts the visor; in the helmet she finds a jewelled skull, resembling the relics of saints.[10] The astronaut's skull is carried off and venerated; it forms the centrepiece of a mystical ritual, in which only women take part. The women form a magic circle.

The scene changes and Bowie appears in extraordinary form. His face is bandaged, and there are buttons where his eyes should be. There is so much here too to explore. In its account of the resurrection of Lazarus, the Gospel of John says: 'The dead man came out... his face wrapped in a cloth.'[11] Blindness and seeing is a theme in Bowie's more explicitly spiritual works, right back to 'Karma Man', through to 'Soul Love', 'Loving the Alien', 'New Angels of Promise' and the artwork for *Heathen*.

Then a different Bowie stands before painted clouds, hand on hip, wind ruffling his hair and blowing the pages of his holy book. It is as if Bowie is atop a mountain; wearing a black jacket and with his elbow bent, it seems to be yet another reference to *Wanderer above the Sea of Fog*. Later in the video, three scarecrow men gyrate like Elvis and writhe in agony as they are crucified.

Like classical depictions of the crucifixion of Christ, it all takes place under an eclipsed sun, or a black star.

The flow of allusions continues. The ★ symbol calls to mind magickal pentagrams, and is imprinted upon the holy book Bowie wields. 'In dealing with elementals or non-human entities the Pentagram, or Pentalapha [sic], is the best weapon,' wrote Dion Fortune.[12]

★'s video was directed by Johan Renck, 'a huge Crowley fan', who talked 'a little bit' with Bowie about Crowley. Renck said of the video: 'On one side of things there is no deliberate, underlying, firm quest to have any references to past times. On the other side of things, a lot of these ideas have been conglomerative of David and I chatting.'[13]

And something else is being reflected and refracted here, intentionally or otherwise – namely, the video for 'Loving the Alien'. Both videos emphasize the artifice of their Middle Eastern–themed sets; both depict figures shaking violently in spiritual fervour; both feature Bowie playing, among other characters, an incongruously smarmy showman; both have women's eyes seen through narrow frames. Both share the same essential concern, only ★ is both more graphic in its imagery and more subtle in its symbolism, and places the conflict between West and East – in broad terms, and between Christianity and Islam, although neither originated in the West – in a wider, wilder, stranger, more primal yet more sophisticated spiritual domain. For whatever reason, the Bowie of 2015 was able to tap into something that just eluded the Bowie of 1984 – something terrifying, vast, overwhelming and maybe even true. ★ the song and ★ the video: magic, and magick, everywhere.

Time now for some stage magic. While working on his new music, Bowie was also working on the realization of a lifetime's dream: a piece of musical theatre. His collaboration with Michael Cunningham had fizzled out, but Bowie persevered. He got in touch with Enda

Walsh, an Irishman whose plays and musicals, including *Disco Pigs*, *Penelope* and *Once*, had by then received countless awards. The result of their efforts was arguably as significant as any of Bowie's other last works: put it together with the touring exhibition and you have a kind of multimedia autobiography.

Agape was still very much on Bowie's mind during his discussions with Walsh. 'There was a lot of talk about the beauty of unconditional love,' Walsh recalled.[14] Elsewhere, Walsh said, 'We looked a lot at stained-glass windows, how a story is told with a central image. How it's all broken and shattered.'[15]

After the false start with Cunningham, Bowie's work with Walsh was showing potential. So in 2014 Bowie asked Ivo van Hove, one of the most decorated theatre directors in Europe, to help take it to the stage. From Bowie's earlier concept, two elements survived: Thomas Jerome Newton, his character from *The Man Who Fell to Earth*, and the poet Emma Lazarus, who was beginning to elide with the resurrected biblical figure. But details remained scarce. 'There should be a killer in it, there should be a girl in it,' was all he told van Hove.

Bowie, Walsh and van Hove met in New York in 2014, along with Corinne 'Coco' Schwab, Bowie's personal assistant and confidante since the mid-1970s. Bowie and Walsh read the script to van Hove, interspersed with songs played on CD. Van Hove thought something was missing, and told Bowie that he needed to write 'the one song in the beginning. We need to know who that guy is. And we need a song that establishes the character within three or four minutes.'[16] So Bowie wrote the song and recorded a demo. The song was called 'Lazarus'.

'It sounded like an immediate Bowie classic, even in a demo version,' said van Hove. 'And I knew: now we have a show. Now we know who the guy is, what he's longing for, what his issue is. It's mysterious at the same time. It's everything.'[17]

Bowie wanted Newton to be played by Cillian Murphy. He was perhaps best known at the time for his role in the BBC series *Peaky*

Blinders, about well-dressed gangsters in England in the aftermath of the First World War. Of course, Bowie loved it. Murphy, a Bowie devotee, attended a workshop for *Lazarus* in New York, but his filming commitments precluded his further involvement. Michael C. Hall, who played the title character in the American drama *Dexter*, took his place.

Bowie called *Lazarus* a 'music theatre piece'. Van Hove is comfortable with a more traditional term: 'It had 19 songs – it's a musical!' Whatever it was, it was taking shape gradually. 'It was very strange, perhaps, but it was not like big existential ideas [at first]. That came together later, and then it became really very deep, but also entertaining.'[18]

Lazarus focuses on Thomas Jerome Newton. Bowie identified so closely with Newton that the two are essentially synonymous on the covers of *Station to Station* and *Low*; Bowie also accidentally referred to Newton as 'I' during rehearsals. Newton is a being from another planet who came to this world to find water, only to be corrupted by alcohol. In *Lazarus*, Newton resides in a New York City tower block, still drinking, barely really living. He is tormented by his past, not by memories of suffering, but by memories of love. He cannot die, and this is a problem.[19]

Much of what happens in *Lazarus* takes place inside a dream. Newton, it seems, is real; but it is unclear to what extent the other characters, and the various strange happenings of the play, are conjured by Newton's mind. The set takes this a step further, with two large rectangular windows giving the appearance of eye sockets. In his own notes for the play, Bowie envisaged the set as 'the inside of Thomas Newton's head – and within it – music, songs and story swirl about'.

Lazarus, as one may expect, is unconventional. It is not a standard jukebox musical. There is no attempt to weave a plot around Bowie's greatest hits. Indeed, eight of its songs were recorded after 2011 and much of the older material is rearranged and rethought, sometimes radically. The music is integral to the show, but rarely in a straightforwardly narrative way. Bowie said that his concerns as a writer were less what he felt about things, and more how things felt; that sense of expressionism is the work's dominant mood.

Newton, now older, still pines desperately for his lost love, Mary Lou, and for his family. He seeks some kind of eternal rest, which is denied him. He is attended by various characters, including a teenager initially known only as Girl, an assistant of sorts named Elly, and a killer, Valentine, familiar from *The Next Day*. The identities of some of these characters are never quite certain; they are fluid, amorphous.

The set too, though sparse, is in flux. Much of the dialogue is stilted and faltering; this is presumably deliberate. 'He understood that what you're putting out there is tone and atmosphere and not the detail of words or even character,' said Walsh. 'It's a real "what does it feel like? What is the big feeling that you're sending people away with?"'[20]

Emma Lazarus's poem 'The New Colossus' was printed in the programme, but the word *Lazarus* appears nowhere in the play. 'It's an existential drama – it's a drama about existence, about life and death. All these things are clearly there,' says van Hove. 'Lazarus is the person who dies but doesn't die. Because he comes back.' In the case of Bowie, that became more meaningful later, van Hove believes, but it also applied specifically to the character of Newton. 'I think that was a very important thing, that idea that you really never die, you will always be or in the memory of somebody, or like Bowie, you're still in the memory of a lot of people.'[21]

Lazarus explores themes that were coming to dominate Bowie's last years. First, there is simple, beautiful, unconditional love. In the opening minutes of the play, Newton recalls a vision: 'It was morning time and I was sitting at home with my wife and son and daughter – and nothing special happened – just small talk between us that I can't remember now – but I was there at home for a few moments with them.' Later, Girl reminds him that he had a teenage daughter, with whom he would walk to a nearby hill and look up at the sky as it filled with stars. They would make up stories about travelling through space. 'And when you paused a little – your daughter would say – "Speak some more – and we'll travel on."'

Relatedly, there is the destruction of love, personified by Valentine. He sings the song 'Valentine's Day'; numerous black balloons are burst, in an imitation of rapid gunfire. Black wings unfurl behind him; his presence is demonic, his personality that of Satan the suave deceiver. During the 'Valentine's Day' section, the stage directions state: *Slowly glides downstage like Fred Astaire – the space around him turning black.* It is an explicitly spiritual framing of the conflict between love and its enemy. When members of the Roman Catholic Church renew their baptismal vows every Easter, the priest asks if they renounce Satan 'and all his empty show'.

And as well as love and its destruction, there is the theme of life itself. Just before Girl appears, early in the play, Newton quotes Hamlet in Shakespeare's eponymous play: 'In this sleep of death – what dreams may come...' The line is from the soliloquy beginning 'To be, or not to be, that is the question'. Van Hove said he himself was interested in 'our existence. Why are we here? Can we make sense of it? We could commit suicide. Why don't we?'[22]

There were four new Bowie songs in *Lazarus*. One of them is called 'When I Met You'; it is the penultimate song of the play, and may well be its dramatic climax. It tells of an encounter that brings redemption. Another is a rageful thing called 'Killing a Little Time'. Another, 'No Plan', could be sung from heaven, or at least from between two worlds. It just – *just* – defies the laws of gravity. The fourth is the song 'Lazarus'.

Newton sings 'When I Met You' to Girl and then he stabs her. Valentine told him to. Valentine turns away and is lost in the darkness. Newton has a kind of epiphany: 'to be up there – and to feel the simple love of family'. Girl, whose name is revealed to be Marley, slowly opens her eyes. They sing 'Heroes',[23] only 'not the big version, not the stadium version, but in a really small version', as van Hove puts it. They splash and slide around in milk, like dolphins.

A shape is drawn on the floor. It promises a means of escape, or a means of enlightenment; perhaps they are the same. We are back in 1975, back with Kabbalah, back with the Tree of Life. The tree here is sharpened into the shape of a rocket. In the production, we see Newton lie in it; a screen shows it lifting off, in silence.

The original production of *Lazarus* was staged in only two cities, first New York and then London, in small theatres. Musically and visually, it was striking: wild visions and sounds transfigured the auditorium; a screen would sometimes relay the action on the stage but a second or two ahead of that in the auditorium, giving the impression that all was preordained. The overall effect was simultaneously engrossing and alienating.

When Bowie saw the premiere of *Lazarus* in New York on 7 December 2015, he witnessed the fulfilment of his most enduring creative ambition. It was a fitting moment for his last public appearance. 'At the opening night there was a picture of it with us on stage, and he's smiling,' says van Hove. 'And a lot of people wrote in the press that he was looking great. But I was there and he said backstage, "Ivo, you have to hold my hand," because he was too weak even to get on stage. It was only a few metres.' When they left the stage, Bowie had to sit down immediately. 'And then we had the most wonderful conversation. And he said "Ivo, let's do the next one."'[24]

'We started talking about escape but we ended up talking about a person trying to find rest,' wrote Enda Walsh on his collaboration with Bowie. 'About dying in an easier way.'[25] The stage directions say only: *Marley leaves. Newton finds rest. Blackout. The end.*

The third of the four last works was 'Lazarus', the song and video. Released as a single on 17 December 2015, 'Lazarus' has a deep and distinctive sound: the bass bubbles and prowls and circles; sharp yowls of guitar slash a charcoal sky; saxophones sigh. They herald Bowie, who, in the first line, tells his listeners to cast their eyes upwards; he is in heaven.[26]

No Bowie song has acquired greater posthumous resonance than 'Lazarus'. That opening line was sung in the play by Newton, in a skyscraper, in the heights of altitude and intoxication. It is sung on the single by Bowie, with strength, resignation and the slightest wheeze. The atmosphere is dark, but lights dart around.

The words of the middle section make little sense outside the play. But that seems not to matter, because by that point the music has found a new vigour that propels the song through the next verse, the saxes now rising defiantly, Bowie raising the pitch, raising the stakes. One way or another, freedom is inevitable; but is it willed or fated? A solo from Donny McCaslin then says all that words cannot, joined by the band as they brew a storm of focused bombast, smashing and raging before all falls back, and there is again space to catch breath.

Then, on 7 January 2016, came the video. The frame is narrowed, creating tension from the outset; a hand tentatively opens a wardrobe from within; and we are taken up to that bandaged and button-eyed face of Bowie in what looks like some kind of desolate institution. He is lying on a bed, and sometimes hovers gently above it; a woman seems to be hunting him, softly and secretly. Then the video snaps into that energetic middle section, and there is Bowie in those dark clothes daubed with white diagonal stripes, the attire from the days when he would scrawl the Kabbalist Tree of Life. Bowie moves half-comically, half-disturbingly. Soon, he is at a desk upon which sits a jewelled skull; he casts around for inspiration, before scribbling furiously. The video ends as he withdraws, backwards, into the wardrobe. The final note is a scythe of guitar, played by Bowie.

In his notes for the video, Bowie called that dark-clothed character the Somnambulist.[27] It refers to *The Cabinet of Dr Caligari*, a seminal work of horror cinema made in Germany in 1920. Somnambulism is the technical term for sleepwalking; the villain of the film enlists a sleepwalker, keeps him in a box resembling a coffin, and makes him kill people. It is easy to see why *The Cabinet of Dr Caligari* might appeal to Bowie: its themes include madness, dual identities and freedom in the face of tyrannical authority, while its aesthetic is highly stylized and non-naturalistic, emphasizing its own artifice in the cause of emotional realism. Bowie's appearance and jerky movements echo those of the somnambulist in the film.

There is also a teasing ambiguity here. Bowie had sung about a particular form of sleepwalking in 'Did You Ever Have a Dream', written in 1967, when his interest in Buddhism was at its peak. The song is concerned with the arcane practice of astral flight, and describes it as a kind of walking while sleeping. Dr Caligari's somnambulist sleeps upright in a box; such behaviour was encouraged at the Buddhist monastery Samye Ling – where Bowie spent some time – supposedly to induce meditative states. It is surely not unduly fanciful to suppose that the Bowie of the mid-1970s, to which his costume in the video alludes, indulged in the odd astral adventure.

The video for 'Lazarus' was again directed by Johan Renck. It was shot in November 2015; while it was being filmed, Bowie learned that his cancer had reached the point where further treatment would be ineffective.[28]

The eighth of January 2016 was David Bowie's 69th birthday, and the day his final album was released. Like the song, it is officially called ★ and typically known as *Blackstar*. Its sleeve is part of its world: shadowy, crypt-like, cryptic, astronomic. There is no picture of Bowie on the cover; his customary place is taken by a five-pointed star. Even the word *Bowie* is absent, at least in that form; it is spelt out abstractly by shards of that star.

The gatefold sleeve of the original vinyl opens to reveal a large image of a starfield and a picture of Bowie looking something between unsettled and contemplative in a setting resembling the ★ video. A few lyrics from the album are arranged and linked like constellations, a fitting image for a time in Bowie's career when so many elements appear connected, and when the listener and viewer is invited to see patterns. The lyric booklet has on its cover a button-eyed Bowie; the words are printed black on black. There is little relief or release.

But that starfield holds a sort of promise, bright blasts in the void; and there are aspects of enchantment, hidden elements that take some time to discover. For example, take out the record, shine a light through the starfield, and that star on the cover sparkles. 'There are a lot of other things going on that aren't completely at the surface, but I do hope people see them – not necessarily straight away,' said Jonathan Barnbrook, the designer, in 2016.[29] 'There's one big thing which people haven't discovered yet. Let's just say, if people find it, they find it. If they don't, they don't.' A decade on, it seems no one has.

★, the album, has instant similarities to *Station to Station*. By modern standards, ★ has few songs – seven, one more than *Station to Station* – but, like those on *Station to Station*, they are relatively long, and the first is a ten-minute track sharing the album's name. These similarities follow the nods to occultism and esotericism in the videos for the singles ★ and 'Lazarus'; the suggestion is of unearthly and forgotten forces being corralled once more.

The lyrics, of course, can be pored over for references to death. Some are now painful to hear. In 'Dollar Days', there are evergreens in England that may never be seen, and faces that cannot be forgotten, no matter how hard one tries. The final song is called 'I Can't Give Everything Away', and we are told in the first line that there is something very wrong. These, in addition to some of the words of ★ and 'Lazarus', coupled with the granite black of the vinyl LP cover, plus what we now know, say that this is an album doubling as an epitaph.

But ★ is foremost a work of music, and the music here is alive, bursting with life. Bowie drove the band – a stellar cutting-edge jazz ensemble comprising McCaslin, keyboardist and pianist Jason Lindner, bassist Tim Lefebvre, drummer Mark Guiliana and guitarist Ben Monder — beyond what even they thought possible. There is abandon and wildness; the frontier of control grows hazy, porous, as instinct, feeling, force, lust, thrust take over; the movement of the moment is all, and this music is happening *now*. It sounds real, too: ★ is a masterpiece of production, engineering and mixing,[30] ensuring clarity and solidity even when the squalls are at their thickest. Only by being so earthed, so earthy, can it touch the stars.

And so the defining moment of ★ may not be a heartbreaking line or even a lifetime of emotion in a sung word. Instead, the defining moment may be one of Bowie's yells of ecstasy in ''Tis a Pity She Was a Whore', his spirit taken up by the music; it may be the moments of extreme noise conjured in 'Sue (or In a Season of Crime)', re-recorded and dangerous; it may be Ben Monder's guitar solo in 'I Can't Give Everything Away', sanguine and serene in its freedom. The defining *sound*, meanwhile, is easier to identify: it is that of the saxophone, an instrument that makes music from breath, and does not smooth or sanitize it but sings out the effort, the struggle, the noise, the dirt. The saxophone, Bowie's first love, propels ★, a thundering, coruscating, tender, beautiful, beautiful final ode to life.

Two days after its release, David Bowie died. Iman posted on Instagram: 'The struggle is real, but so is God.'

Bowie asked in his will for his ashes to be scattered in Bali, Indonesia, where he and Iman had their honeymoon. He stipulated that the ceremony was to be held 'in accordance with the Buddhist rituals' of the island.

'I'm going to pray something for him,' said Lama Chime Youngdong Rinpoche, after receiving news of Bowie's death. 'I'll meet him again, in the next life.'[31]

In one of his final photographs, Bowie looks like a magician. He is in a bright white shirt and a bright white jacket, but his arms are not in their sleeves: they are instead caught in a blur, as if in the midst of some sleight of hand, or mystical ritual. Bowie is pictured in front of what appears to be a medical scan or X-ray, evidently organic but unrecognizable. The photograph was taken in 2015 by Jimmy King: his images of Bowie are never candid, but this may be the most impenetrable of all. What magic is this?

Magic has what are known as 'allied arts'. One of these is escapology. Bowie was a dab hand, and showed us three escapes. The first is at the end of *Lazarus*, in which Newton, a kind of proxy for Bowie, draws shapes on a floor and flies away. The second is at the end of the music video for the song 'Lazarus', in which Bowie edges back tremulously into a wardrobe and closes the door. The third, perhaps less deliberate and more complex, is at the end of ★, the album: the music hangs on the same chord for a few bars, conveying release, contentment and excitement, before shifting to a final chord that sounds like a cosmic question mark. Where did he go?

The Church has a long history of suspicion, if not persecution, of those it suspects of practising real magic. The New Testament has a story about a magician called Simon. He made out that he was great, and he was lauded by the people, who believed he had the power of God. He converted to Christianity, and was amazed by the miracles performed by the Christian apostles. He saw them lay hands on the people, who were then gifted with the Holy Spirit; he wanted to know how to do this, so he offered money to the apostles, that they might give him this power.

But the apostles were appalled: 'May your silver perish with you, because you thought you could obtain God's gift with money!' said Peter, who ordered him to repent. Simon seems contrite, and we read no more about him – at least, not in the Bible.[32] But legends grew up around him, and within a couple of hundred years he was regarded by the early Church fathers as the founder of Gnosticism and the archetypal heretic.

The Church's hostility to magic is understandable, at least to some extent: if the laws of nature are written by God, then flouting them is a grievous crime indeed. Magic is also, to put it tamely, cheating – it circumvents reality. But there are those who practised magic who might have been open to the message of Jesus, yet have been pushed away, or worse, by the zeal of the Church.

Moreover, those honest magical entertainers and their allied artists have been among the fiercest denouncers of religion and debunkers of the supernatural. Harry Houdini made assiduous efforts to expose fraudulent mystics. Scepticism is fundamental to the work of the American double act Penn & Teller. In 1964, the Canadian–American magician and author James Randi bet a thousand dollars that no one could demonstrate supernatural or paranormal abilities under mutually agreed scientific conditions. The sum rose over time to a million dollars. Randi died in 2020 without ever having had to pay out.

Between, among and around all this, living in the tension of the religious and the magical and the material, was David Bowie. On stage and in his music, he invoked Lazarus, the man who died and came back to life. In his will, he left shares for Coco Schwab in something called Opossum Inc: what this company does is a mystery, but it is named after an animal that can look like the very image of death before it gets up and scurries off. That Buddhist ritual in Bali will have been based on the belief that the soul lives on. Bowie's vision for the play *Lazarus*, recorded in his notes, was that Newton and Marley 'will live eternally – and always in imagination – always in space and dreams – always in restful delusion – and always with simple song'. But there is nothing complacent or blasé about Bowie's last works. He made art like a man who knew he had only a certain number of days left on earth, like a man who knew the end was real, like a man who knew the truth of death; and that is surely why these last works exude so much life. Abracadabra. The dead man sings.

CONCLUSION

In 2004, David Bowie gave an account of his spiritual adventure. 'Tibetan Buddhism appealed to me – I thought, there's salvation. It didn't really work. Then I went through Nietzsche, Satanism, Christianity, er, pottery – and ended up singing. It's been a long road.'[1]

He gave that account on *The Ellen DeGeneres Show* in 2004. It was hardly the most serious interview, so his answer was appropriately flippant, and he obviously missed out a fair bit. But now we are at the end of that long road, we can see he got the essence of the thing across, its movement and its pace. His sheer perseverance is something to behold. The adventure entailed great misery, disenchantment and despair, but he never gave up. He would doubtless say that he was just stubborn, but there was plainly more to it than that.

Indeed, follow him along that road closely, as we have, and we can even discern sense in it all. If we just take Bowie's words and interpret them as taking us up to 1976, the path now looks remarkably logical.

Shifting metaphors from roads to rivers, we can see that there were a few currents flowing together. One was Christianity: Bowie's first real encounter with religion was at St Mary's, Bromley. This may not have been particularly meaningful spiritually, but we can surmise he found something there of value, as he maintained an interest in Christianity for the rest of his life. Another current was Buddhism: aside from its spiritual insights, it gave him licence to explore and experiment.

To this we can add early childhood experiences. There was the transfiguring force of rock and roll. There was also the heartbreaking sight of bombed-out homes, and the chill of his family life. From an early age, he was sensitive to the oppression of the vulnerable and marginalized. His sympathy for the people of Tibet ran alongside his interest in Buddhism. We can see how this led to his dalliance with hippiedom, and how he became disillusioned with it. A natural recourse was Friedrich Nietzsche, with his atheistic existentialism and heroic individualism; blend that with the enticing darkness of Aleister Crowley, and you have whole new dimensions to escape to. But you can stay too long there and it can get pretty scary, so you might want to ask Jesus to help you. And look, it's 1976. From this view, we can see that although the river meanders, its movements follow an intelligible course, and it remains one river.

And we can see what this meant for Bowie's work. His first album was generally parochial and suburban, as befitted a chap from Bromley; but one song, 'Silly Boy Blue', showed the influence of Buddhism. Existentialism came through in 'Space Oddity', while his fury with hippies was evident in 'Cygnet Committee'. Crowley and occultism more generally began to make their presence felt on the single 'Holy Holy' and the album *The Man Who Sold the World*, which incorporates some Nietzsche, whose ideas also fed into *Hunky Dory*. In the character Ziggy Stardust, Bowie brought together his views on religion, politics and art. Ziggy bled into the more troubled *Aladdin Sane* and a deeper examination of messianic figures. This, via cocaine and worsening psychological torment and Los Angeles generally, led to 'Station to Station' and 'Word on a Wing'. Terrified of what he saw as the spiritually dark elements of rock and roll, he emphasized a European aesthetic, and so we have the Thin White Duke and his tour in 1976. Of course there was more going on – not least a desire for sex and money – and there are individual songs that have apparently little or nothing to do with anything spiritual or philosophical. But all was borne on those great tides, which kept rolling and surging for another 40 years.

Bowie had another metaphor. He spoke of being driven, or of having a drive. Whoever was at the wheel must have had an uncanny sense of direction, because Bowie ended up somewhere beautiful. His final works derive their force from two essential sources.

One is love. Bowie tried hard over the years to work through his feelings about love, and his efforts were not helped by the English language, in which the word 'love' has various meanings. 'Love,' said Bowie in 1976, 'is a disease that breeds jealousy, anxiety and brute anger. Everything but love. It's a bit like Christianity.'[2] So much of Bowie's thinking about love and religion is encapsulated in those three sentences. By the end, Bowie had evidently come to know love of the highest and deepest kind.

The other is life, which Bowie never took for granted. He understood its fragility and knew it was precious, even holy. 'Do you indulge in any form of worship?' he was asked in 1973. 'Er... life,' Bowie replied. 'I love life very much indeed.'[3] Zowie, a middle name of his son Duncan, is a variation on the Greek name Zoe, which means 'life'. Bowie described the album *Heathen* as expressing a 'head-spinning dichotomy of the lust for life against the finality of everything'.[4] On *Heathen*, this leads to doubt and anger; by the time of ★, there is a kind of purity, an undimmable brilliance shooting through every moment.

★ radiates life in its *nowness*. In this way, it sounds like the experiences of others who have confronted death. One such figure is Wilko Johnson, a guitarist, singer and songwriter, perhaps best known for his work with the 1970s British R&B band Dr Feelgood. Johnson was diagnosed in 2013 with late-stage pancreatic cancer, and chose not to receive chemotherapy. He embarked on a farewell tour and his experiences were made into a film, *The Ecstasy of Wilko Johnson*.[5] In the film, Johnson says: 'The idea that death is imminent really makes you realize what a wonderful thing it is to be alive. I felt this elation. I was almost euphoric. Suddenly everything lifted off of me. Present, future, past – it was all concentrated down into the moment. I'm alive!'

Another account of this phenomenon came from the British screenwriter Dennis Potter. Among his works was *The Singing*

Detective, a BBC series about an ill man whose way to redemption involves escaping into fantasies of stories and music; Bowie's notes show that he wanted the play *Lazarus* to be 'like a swaggering *Singing Detective*'. In 1994, when Potter had cancer and knew he had only a few weeks to live, he said: 'We're the one animal that knows we're going to die. And yet we carry on paying our mortgages, doing our jobs... Unfortunately for most people most of the time, it's too predictable – they're locked into whatever situation they're locked into... And we forget or tend to forget that life can only be defined in the present tense. It *is*, *is*, *is*, and it is now, only.' He talked about the plum blossom in his garden: 'Last week, looking at it through the window as I'm writing, I see it is the whitest, frothiest, blossomest blossom that there ever could be.'[6]

He continued: 'The nowness of everything is absolutely wondrous. And if people could see that... there's no way of telling you. You have to experience it. But the glory of it, the comfort of it – the fact is that if you see the present tense, boy, do you see it. And boy, can you celebrate it.'[7]

A photograph of blossom appears on the cover of a book called *Life with Full Attention*. It is written by Maitreyabandhu, a Buddhist writer and poet, and its introduction quotes Potter's words. The book is a course in mindfulness, a concept that has become fashionable in recent years and which, like 'spirituality', is in danger of becoming cheapened by those wishing to market it as just another aspirational lifestyle product. But its history reaches back thousands of years, and it has long been integral to Buddhist practice, offering sublime insights into reality.

But it is not just Buddhism that teaches attentiveness to *now*, to *life*. So does Christianity, although the average reader could be forgiven for not knowing this, such have been the misguided preoccupations of churches through the centuries. The Gospel of John recounts Jesus saying: 'I came that they may have life, and have it abundantly.'[8] There is the concept of a dimension that transcends time, a heavenly realm that is 'near', that abuts our own. Jesus talks of the Kingdom of

Heaven being like various ecstatic experiences, like finding treasure in a field, or like finding a valuable pearl.[9] With God, 'one day is like a thousand years, and a thousand years are like one day'.[10] There is a sense of the eternal as *now*, a mind-warping collision of tenses. In John's Gospel, Jesus says: 'Before Abraham was, I am.'[11] This in turn echoes the moment in the Hebrew Bible – known to Christians as the Old Testament – when God reveals God's divine name: I AM.[12] Strip away all the accretions, some beautiful, some appalling, that religions have built up around God over the centuries – accretions that themselves have been called God – and we might be close to something like Bowie's God beyond God. God simply *is* – as in the essence of being and as in now, the present tense. Add in Bowie's ideas about love, as expressed at least quasi-spiritually on *The Next Day* and then explicitly spiritually in the play *Lazarus*, and we may get closer still.

We cannot know if Bowie ever found this God. But we do know that, in searching for God, Bowie made art that shook the world and changed lives. One of those lives was mine. When I pressed play on my clunky old personal stereo that evening in 1996, I had no idea what I was letting myself in for. Now, 30 years later, here I am, and so is he. He's been with me through so much and taught me so much and, goodness, I'm still learning. I can only hope that you have learned as much from reading this book as I have from writing it.

'Searching for music is like searching for God,' said Bowie. 'They're very similar. There's an effort to reclaim the unmentionable, the unsayable, the unseeable, the unspeakable, all those things, comes into being a composer and to writing music and to searching for notes and pieces of musical information that don't exist.'[13]

'Where are we now?' Bowie asked. After all that questing and journeying and searching and searching, maybe we have an answer. We are *here*.

ACKNOWLEDGEMENTS

I am indebted to the following:

To the wonderful team at Bloomsbury Continuum, including my editor Octavia Stocker, for your alchemical gifts, and Tomasz Hoskins, for your belief and trust, as well as Sarah Jones, Sarah Head and Cathleen Bradford-McCormac. Mandy Woods made the copyediting process as painless as it could be.

To Philip Gwyn Jones, for your email, and to my proofreaders, especially Richard Howarth.

To Leah Kardos: your support and enthusiasm for this project was crucial to my persevering with it, and your book, *Blackstar Theory: The Last Works of David Bowie* (Bloomsbury, 2022) lit a flame that gave form and energy to my hitherto vague musings. It also alerted me to Bowie's interest in Dennis Potter. Thanks too to Nicholas Pegg and David Buckley. Barney Hoskyns deserves at least a knighthood for running the rocksbackpages.com website. Paul Kinder's bowiewonderworld.com showed me I was not alone.

To George Underwood, Mary Finnigan and Ivo van Hove; and to Maria Beale and all at St Mary's, Bromley. You've all been so generous. To the staff at the V&A's David Bowie Centre, for your helpfulness and efficiency.

To everyone who has supported my writing on this subject from the start, especially Susan Belanger, Amber Bird, Sean MacGabhann and S. C. Skillman.

To Brighid, Sarah Proudfoot, Anna Potts, Georgi Poulter, Andrew Shepherd, Rob Hudson, Pete Bunten and Trevor Bannister. You've all played your part.

To my mother Priscilla, my sister Sarah, and my brother Michael (whose copy of *Hunky Dory* I borrowed, thus starting this whole business); to my late father Henry, and my late grandfather, Theodore.

To my godchildren, Harry, Willow and Mary, for bringing brightness and joy to my life; I hope you take something of lifelong value from this book.

To Rob Walker: I don't have to tell you. You already know.

To Emma: as long as there's —

NOTES

INTRODUCTION

1. 2021 edition.

1. CHOIRBOY

1. Currie, R., A. D. Gilbert and L. Horsley, *Churches and Churchgoers: Patterns of Church Growth in the British Isles since 1700*. London: Oxford University Press, 1978.
2. Gilbert, Alan D., *The Making of Post-Christian Britain: A History of the Secularization of Modern Society*. London: Longman, 1980.
3. https://www.churchofengland.org/media/press-releases/church-england-attendance-rises-fourth-year.
4. This would be worth about £180,000 today, according to the Bank of England (https://www.bankofengland.co.uk/monetary-policy/inflation/inflation-calculator).
5. Trynka, Paul, *Starman: David Bowie – The Definitive Biography*. London: Sphere, 2011, p. 17.
6. Tucker, Carol, 'The 1950s – Powerful Years for Religion'. News release, University of Southern California, 16 June 1997.
7. Gillman, Peter, and Leni Gillman, *Alias David Bowie*. London: Hodder & Stoughton, 1986, p. 57.
8. MacCormack, Geoff, *David Bowie: Rock 'n' Roll with Me*. Melton Woodbridge, Suffolk: ACC Art Books, 2023, p. 16.
9. BBC Radio 1 interview, January 1997.
10. Judge's verdict: 'A singer devoid of personality. Sings wrong notes and out of tune.'
11. The song was called 'The London Boys'.
12. Produced, incidentally, by Tony Hatch, whose songwriting credits range from Petula Clark's hit 'Downtown' to the theme tunes for the soap operas *Crossroads*, *Emmerdale Farm* and *Neighbours*.

13. *There is a Happy Land* is also the title of the first novel by British author Keith Waterhouse, of whom Bowie was an admirer; the book is inspired by Waterhouse's own childhood, and was first published in 1957.

2. BUDDHIST

1. https://bowiesongs.wordpress.com/2013/06/18/seven-years-in-tibet/
2. MTV interview, 1997.
3. Brunton, Paul, *The Quest of the Overself*. London: Rider & Co, 1951, p. 194.
4. The significance of 'Blue' is unclear, but it was evidently a meaningful colour to Bowie, who used it throughout his career in numerous songs and images and in the name of a girl whose murder is the ostensible subject of a later album. He instructed his band at Live Aid in 1985 to 'be lucky' and 'wear blue'.
5. MTV, 1997.
6. *Melody Maker*, 26 February.
7. Gillman and Gillman, *Alias David Bowie*, p. 137.
8. For example, 'Within You Without You', a song on the album *Sgt. Pepper's Lonely Hearts Club Band*, which was released on the same day as Bowie's debut album.
9. Welch, Chris, *David Bowie: The Ken Pitt Interview*, 2004, unpublished (accessed via rocksbackpages.com).
10. 'Why do Buddhist monks sleep upright?', bbc.co.uk, 22 June 2009. Some Buddhists are known to sleep in boxes, and Bowie is speculated to have done this, but there is no firm evidence that he did.
11. It ought also to be said that Bowie was not always the most reliable narrator of his own story. Other accounts circulate claiming that his decision was rather more considered, and was taken after Chime Youngdong Rinpoche advised him to pursue a career in music, as he 'wasn't going to make a great monk'. One of the people who has circulated such an account is David Bowie.
12. A teacher at Burnt Ash Junior School described it as 'astonishing' for a nine-year-old and recalled his 'quite vividly artistic' interpretation of music. See: Sandford, Christopher, *Loving the Alien*. New York: Warner Books, 1997, p. 19.

13. Visconti, Tony, *Bowie, Bolan and the Brooklyn Boy: The Autobiography*. London: HarperCollins, 2007, p. 121.
14. Bowie, David and Rock, Mick, *Moonage Daydream: The Life and Times of Ziggy Stardust*. Guildford, Surrey: Genesis Publications, 2002.
15. June 1968.
16. Personal communication.
17. Finnigan gives a full account of this period in her book *Psychedelic Suburbia: David Bowie and the Beckenham Arts Lab* (Portland, Oregon: Jorvik Press, 2016).
18. *Jackie* magazine, 10 May 1970.
19. Ibid.
20. *Moonage Daydream* (film), Universal Pictures, 2022.
21. MTV interview.

3. OCCULTIST

1. Hollywood Online live chat, 1 July 1994.
2. Cann, Kevin, *Any Day Now: David Bowie – The London Years 1947–1974*. Croydon: Adelita, 2010, pp. 133–4.
3. Song titles included 'Silver Tree Top School for Boys' and 'The Reverend Raymond Brown (Attends the Garden Fête on Thatchwick Green)'. The latter can be seen as an early example of Bowie's cynicism concerning the clergy, the cleric in question trying to hide his amorous interest in the local beauty queen.
4. The supposed 'rock opera', called *Ernie Johnson*, amounted to nothing more than a tape of scratchy demos.
5. *Playboy* magazine, September 1976.
6. Cann, *Any Day Now*, p. 121.
7. *Cracked Actor: David Bowie* (television documentary), BBC, 1975.
8. 'Changes: Bowie at 50' (television interview), BBC, 1997.
9. *New Musical Express (NME)*, 27 January.
10. The puppet, Zig, achieved fame in the UK with his partner Zag on the Channel 4 programme *The Big Breakfast* (Bowie had a fondness for anarchic television). This encounter took place on MTV in 1995.
11. Cann, *Any Day Now*, p. 140.
12. https://www.davidbowie.com/blog/2019/8/5/remembering-haywood-stenton-john-jones
13. Visconti, *Bowie, Bolan*, pp. 137–9.

14. Cann, *Any Day Now*, p. 153.
15. 11 October 1969
16. The clearest influence on 'Space Oddity' is probably 'New York Mining Disaster 1941' by the Bee Gees. It was their first hit in the UK and the USA; aside from similarities in sound and mood, it alludes to the protagonist's wife, refers to a Mr Jones and, as with 'Space Oddity', makes no mention of the song title in the lyrics.
17. He performed a startling stripped-back version for *The Kenny Everett Show* on BBC television in 1979, as a one-off.
18. Cann, *Any Day Now*, p. 147.
19. The word describes a kind of knowledge understood by only a few.
20. Pauwels, Louis and Bergier, Jacques (Éditions Gallimard, 1960).
21. As opposed to seeing mankind and the divine as fundamentally separate, as is the case with Judaism, Christianity and Islam.
22. Hamann, Brigitte, *Hitler's Vienna: A Dictator's Apprenticeship*. Oxford: Oxford University Press, 1999, p. 74.
23. https://plato.stanford.edu/entries/nietzsche-life-works
24. Hollingdale, R. J., *Nietzsche the Man and His Philosophy*. Cambridge: Cambridge University Press, 1999.
25. Nietzsche, Friedrich, *Beyond Good and Evil*. New York: Modern Library, first published 1886, p. 87.
26. Nietzsche, Friedrich, *Thus Spoke Zarathustra*. London: Penguin Classics, 2003 edn, p. 90.
27. Ibid., p. 173.
28. Ibid., p. 288.
29. https://www.rollingstone.com/music/music-news/how-david-bowie-realized-theatrical-dreams-on-the-man-who-sold-the-world-121178/
30. A properly mind-expanding visit, which included a meeting with Andy Warhol.
31. Cann, *Any Day Now*, p. 235.
32. recordcollectormag.com/articles/the-making-of-hunky-dory-part-2-song-by-song
33. The Bulwer-Lytton Fiction Contest was established in 1982 and continued to run until 2024. It invited entrants to 'compose the opening sentence to the worst of all possible novels', in dubious honour of Edward Bulwer-Lytton's novel *Paul Clifford*, which was published in 1830 and began: 'It was a dark and stormy night'. Bowie often showed interest in writers and others whom critics scorned.

34. Released on *The Beatles (White Album)*, 1968.
35. The final line of Clarke's novel *2001: A Space Odyssey* (London: Hutchinson, 1968).

4. MESSIAH

1. This is the earliest known use, according to the *Oxford English Dictionary*.
2. 'Changes: Bowie at 50', BBC interview, broadcast January 1997.
3. *Melody Maker*, 9 February 1957.
4. Matthew 9:21 (NRSV)
5. 22 January edition.
6. Bowie, Angela, with Patrick Carr, *Backstage Passes: Life on the Wild Side with David Bowie*. New York: Cooper Square Press, 2000, pp 160–1.
7. Compare with, for example, Rembrandt's *Adoration of the Shepherds* (1646).
8. There was also a religiosity to some of the most popular songs of the early 1970s, including 'Let It Be' by The Beatles, 'Bridge Over Troubled Water' by Simon & Garfunkel, 'My Sweet Lord' by George Harrison and an actual Christian hymn, 'Morning Has Broken', recorded by the artist known then as Cat Stevens. The best-selling single in 1972 in the UK was 'Amazing Grace', played by The Pipes and Drums and the Military Band of the Royal Scots Dragoon Guards.
9. Duncan also introduced Bowie to the music of Scott Walker and Jacques Brel, whose influence endured over decades.
10. David and Angie Bowie were in an open relationship. Incidentally, there is yet another connection: the first man cast as Jesus in the London production was Paul Nicholas, who had covered an obscure Bowie novelty, 'Over the Wall We Go', in 1967.
11. Nietzsche, Friedrich, *The Joyous Science*. London: Penguin Classics, 2018 edn (first pub. 1882), p. 133.
12. Cann, *Any Day Now*, p. 260. The plan did not come to fruition. There is another connection to Aylesbury: Stanley Kubrick shot some scenes there for *A Clockwork Orange*, although these were not used in the film.
13. Matthew 19:14 (NRSV)
14. There may be a hint too of Crowley, who wrote: 'Every man and every woman is a Star.'

15. Nietzsche, *Zarathustra*, p. 39.
16. A translation of Sanhedrin 98b.
17. Bowie, *Backstage Passes*, pp. 167–8.
18. Cann, *Any Day Now*, p. 258.
19. Doggett, Peter, *The Man Who Sold the World: David Bowie and the 1970s*. London: Bodley Head, 2011, p. 151.
20. Played by the band that appeared on the previous album, with the addition of Mike Garson, an outré jazz pianist whose playing defines much of the record.
21. *Cracked Actor*.
22. Underwood helped recolour Brian Ward's photograph. Underwood had performed the same role for the cover of *Hunky Dory*.
23. Personal communication.
24. This is officially known as 'Alternative Candidate', and is quite different from the song named 'Candidate' that appears on the *Diamond Dogs* album. 'Alternative Candidate' was not released officially until 1990.
25. https://www.shortlist.com/news/ricky-gervais-on-david-bowie

5. LOST

1. *Storytellers*, VH1, 1999.
2. *Planet Rock Profile*, VH1, 1997. 80lbs is 5.5 stone or 36kg.
3. *Melody Maker*, 29 October 1977.
4. A play on *Jacques Brel is Alive and Well and Living in Paris*, the musical revue of Brel's songs.
5. *Cracked Actor*.
6. He also arranged the strings for the song '1984'.
7. *Playboy* magazine, 1976.
8. https://time.com/archive/6738782/the-genius-of-brother-ray
9. Cited in *American Heritage* magazine, October 2005.
10. Bowie, *Backstage Passes*, pp. 293–5.
11. Ibid., p. 299.
12. Ibid., p. 305.
13. *NME*, 1 February 1997.
14. MacCormack, *David Bowie: Rock 'n' Roll with Me*, p. 148.
15. Bowie liked anagrams and puns, so it is notable that Isolar also happens to be an anagram of Sailor, the pseudonym Bowie used in online chats on his website, and a word that appears in various songs of his; he also wore a sailor's cap on his 1978 tour.

16. Published on 12 February 1976.
17. Among her various activities, Fortune was part of a small group of occultists who sought to defend the UK from what they regarded as the nefarious mystical forces of Nazi Germany during the Second World War.
18. The word, being Hebrew, has various spellings in English; 'Qabalah' is sometimes used to describe the more occult uses of Kabbalah.
19. *Crawdaddy* magazine, February.
20. *NME*, March 1993.
21. As well as *A Hard Day's Night* (1964) and *Help!* (1965), there was the television film *Magical Mystery Tour* (1967), the animation *Yellow Submarine* (1968) and the documentary *Let It Be* (1970).
22. *Rolling Stone*, 12 May 1983.
23. He wanted to fly, so he made wings of feathers and wax; but he flew too high, and the sun melted the wax, so Icarus fell.
24. 12 February 1976.
25. Crowe's suspicions proved correct: there exists apparently only one chapter of it, and it is kept at the library and archives of the Rock and Roll Hall of Fame in Cleveland, Ohio.
26. *Melody Maker*, 13 March 1976.
27. Pegg, Nicholas, *The Complete David Bowie*. London: Titan, 2016 edn, p. 381.
28. *Q* magazine, February 1997.
29. See n.18.
30. *Q* magazine, February 1997.
31. There are usually 14 images, although there is sometimes added a 15th, depicting the resurrection of Jesus.
32. Schapiro, S., *Bowie: Photographs by Steve Schapiro*. New York: PowerHouse Books, 2016.
33. *NME*, February 1997.
34. Bowie said in 1997: 'I always thought Crowley was a charlatan.' Evidence from Bowie's life and work suggests that he did not always think this.
35. https://www.bowiebible.com/gallery/lyrics/#jp-carousel-5732
36. *Storytellers*.
37. *NME*, 13 September 1980.
38. https://www.bowiebible.com/gallery/lyrics/#jp-carousel-10720
39. 1 Corinthians 1:23 (KJV).
40. At around 1:08.

41. The sound in fact comes from a Chamberlin, a primitive kind of sampler; press a note on its keyboard, and it plays a tape.
42. *NME*, 13 September 1980.
43. Bowie, *Backstage Passes*, p. 282.
44. Published 12 February, 1976
45. 'I Pity the Fool' (composed by Joe Medwick and Don Robey), 1965.
46. Bowie, *Backstage Passes*, p. 283.
47. Bowie's first exposure to this form of lighting came in 1968, when he saw a production of the musical *Cabaret*: 'It was just stark white light. I'd never seen that before in my life, and that became a central image for me of what a stage should look like.' He used a similar style for the first few shows on the Ziggy Stardust tour.
48. From the song 'Quicksand', which could be regarded as a younger brother of 'Station to Station'.
49. Bowie addressed the audience with the words 'Ladies, and gentlemen, and others.'
50. 12 February 1976
51. From the hymn 'Jerusalem'; the words are by William Blake.
52. Samhain edition, 1998.
53. *Planet Rock Profile*.

6. VANQUISHER

1. *Melody Maker*, 13 March 1976.
2. Bowie, *Backstage Passes*, p. 317.
3. This was finalized in 1980.
4. *Uncut*, April 2001.
5. *Uncut*, February 2001.
6. As with his previous references, this appears in the chapter named 'The Risks Incidental to Ceremonial Magic', and is part of the same story in which a man falls from a window.
7. The song was released as a single and reached number three in the UK charts, having been used as a backing track for trailers on BBC One.
8. *Storytellers* (audience recording).
9. Ibid.
10. Ibid.
11. *Record Mirror*, 24 September 1977.
12. Bowie invented them.

13. The album is called *ForeverAndEverNoMore*.
14. BBC Radio 6 Music interview.
15. *Uncut*, February 2001.
16. An insight into Tillich's thinking can be gained from his description of Pablo Picasso's great work Guernica as 'the greatest religious painting of the twentieth century'.
17. *Record Mirror*, 24 September 1977.
18. *Uncut*, February 2001.
19. *Melody Maker*, 18 February 1978.
20. The cover was designed by George Underwood.
21. A growing problem, however, was alcohol. Bowie's alcoholism typically receives less attention than his cocaine addiction, and its effects on his work and appearance were less pronounced. But it evidently wrought its own kind of destruction.
22. *Uncut*, February 2001.
23. *Creem* magazine, May 1976.
24. *Storytellers*.
25. *Uncut*, February 2001.
26. Held by the Metropolitan Museum of Art in New York.
27. Held by the Brücke Museum in Berlin.
28. Interview with Rune Koldborg J. for Danish radio.
29. https://daily.redbullmusicacademy.com/2013/02/key-tracks-tony-visconti-on-heroes
30. Tillich, Paul, *The Courage to Be*. New Haven, Connecticut: Yale University Press, 2000, p. 174.
31. Zowie, a middle name of his son Duncan, is a variation on the Greek name Zoe, which means *life*.
32. *Uncut*, February 2001.
33. *Guardian*, 13 January 2016.
34. Ibid.
35. *Rolling Stone*, 12 February 1976.
36. *Creem*, May 1976.
37. *Crawdaddy*, February 1978.
38. *Rock Australia* magazine, 26 July 1975.
39. *Playboy* magazine, September 1976.
40. *NME*, 13 September 1980.
41. *NME*, 20 March 1993.
42. *Uncut*, January 2017.
43. Bowie, *Backstage Passes*, p. 320.

44. An example of this is his performance of 'Starman' on *Top of the Pops* in 1972.
45. On Nicky Horne's *Your Mother Wouldn't Like It*, 14 May.
46. Bowie performed 'Space Oddity' in stark and pared-back form on the ITV show *Will Kenny Everett Make It To 1980?*, and mimed to the original track on the US show *Dick Clark's Salute to the Seventies*, both broadcast on New Year's Eve, 1979.

7. GNOSTIC

1. It reached number one in the UK charts, his first album to do so since *Diamond Dogs* in 1974.
2. Bowie's 'going mainstream' is treated with particular disdain in the 1998 film *Velvet Goldmine*.
3. He makes this claim in his 1971 song 'Kooks'.
4. https://www.kut.org/life-arts/2016-01-11/david-bowie-the-boxer-former-pro-recalls-training-the-musician-in-dallas
5. See chapter four.
6. A Christian poem called 'Footprints', written anonymously, became popular in the 1970s. It tells of a person walking along a beach with God; looking back, the person is aghast at God's footprints apparently disappearing at times of difficulty, to which God replies: 'It was then that I carried you.' The image seemed to remain in Bowie's consciousness for decades.
7. There is an obvious allusion to the song 'Get Me to the Church on Time' from the musical *My Fair Lady*, but only its title seems significant here.
8. The story that opens this chapter is taken from that book.
9. *Lola Da Musica*, VPRO (Netherlands), broadcast January 1996.
10. See chapter three.
11. Pagels, Elaine, *The Gnostic Gospels*. London: Weidenfeld & Nicolson, 1980, p. 27.
12. Ibid., p. 31.
13. Ibid., p. 149.
14. *Lola Da Musica*.
15. 'Pilgrimage to Nonviolence' (article for *Christian Century* magazine), 1960.
16. See the website of The Martin Luther King, Jr Research and Education Institute at Stanford University (kinginstitute.stanford.edu)

17. *Storytellers*.
18. *Countdown* (Australian television programme), March 1983.
19. There may be another echo of the past here, a voice we have not heard for a while. There is a poem that is similar to the words of 'Let's Dance': it is called 'Lyric of Love to Leah', and it was written by Aleister Crowley.
20. Song of Songs 8:6 (NRSV).
21. John 4:18 (NRSV).
22. Nietzsche, *Zarathustra*, pp. 40, 68.
23. Pegg, *Complete David Bowie*, p. 577.
24. O'Regan, Denis, *Ricochet: David Bowie 1983: An Intimate Portrait*. London: Particular Books, 2018.
25. Reprinted in O'Regan, *Ricochet*.
26. *Rolling Stone*, 12 May 1983.
27. Interview with Mark Goodman, 1983.
28. Pagels, *Gnostic Gospels*, p. 154.

8. DENIER

1. *Planet Rock Profile*.
2. *NME*, 29 September 1984.
3. *Q magazine*, June 1989.
4. *David Bowie: A Reality Tour*, DVD, 2004.
5. 29 September 1984. Bowie is on the cover and looks like he would rather be anywhere else.
6. Pegg, *Complete David Bowie*, p. 177.
7. Ibid.
8. And there is a further oddity, in that 'Loving the Alien' seems to quote the biblical book of Leviticus: 'The alien who resides with you shall be to you as the citizen among you; you shall love the alien as yourself.' However, this particular translation – the New Revised Standard Version – was not published until 1989.
9. This was later edited out.
10. George Underwood: 'One memory comes to mind when David was living in Berlin [in 1976–7] – we used to send each other mixtapes of music which we thought the other would like. On one of my tapes was "Real Wild Child" by the Crickets. David phoned me asking if I knew who wrote it. He was recording Iggy Pop at the time. The rest is history.'

11. The notes went on display in 2013 and are archived online at https://davidbowieautograph.com/evaluation%2Fhelp/f/the-last-temptation-of-christ
12. *Planet Rock Profile*.
13. *Guardian*, 18 July 2001.
14. *Planet Rock Profile*.
15. Berklee Commencement Address, Berklee College of Music, 1999.
16. *Planet Rock Profile*.
17. They are not mentioned in *Moonage Daydream*, the 2022 film sanctioned by Bowie's estate.

9. HOLY MAN/SHAMAN

1. MTV interview, 1997.
2. *Hello!* magazine, 19 September 2000.
3. BBC Newsnight, 1997.
4. On its website, Alcoholics Anonymous says: 'It's important here to say that you do not have to be religious or believe in God to go to AA meetings. The purpose of ending the meeting with a prayer is to think of a higher power, such as nature, or simply the collective energy of people coming together to help each other.'
5. BowieNet online chat, 1998.
6. *Uncut*, October 1999.
7. *Q magazine*, July 2000.
8. *Hello!* magazine, June 1992.
9. King James Version.
10. David Bowie (1995) [transcript], *Rock's Backpages* transcripts.
11. *Hello!* magazine, 13 June 1992.
12. 10 June 1993.
13. Spring/Summer 1993.
14. 10 June 1993
15. Hollywood Online chat, 1 July 1994.
16. *Record Collector*, May 1993.
17. *NME*, 27 March 1993.
18. Wells was not fond of the place. When offered the honour of the freedom of the borough, he responded: 'Bromley has not been particularly gracious to me nor I to Bromley and I don't think I want

to add the freedom of Bromley to the freedom of the City of London and the freedom of the City of Brussels – both of which I have.'
19. Reissues rectified this failing.
20. John 12:31 (NRSV).
21. 2 Corinthians 4:4 (NRSV).
22. Galatians 5:17 (NRSV).
23. Quoted in Paytress, Mark and Steve Pafford, *BowieStyle*. London: Omnibus Press, 2000, p. 146.
24. Interview with Kim Hughes of CFNY-FM, 1997.
25. Ibid.
26. *IKON*, October 1995.
27. Bowie wrote about him in 'Joe the Lion', a song on *'Heroes'*.
28. Interview with Kim Hughes.
29. Interview with Kurt Loder, MTV, 1995.
30. 'Dead Man Walking', 1997.
31. *IKON*, October 1995.
32. Eno gave a lecture later in 1992 titled 'Perfume, Defence, and David Bowie's Wedding', in which the ceremony was analysed as a postmodern spectacle, somehow unreal yet 'lovely'.
33. 19 April 1995.
34. MTV, 1997.
35. Buckley, David, *Strange Fascination: David Bowie: The Definitive Story*. London: Virgin Books, 1997, p. 447.
36. Yle (Finnish TV station), 16 January 1996.
37. 'I'm Afraid of Americans', a track on *Earthling*.
38. MTV, 1997.
39. Musicians in the USA and the UK perceived Bowie in subtly different ways during the 1990s, with Nirvana covering 'The Man Who Sold the World', and with Nine Inch Nails performing joint headline sets with Bowie.
40. In fact, two were significant, for reasons that will become clear.
41. On the *1. Outside* track 'Segue – Algeria Touchshriek'.
42. *Melody Maker*, 13 March.
43. *New York Times*, 14 June.
44. 'Little Wonder', 1997.
45. The USA version had the prefix Omikron.
46. Indeed, arguably beyond them: there were complaints that it took tiresomely long for its various parts to load.

47. The lower-case 'h', the inverted commas and the ellipsis were deliberate.
48. *Rock's Backpages* audio, 29 July 1999.
49. Matthew 6:34: 'Do not worry about tomorrow, for tomorrow will bring worries of its own. Today's trouble is enough for today' (NRSV).

10. DOUBTER

1. *SOMA* magazine, October 1999.
2. *Front Row*, BBC Radio 4, June.
3. Psalm 13, attributed to King David (NRSV).
4. 19 September 2000.
5. Eventually released as a bonus track in 2002 with the title 'Safe'.
6. Interview for *Heathen* electronic press kit, 2002.
7. Pegg, *Complete David Bowie*, p. 442.
8. *Performing Songwriter*, 2003.
9. *Q Magazine*, June 2002.
10. Bowie adopted a pose similar to that in the painting for the cover of *Earthling*, and for a photograph taken in 2013 by Jimmy King.
11. As mentioned in Bowie's interview with Russell Harty discussed in chapter five.
12. *Interview* magazine, June 2002.
13. *Front Row*, BBC Radio 4, June. Bowie opened the fundraising Concert for New York City at Madison Square Garden on 20 October 2001, singing an intimate and affecting version of the Simon & Garfunkel song 'America' and a full-blooded 'Heroes'.
14. *Heathen* electronic press kit.
15. The designer was Jonathan Barnbrook, who went on to design the packaging for Bowie's next three albums.
16. Pegg, *Complete David Bowie*, p. 448.
17. Interview with Guillaume Durand, France 2 (French TV channel), 2002.
18. Pegg, *Complete David Bowie*, p. 448.
19. *Hypershow*, Canal+ (French TV channel), 18 September 2002.
20. Ibid.
21. Published in 1818: 'On the pedestal, these words appear: My name is Ozymandias, King of Kings; Look on my Works, ye Mighty, and despair! Nothing beside remains.'

22. The song was 'The Width of a Circle'. 'On Love' was published in 1923, the relevant lines being: 'But if in your fear you would seek only love's peace and love's pleasure…'
23. *Interview* magazine, June 2002.
24. *Guardian*, 5 June 2002.
25. *LiveWire*, 16 June 2002.
26. *Billboard*, 1 June 2002.
27. BBC Radio 4 interview with John Wilson, 2002.
28. National Public Radio (NPR), interview with Terry Gross, 2002.
29. Ibid. Compare with this, just three years earlier: 'I think we are intelligent animals and we can quite simply see it's not right to hurt others. It's quite easy to develop a social morality that comes through a consensus of behaviour and opinion' (*Uncut*, October 1999).
30. *Hypershow*, 18 September 2002.
31. Beliefnet (online publication), 2003.
32. BBC Radio 2, 15 June 2004.
33. BowieNet, 20 July 2003.
34. Beliefnet, 2003.
35. These songs seem related to 'Cracked Actor', a track on *Aladdin Sane* recorded 30 years earlier; it tells of a seedy, priapic, useless old movie star living and dying off his past.
36. Pegg, *Complete David Bowie*, p. 172.
37. July 2003.
38. Ibid.
39. *Yeah Yeah Yeah* magazine, 23 July 2003.
40. *Vatican News* (vaticannews.va), 28 February.
41. *National Catholic Reporter* (ncronline.org), 12 December.
42. Beliefnet, 2003.

11. LOVER

1. *GQ*, 9 January 2017
2. *Performing Songwriter*, 2003
3. Interview with Nicky Horne, Talk Radio, January 1999.
4. A re-recording of 'I Can't Read', with synths and acoustic guitars.
5. Farthingale performed in the musical *Song of Norway* shortly after ending her relationship with Bowie.
6. Interview with Mary Anne Hobbs, BBC Radio 1.

7. Its music was written by Alan Winstanley, who co-produced 'Dancing in the Street' and 'Absolute Beginners'.
8. Lady Manners inspired Waugh's character Mrs Stitch, who appears in various novels of his.
9. Visconti said the title 'is part of a chant that they're taught as they plunge their bayonets into a dummy' (*Rolling Stone*, 15 January 2013).
10. Compare with the song 'Shopping for Girls' from the album *Tin Machine II*.
11. Compare with 'Crack City' from the album *Tin Machine*.
12. It drew a response from a former Archbishop of Canterbury, George Carey. 'I doubt that Bowie would have the courage to use Islamic imagery – I very much doubt it,' he wrote in the *Telegraph*. 'Frankly, I don't get offended by such juvenilia – Christians should have the courage to rise above offensive language, although I hope Bowie will recognise that he may be upsetting some people.'
13. Pegg, *Complete David Bowie*, p. 776.
14. van Beneden, Benjamin and Nicola Jennings (eds), *David Bowie's Tintoretto: Angel Foretelling the Martyrdom of Saint Catherine of Alexandria*. London: Colnaghi Foundation, 2017, p. 166.
15. Ibid., p. 167.

12. MAGICIAN

1. *Reality* electronic press kit, 2003
2. 'Holy Holy'.
3. Billboard, 1 March 2018.
4. A line from 'Sunday', from the album *Heathen*; the lower-case 'h' and 'c' and full stop are deliberate.
5. MacCormack, *David Bowie: Rock 'n' Roll with Me*, p. 235.
6. *Rolling Stone*, 23 November 2015.
7. *Guardian*, 20 November 2014.
8. *Global-e* journal, 14 September 2017.
9. BBC Online, 12 December 2017.
10. See *Beauty from the Crypt: Mystery of Europe's Jeweled Skeletons*, CNN.com, 29 June 2015.
11. John 11:44 (NRSV).
12. *Psychic Self-Defence*, p. 153.
13. Vice.com, 19 November 2015.
14. Programme notes for *Lazarus*, 2015.

15. *Financial Times*, 21 October 2016.
16. Personal communication.
17. Ibid.
18. Ibid.
19. There are echoes here of Bowie's song 'The Supermen' and relatedly of *Thus Spoke Zarathustra*, in which the prophet lives high up, in solitude. Zarathustra revels in being alone. Van Hove says of *Lazarus*: 'It's about someone who is lonely but doesn't have a big problem with it. So the power of loneliness, perhaps – the power of being alone' (personal communication).
20. Interview with Dave Fanning, RTE 2FM, 1 May 2016.
21. Personal communication.
22. *Guardian*, 6 November 2016.
23. It seemed an obvious choice to van Hove, but not to Bowie, who wanted a more obscure song – one of the few Bowie songs that van Hove did not know, from the only Bowie album he did not possess. 'Why was it that he really wanted this particular song?' wonders van Hove. 'It's clearly a song that's not so famous, but that really meant a lot to him, which I still don't understand. It's something very personal' (personal communication). Van Hove convinced Bowie that 'Heroes' was the better choice. Respecting Bowie's desire for secrecy, van Hove will not reveal Bowie's choice of song.
24. Personal communication.
25. Bowie, David and Enda Walsh, *Lazarus: The Complete Book and Lyrics*. London: Nick Hern Books, 2016.
26. There is another Lazarus in the gospels. He appears in a parable told by Jesus (Luke 16:19–31). This Lazarus was a beggar, covered with sores. His fate is contrasted with that of a rich man; the rich man is sent to Hades, while Lazarus is in heaven. The name Lazarus means *God has helped*.
27. https://davidbowieautograph.com/evaluation%2Fhelp/f/lazarus
28. *Guardian*, 6 January 2017.
29. https://www.nme.com/news/music/fans-share-secrets-found-david-bowies-blackstar-album-artwork-1857821
30. It was produced by Bowie and Tony Visconti, engineered by Kevin Killen, Kabir Hermon and Erin Tonkon and mixed by Tom Elmhirst. The album was recorded in New York at a studio called The Magic Shop.

31. lionsroar.com website, 12 January 2016.
32. The story appears in Acts 8:9–24.

CONCLUSION

1. *The Ellen DeGeneres Show*, NBC, 23 April 2004.
2. *Rolling Stone*, 12 February 1976.
3. *Russell Harty Plus*, ITV, 1973.
4. *Interview* magazine, June 2002.
5. It was directed by Julien Temple, who had directed the videos for Bowie's singles 'Blue Jean' and 'Day-In Day-Out' and the film *Absolute Beginners*, in which Bowie performed and for which Bowie wrote the title song.
6. Interview with Melvyn Bragg, Channel 4, broadcast on 5 April 1994. Potter died on 7 June that year.
7. Ibid.
8. John 10:10 (NRSV).
9. Matthew 13:44–6 (NRSV).
10. 2 Peter 3:8 (NRSV).
11. John 8:58 (NRSV).
12. Exodus 3: 13–14.
13. *60 Minutes*, CBS, 2003.

INDEX

1. *Outside* 150–4, 157, 158, 164, 193, 235n40
'5:15 The Angels Have Gone' 169, 170–1
9/11 (terrorist attacks) 166, 171, 174, 236n13
50th birthday concert (1997) 35, 156–7
1001 Albums You Must Hear Before You Die 2
2001: A Space Odyssey (film; 1968) 29, 41, 45–6, 50

ABC (band) 2
Abraham (biblical figure) 31–2, 221
Absolute Beginners (film; 1986) 126, 240n5
'Absolute Beginners' (song) 126, 147, 237n7
Adam Ant 56
Adams, Bryan 159
Adams, John 183
'After All' 42
Agnus Dei (prayer) 76
Al B. Sure! 145
Aladdin Sane (album) 57–8, 64, 129, 189, 218, 237n35; *see also* 'The Jean Genie'
Aladdin Sane (character) 57, 74
'Aladdin Sane (1913–1938–197?)' (song) 57
alcoholism 132, 137–8, 231n21, 234n4
Alford, Zack 154, 187
'Ali al-Samman, Muhammad 105, 117
Alomar, Carlos 65–6, 74, 86, 153
'Alternative Candidate' 228n24

'Always Crashing in the Same Car' 30, 88
Andersen, Hans Christian, 'The Red Shoes' 112
Anderson, Brett 144
'Angel, Angel, Grubby Face' 170
Anglicanism 8–9, 10, 14–15, 17, 97, 101, 141, 217
Arcade Fire 2, 182
Arena (magazine) 142–3
'As the World Falls Down' 127
'Ashes to Ashes' 101–2, 124
atheism 173–4, 218
Austin, Texas 107
Aylesbury 53, 227n12

Baal 106
'Baby Loves That Way' (Davy Jones & The Lower Third) 21
Bali 213, 215
Bandslam (film; 2009) 182
Bangkok 114, 115
Barnbrook, Jonathan 212, 236n15
Barnett, Angela *see* Bowie, Angie
'Be My Wife' 89
Beat Room, The (television programme) 12
Beatles, The 13, 72, 229n21; 'Let It Be' 227n8; 'Martha My Dear' 45; *Sgt. Pepper's Lonely Hearts Club Band* 14, 36, 224n8; 'Tomorrow Never Knows' 22–3
Beckenham 24; Arts Lab 25, 39; Free Festival 25; Haddon Hall 38, 58
Bee Gees 226n16
Benjamin, Floella, Baroness 52

Berlin 85, 88, 91, 92–4, 95, 100, 110, 146, 178, 181, 184–6, 233n10
Berman, Siegrid 22
'Better Future, A' 169, 171
'Bewlay Brothers, The' 175
Bittan, Roy 74, 79
Black, Frank 157
Black Ball gala, New York (2006) 182
Black Sabbath 40
Black Tie White Noise (album) 143–6, 177; *see also* 'The Wedding Song'
'Black Tie White Noise' (song) 144–5
Blackburn, Tony 50
Blackstar (album) 211–13, 214, 219
'Blackstar' (song) 200–4, 211, 212, 214
Blaine, David 197
Bloom, Harold, *The American Religion* 156
'Blue Jean' 120–1, 240n5
Blur 2
Bolan, Marc 24, 39, 43, 56
Bolder, Trevor 46, 50
'Bombers' 189
Book of Common Prayer 8, 101
'Boss of Me' 190–1
Bowie, Angie 38–9, 45, 51, 55, 58, 67–8, 80, 85, 92, 99, 227n10
BowieNet (internet service provider) 157–8
Boy George 56
Boyle, Danny 184
'Boys Keep Swinging' 190
Bramble, Derek 122
'Breaking Glass' 87–8, 92, 187
Brecht, Bertolt 81; *Baal* 106; 'Contemplating Hell' 67

Brel, Jacques 227n9, 228n4
Briggs, Raymond 127
'Brilliant Adventure' 94
'Bring Me the Disco King' 175, 198
Brit Award for Outstanding Contribution to Music 2
Brixton 8
Broackes, Victoria 199
Bromley 7–8, 17, 146–7, 234n17; Register Office 38; St Mary's Church 7–8, 15, 53, 72, 141, 200, 217
Brown, Dan, *The Da Vinci Code* 116–17
Brown, James 66
Browning, Robert 200
Brücke, Die (artists group) 94
Buckley, 'Lord' Richard, 'The Nazz' 54–5
Buckmaster, Paul 33–4
Buddha of Suburbia, The 147–9
Buddhism 17–26, 42, 44, 87, 94, 100, 105–6, 115, 137, 148–9, 155, 161, 211, 213, 215, 217, 218, 220, 224n10
Bulwer-Lytton, Edward 44–5; *The Coming Race* 45; *Paul Clifford* 226n33; *Pelham* 44; *Zanoni* 44–5, 73
Buñuel, Luis 81
Burden, Chris 151
Burns, Terry (DB's half-brother) 9, 11, 145
Burretti, Freddie 165
Burroughs, William S. 65; *Naked Lunch* 77
Bush, Kate 2, 138

Cabaret (musical) 93, 230n47
Cabinet of Dr Caligari, The (film; 1920) 210–11
Cambridge, John 39, 40
Campbell, Sterling 187
Can (band) 86
'Candidate' 60, 228n24
'Can't Help Thinking About Me' 11, 13, 14, 15
Capital Radio 100
Carey, George 238n12
Cars, The, 'Drive' 133
'Cat People (Putting Out the Fire)' 126

Catherine of Alexandria, St. 161
Catskill Mountains, New York 165–6
Cave, Nick 2
Cavett, Dick 67
'Changes' 50, 182
Changesbowie 199
Changesonebowie 199
Changestwobowie 199
Charles, Ray 66
Chemical Brothers 154
Cher 82
Cherry, Ava 66
Chien Andalou, Un (film; 1929) 81
'China Girl' 111–12, 116, 124, 192
Church of England *see* Anglicanism
Clark, Robin 66
Clarke, Sir Arthur C., *2001: A Space Odyssey* 29, 46, 227n35
Clash, The 133
Clockwork Orange, A (film; 1971) 50, 152, 227n12
cocaine 58, 63, 68, 92, 218, 231n21
Cockney Rebel 56
Collings, Matthew 196
Collins, Phil 119
Cooke, Sam 66
Cool World (film; 1992) 143
Cork Street, London, The Gallery 153
Costello, Elvis 189
'Crack City' (Tin Machine) 238n11
'Cracked Actor' (song) 237n35
Cracked Actor (television documentary) 65, 73, 197
Crickets, 'Real Wild Child' 233n10
Crowe, Cameron 69–70, 73, 93, 229n25
Crowley, Aleister 2, 36–7, 38, 42, 44, 76, 77, 116, 197, 204, 218, 227n14, 229n34; *The Book of the Law* 37; 'Lyric of Love to Leah' 233n19; *The Star Sapphire* 201; *White Stains* 76, 201

Culture Club 2
Cunningham, Michael 183, 204, 205
Cure, The 2, 157
Curtis, Ian 56
cut up (writing technique) 65
'Cygnet Committee' 39–40, 60, 194, 218

Dalai Lama 20, 155
Dalí, Salvador 81
'Dancing in the Street' 126, 237n7
Daniels, Paul 197
David Bowie (1967 album) 14–15, 17, 19–20, 24, 28, 218; *see also* 'Please Mr. Gravedigger'; 'Silly Boy Blue'
David Bowie (1969 album) 32–3, 39–40; *see also* 'Cygnet Committee'; 'Memory of a Free Festival'; 'Space Oddity'
David Bowie Is (exhibition) 199, 205
Davie Jones & the Manish Boys 12–13
Davies, Ron 54
Davis, Dennis 74, 86, 90
Davy Jones & The Lower Third 13–14, 21
Dawkins, Richard 173
'Day-In Day-Out' 129, 133, 240n5
'Days' 175
Decca Records 12
Deep Purple 40
Deloria, Vine Jr. 84
Dennett, Daniel 173
Denti di Pirajno, Alberto, *A Grave for a Dolphin* 138
Depeche Mode 2
Derrida, Jacques 38
Diamond Dogs (album) 64, 65, 152, 187, 228n24, 232n1
Diamond Dogs tour (1974) 63–5, 131
Dick Cavett Show (television programme) 67
'Did You Ever Have a Dream' 22, 211
Dietrich, Marlene 46
'Dirty Boys' 190

INDEX

Disc and Music Echo (magazine) 34, 43
Dolci, Carlo, *The Magdalene* 167
'Dollar Days' 212
Dominion Theatre, London 134
Donovan (singer-songwriter) 23
Dorsey, Gail Ann 152, 154, 187
Dr Feelgood 219
Duccio di Buoninsegna, *Madonna and Child* 167
Duncan, Lesley 52, 227n9
Duran Duran 2
Dylan, Bob 133, 158–9, 183; *Time Out of Mind* 159

Earth Mysteries Movement 36
Earthling 154–5, 158, 159, 160, 161, 164, 196, 200, 235n36, 236n10
Echo & The Bunnymen 56
Eckhart, Meister 195
Edwardsville, Illinois 49
Einstein, Albert 167–8
Elephant Man, The (play) 106
Ellen DeGeneres Show (television programme) 217
Elson, Steve 187
Eno, Brian 2, 86, 89, 90, 91, 93, 100, 147, 148, 149, 153, 235n31
esotericism 4, 35–8, 42–3, 44–5, 63, 67–8, 212
Essex, David 72
existentialism 31, 110–11, 203, 218
Extras (television series) 182

Faithfull, Marianne 12
Falcon and the Snowman, The (film; 1985) 126
'Fame' 66, 82
'Fantastic Voyage' 99, 127, 182
Farthingale, Hermione 28, 32–3, 188, 192, 237n5
fascism 37–8, 98
Fashion Rocks (2005) 181–2
Feathers (trio) 28–9

Finnigan, Mary 24–5, 38, 225n17
'Five Years' 52–3, 55, 193
Flaming Lips, The, 'Is David Bowie Dying?' 183, 187
Florence, St James Episcopal Church 141–2
Foo Fighters 157
'Footprints' (Christian poem) 169–70, 232n6
Fortune, Dion 70–2, 75, 77, 87–8, 197, 204, 229n17
Frampton, Peter 39
Francis, Pope 180
Franklin, Aretha 66, 81
Fraser, Giles 97
Freud, Sigmund 167–8, 192
Friedrich, Caspar David, *Wanderer above the Sea of Fog* 166, 196, 203
Fripp, Robert 94
Führerling (character) 60
Fuller, Paul 19

Gabrels, Reeves 134, 153, 154, 158, 160
Gadzooks! It's All Happening! (television programme) 13
Gardiner, Ricky 93–4
Gardner, Gerald 36
Garson, Mike 153, 154, 175, 228n20
Gay Pride march (1972) 56
Gaye, Marvin 116
Geldof, Bob 133
Generation X (band) 146
Gerry & The Pacemakers 12
Gervais, Ricky 61, 182
Gibran, Kahlil, 'On Love' 169, 236n22
Gilbert & George 120
Gillespie, Dana 52
Gilmour, David 182
Ginsberg, Allen 17
'Glass Spider' (song) 130, 176
Glass Spider tour (1987) 35, 130–1, 134, 138
Glastonbury 98; Festival 163–4
Gnosticism 105–6, 108–10, 111, 116–17, 148–9, 156, 173, 214
'God Bless the Girl' 191, 192

Godspell (musical) 52
Goebbels, Joseph 98
Golden Dawn *see* Hermetic Order of the Golden Dawn
'Golden Years' 77–8, 82, 170
Grammy Awards 81–2
Greek mythology 73, 83, 145, 152, 229n23
Guiliana, Mark 213
Guns N' Roses 33
Gysin, Brion 65

Haggerty, Mick 120
Haley, Bill 49, 55
Hall, Michael C. 206
Hamburg 179
Harley, Steve 39, 56
Harrer, Heinrich, *Seven Years in Tibet* 18, 155
Harris, Sam 173
Harrison, George 23, 227n8
Hartley, Liz 38, 39
Harty, Russell 82–3, 236n11
Hatch, Tony 223n12
'Hearts Filthy Lesson, The' 149–51
'Heat' 196
Heathen (album) 166–73, 174, 176, 177, 186, 203, 219, 238n4
'Heathen (The Rays)' 169, 171–2, 183, 198
Heathen tour (2002) 177–8
Heckel, Erich 94
Hello! (magazine) 146, 164
Henry VIII, King 10
Hermetic Order of the Golden Dawn 1, 36–7, 42, 44, 45, 75, 77
'*Heroes*' (album) 93–6, 100, 102, 115, 129, 159, 186
'Heroes' (song) 95–6, 103, 112, 126, 127, 138, 140, 179, 184, 208, 236n13, 239n23
heroin (smack) 28
Himmler, Heinrich 44, 97
Hinduism 23, 36, 75
Hitchens, Christopher 173–4
Hitler, Adolf 36, 37, 60, 98
Hoffman, Abbie 161
Holly, Buddy, 'Peggy Sue Got Married' 102

Holy Grail 97, 98
'Holy Holy' 42–3, 218
Hong Kong 114
Horton, Ralph 18
Houdini, Harry 215
'hours...' 160–2, 170, 175, 235n46; see also 'New Angels of Promise'
'How Does the Grass Grow?' 189–90
Hughes, Kim 156
Hull 39, 40
Hunger, The (film; 1983) 106
Hunger City (stage set) 63–4
Hunky Dory 1–2, 43–7, 49, 50, 54, 55, 158, 175, 218, 228n22; see also 'Life on Mars?'; 'Quicksand'
Hurricane Festival, Germany 178–9
Hutchinson, John 28
Huxley, Aldous 67
hymns 8, 14, 72, 200, 227n8, 230n51
Hynde, Chrissie 56
Hype, The (band) 39–40

'I Can't Give Everything Away' 212, 213
'I Can't Read' (Tin Machine) 135–6, 237n4
'I Pity the Fool' (Davie Jones & the Manish Boys) 13
'I Would Be Your Slave' 169–70
ICA (Institute of Contemporary Arts) 134
Icarus (mythological figure) 73, 101, 229n23
Ice Storm, The (film; 1997) 187
i-D (magazine) 129
'I'd Rather Be High' 189
Idol, Billy 146–7
'If You Can See Me' 60, 194
'I'll Take You There' 191
'I'm Afraid of Americans' 164, 235n36
'I'm Deranged' 152
Iman (Iman Abduljamid) 123–4, 125, 137, 138, 141–2, 143, 144, 164, 213
International Times (journal) 24
internet 150, 157–8, 184

iSelect (compilation album) 182
Isherwood, Christopher 93
Islam 32, 123, 202, 204
Isley Brothers 116
Isolar tour (1976) 69, 81, 83, 86, 218, 228n15
'It Ain't Easy' 54, 126, 166

Jackson, Mahalia 66
Jagger, Sir Mick 72, 126
'Jean Genie, The' 86
'Jerusalem' (hymn) 72, 230n51
Jesus Christ 14, 19, 31, 49, 51–5, 76, 78, 109, 117, 123, 128, 149, 156, 160–1, 166, 204, 215, 220–1
Jesus Christ Superstar (rock opera) 52
Jesus People movement 52
Jews and Jewish traditions 45, 55, 69, 70–1, 98, 156; see also Judaism; Kabbalah
John, Sir Elton 33
John, St. 113, 128, 181, 194, 203, 220, 221
Johnson, Wilko 219
Jonas, Hans 110
Jones, Alexandria Zahra 'Lexi' (DB's daughter) 164, 166, 177, 196
Jones, Davy 13
Jones, Duncan Zowie (DB's son) 45, 58, 68, 85, 188, 203, 219
Jones, John (DB's father) 8, 9–10, 18, 28, 177; death 33
Jones, Margaret 'Peggy' (DB's mother) 8, 9, 38; death 165
Jones, Robert Haywood (DB's grandfather) 190
Jones, Tricia 129
Joy Division 2, 56
Joyce, Donovan, The Jesus Scroll 123
Judaism 32, 52, 105, 113, 226n21
'Julie' 192–3
'Jump They Say' 145
Jung, Carl 110

Kabbalah 45, 70–1, 75–6, 87, 143, 154, 209, 210, 229n18; see also Tree of Life
'Karma Man' 21, 22, 203
Katz, Dennis 50
Kemp, Lindsay 24, 28
Kent, Andy 98, 99
Kerouac, Jack: The Dharma Bums 17; On the Road 12, 17, 67
Khan, Chaka 127
Kierkegaard, Søren 31, 91, 110, 198; Fear and Trembling 31–2
Killers, The 2
'Killing a Little Time' 208
King, Jimmy 196, 214, 236n10
King, Martin Luther 111
King Bees 12
Kinks, The 12, 13; The Kinks Are the Village Green Preservation Society 14; 'Waterloo Sunset' 189
Kirlian photography 72
Kızılçay, Erdal 131–2, 147
Konrads, The 12
'Kooks' 232n3
Korniloff, Natasha 28
Kraftwerk 81, 86, 90, 148
Kubrick, Stanley: 2001: A Space Odyssey 29, 41, 45–6, 50; A Clockwork Orange 50, 152, 227n12
Kureishi, Hanif, The Buddha of Suburbia 147
Kyoto 94

La La La Human Steps (dance company) 134
Labyrinth (film; 1986) 127
Lady Gaga 2
Last Temptation of Christ, The (film; 1988) 127–8, 234n11
'Law (Earthlings on Fire)' 154
Lazarus (biblical figure) 203, 205, 215, 239n26
Lazarus (musical) 183, 204–9, 210, 220, 221, 239n19
'Lazarus' (song) 205, 208, 209–12, 214

INDEX

Lazarus, Emma 183, 205; 'The New Colossus' 183, 188, 193, 207
Leamington Spa 36
Lean, Sir David 20
Lecavalier, Louise 134
Led Zeppelin 80–1
Lefebvre, Tim 212–13
Lennon, John 23, 66, 133, 164; 'Love' 192
Lennox, Annie 140
Leonard, Gerry 187
Let's Dance (album) 107–8, 111–14, 116, 120, 126, 129; *see also* 'China Girl'; 'Modern Love'
'Let's Dance' (song) 112–13, 116, 124, 126, 127, 233n19
'Letter to Hermione' 32–3
ley lines 36
Lhasa, Tibet 20, 166
'Life on Mars?' 46–7, 54, 96, 181–2
'Like a Rolling Stone' 159
Lindner, Jason 212
Little Richard 12, 49, 108; 'Tutti Frutti' 10
Live Aid (1985) 96, 126, 132–3, 140, 224n4
'Liza Jane' (King Bees) 12, 199
Lloyd Webber, Andrew, Baron 52
Loach, Ken 99
Lock, Édouard 134
Lodger 99–100, 102, 153, 170, 182, 186; *see also* 'Boys Keep Swinging'; 'Fantastic Voyage'; 'Repetition'
'London Boys, The' (Davy Jones & The Lower Third) 13, 223n11
London Palladium 59
'Look Back in Anger' 170
'Looking for Satellites' 154
'Looking for Water' 175–6
Lord, Richard 107
Lord's Prayer 140–1, 142
Los Angeles 67–8, 85, 92, 93, 144–5, 146, 218; Cherokee Studios 74; Doheny Drive 68–9
'Love is Lost' 191–2

'Love Song' 52
'Loving the Alien' 121–5, 202, 203, 204, 233n8
Low (album) 86–92, 93, 94, 100, 102, 125, 158, 178, 182, 186, 192, 200, 206; *see also* 'Always Crashing in the Same Car'; 'Breaking Glass'; 'Subterraneans'
Lower Third, The 13–14, 21
Lynch, David 99

MacCormack, Geoff 11, 69, 141–2, 200
Macmillan, Harold 8
Madonna 2, 114
'Maggie's Farm' (Tin Machine) 159
Mail on Sunday (newspaper) 182
Maitreyabandhu, *Life with Full Attention* 220
Man Who Fell to Earth, The (film; 1976) 30, 72–4, 78, 92, 121, 176, 183, 205
Man Who Sold the World, The (album) 40–2, 43, 218; *see also* 'Running Gun Blues'; 'The Supermen'; 'The Width of a Circle'
'Man Who Sold the World, The' (song) 235n38
Manic Street Preachers 2
Manish Boys, The 12–13
Mann, William 172
Marquee Club, London 39
Mary Magdalene (biblical figure) 52, 128
Maslin, Harry 74
McCartney, Sir Paul, 'Martha My Dear' 45
McCaslin, Donny 202, 210, 212
McCulloch, Ian 56
McQueen, Alexander 154
Meher Baba 23
Melody Maker (magazine) 21, 49, 50, 139, 147
'Memory of a Free Festival' 25, 39
Mercury, Freddie 56, 139; Tribute Concert (1992) 139–41

Mercury Music Prize 177
Merry Christmas, Mr. Lawrence (film; 1983) 106
Metheny, Pat 126
Michell, John, *The View Over Atlantis* 36
Minotaur (mythological creature) 149–50, 152, 153
'Miracle Goodnight' 144
'Modern Love' 108, 111, 142
Moldavi, Sharon 155
Monder, Ben 213
Monkees, The 13
Moody, Rick 187
Moon (film; 2009) 188, 203
moon landing (1969) 33
Moonage Daydream (film; 2022) 234n17
'Moonage Daydream' (song) 53
Moroder, Giorgio 126
Morrissey 56
'Moss Garden' 94
'Mother' 164
MTV (television channel) 54, 112, 116
Murphy, Cillian 205–6
Murray, Charles Shaar 122–3
Murray, George 74, 86
Muslims 121, 123–4; *see also* Islam
Mussolini, Benito 37–8
Mustique 146
My Fair Lady (musical) 232n7

Nazism 37–8, 44, 45, 97–9, 229n17
Neu! (band) 86, 148
'Neuköln' 95
'Never Get Old' 175
Never Let Me Down 126–32, 145; *see also* 'Day-In Day-Out'; 'Too Dizzy'
'New Afro-Pagan and Work 1975–1995' (exhibition) 153
'New Angels of Promise' 170, 203
New Musical Express (NME) 71, 122–3, 144
New York 146, 174, 182, 187, 196, 209; Apollo Theater, Harlem 66; Madison

Square Garden 157, 236n13; Statue of Liberty 183, 188; Tibet House 21, 122; World Trade Center 166, 174
Newley, Anthony 12
Next Day, The (album) 186–96, 199, 200, 207, 221; *see also* 'If You Can See Me'; 'Valentine's Day'; 'Where Are We Now?'
'Next Day, The' (song) 187–8, 193–4, 196
Ng, Geeling 112
Nicholas, Paul 227n10
Niebuhr, Reinhold 138
Nietzsche, Elisabeth 37
Nietzsche, Friedrich 26, 37–8, 40–2, 44, 53, 60, 165, 167–8, 217, 218; *Beyond Good and Evil* 40; *The Gay Science* 167; *Thus Spoke Zarathustra* 40–2, 54, 113, 239n19
Nine Inch Nails 2, 235n38
Nineteen Eighty-Four: The Musical 59–60, 64, 187; see also *Diamond Dogs*
Nirvana 2, 235n38
Nitsch, Hermann 151
'No Plan' 208
Nolan, Sir Christopher 182
Nomad Soul, The (video game) 160
Nothing has changed (compilation album) 199–200
nuclear weapons 99, 127, 129–30, 168
Numan, Gary 2

Oasis 2
Oblique Strategies (creative technique) 86, 147, 149
occultism 4, 35–8, 43, 44–5, 47, 63, 67–72, 97, 197, 212
'Oh! You Pretty Things' 44, 45–6
O'Jays 65
Old Grey Whistle Test, The (television programme) 51
Olympic Games (London; 2012) 184

Opossum Inc. (company) 215
O'Regan, Denis 114–15
Orwell, George, *Nineteen Eighty-Four* 59–60, 64, 83, 187
Outside tour (1995–96) 153–6
Oy Vey, Baby (Tin Machine) 139

Padgham, Hugh 122
paganism 84, 128, 137, 152–3, 167, 172
Page, Jimmy 13, 80
Pagels, Elaine, *The Gnostic Gospels* 109, 110, 117, 123
'Pallas Athena' 145
paranormal activity 12, 67–70, 215
Parlophone (record label) 13
Parsons, Tony 142–3
Partch, Harry 148
Pat Metheny Group 126
Paul, St. 78, 149
Pauwels, Louis and Bergier, Jacques, *The Morning of the Magicians* 35–6, 45
Peaky Blinders (television series) 205–6
Penn & Teller (illusionists) 215
Performance (film; 1970) 72
Pet Shop Boys 2, 56
Peter, St. 214
Philadelphia 65
Philips (record label) 34
Picasso, Pablo, *Guernica* 231n16
Pickett, Wilson 65
Pierrot (character) 102
Pilate, Pontius 127–8
Pin Ups 64
Pine, Courtney 182
Pink Floyd 182
Pitney, Gene 12
Pitt, Kenneth 13, 23, 29
Pixies 2, 157
Placebo 2
Playboy (magazine) 32
'Please Mr. Gravedigger' 192, 200
Pop, Iggy 2, 85–6, 93, 127, 233n10; *Blah-Blah-Blah* 127; *The Idiot* 85–6, 111, 127; *Lust for Life* 127, 134

Porete, Marguerite 194–5
Potter, Dennis 219–20, 240n6
Prague 178
Presley, Elvis 11, 49, 72, 107, 203; 'Heartbreak Hotel' 190; 'Hound Dog' 11
Prestige, The (film; 2006) 182
Pretenders (band) 56
'Prettiest Star, The' 39
Prince 2, 114, 116
Prodigy, The 154, 159
Psalm 13 163
Psalm 121 141–2
psychedelic drugs 22, 36
'Pug Nosed Face' 182
Pulp 2
Pye (record label) 13

Quebec 120
Queen (band) 106, 120, 132
'Quicksand' 43–4, 230n48

racism 98, 116
Radiohead 2
Randi, James 215
'Rave Uncle' phase 154
RCA Records 50, 91
Ready Steady Go! (television programme) 12
'Real Cool World' 143
Reality (album) 174–7; see also 'Bring Me the Disco King'; 'She'll Drive the Big Car'
'Reality' (song) 175
Reality Tour, A (2003–04) 178–9
'Rebel Rebel' 64
Redding, Otis 66
Reed, Lou 2, 157, 187
Renck, Johan 204, 211
Reni, Guido, *Massacre of the Innocents* 167
'Repetition' 99, 182, 187, 192
Return of the Thin White Duke, The (autobiography) 73
Rice, Sir Tim 52
Richard I 'the Lionheart,' King 121
Richards, David 147
Ricochet (documentary film; 1984) 114–16

INDEX

'Ricochet' (song) 116
Rinpoche, Chime Youngdong 18–19, 22, 24, 26, 155, 213, 224n11
Rise and Fall of Ziggy Stardust and the Spiders from Mars, The 49–51, 52–5, 58, 59, 107, 193; *see also* 'Soul Love'; 'Starman'
Roberts, Chris 161
'Rock 'n' Roll Suicide' 193
'Rock 'n' Roll with Me' 64
Rodgers, Nile 108, 120, 143
Roe, Anthony 84
Roeg, Nicolas: *The Man Who Fell to Earth* 30, 72–4, 78, 92, 121, 176, 183, 205; *Performance* 72
Rolling Stone (magazine) 69, 73, 80, 82, 142, 144
Rolling Stones 33, 86
Ronson, Mick 39, 40, 50, 55, 56, 140, 158–9
Rosicrucians 45
Rot, Dieter 149
Roundhouse, London 39
Rowlands, John 83
Roxy Music 86, 148
Royal Albert Hall, London 182
Royal Festival Hall, London 24
Rubens, Peter Paul, *Christ and St. John with Angels* 167
Rugrats Movie, The (film; 1998) 164
'Running Gun Blues' 189
Russell, Bertrand 154

'Safe' (song) 236n5
Sales, Hunt 134, 139
Sales, Tony Fox 134
Samye Ling monastery 23, 25, 211
San Diego 100
Sanzio, Raffaello, *Saint Sebastian* 167
Satan and satanism 37, 40, 67, 68, 149, 208, 217
Scary Monsters (and Super Creeps) 102, 106, 120, 129, 186, 187; *see also* 'Ashes to Ashes'
Schapiro, Steve 71, 76–7, 92

Schneider, Maria 200
Schrader, Paul 128
Schwab, Corinne 'Coco' 205, 215
Scorsese, Martin 128
Scott, Ken 46
'Segue – Algeria Touchshriek' 235n40
'Sense of Doubt' 115
'Seven' 161, 175
Seven Years in Tibet 155
Severin, Steven 146–7
'Sex and the Church' 148–9
Sex Pistols 2
Shadows, 'Apache' 190
Shakespeare, William: *Hamlet* 208; *The Tempest* 75
'She'll Drive the Big Car' 30
Shelley, Percy Bysshe, 'Ozymandias' 168, 171, 236n21
'Shopping for Girls' (Tin Machine) 238n10
Siddhartha Gautama (the Buddha) 19, 42
Siegfried & Roy (illusionists) 197
'Silly Boy Blue' 17, 20–1, 24, 218
Simon (biblical figure) 214
Simon & Garfunkel: 'America' 236n13; 'Bridge Over Troubled Water' 227n8
Simone, Nina 80
Simple Minds 2
Simply Red 2
Sinatra, Frank 177
Sinclair, David 144
Singapore 114, 115
Singing Detective, The (television series) 219–20
Siouxsie and the Banshees 2, 146
Slick, Earl 74, 79, 186–7
Smashing Pumpkins 2
Smith, Pamela Colman 77
Smith, Robert 157
Smiths, The 2, 56
Snowman, The (film; 1982) 127
Snyder, Gary 17
Soft Cell 2
Soma (magazine) 176
'Some Are' 182

'Somebody Up There Likes Me' 60
'Song for Bob Dylan' 158
Song of Norway (film; 1970) 33, 188, 237n5
Sonic Youth 157
'Soul Love' 53, 108, 194, 203
Soul Train (television programme) 82
'Sound and Vision' 88–9
Sound+Vision tour (1990) 138–9
'Space Oddity' 27–32, 33–5, 39, 46, 54, 72–3, 101, 218, 226n16, 232n46
Spandau Ballet 2
'Speed of Life' 87
Speer, Albert 98
Spiders from Mars 50–1, 64, 158
Spinners (band) 65, 116
SpongeBob SquarePants (television series) 182
Springsteen, Bruce 74
Sri Yukteswar Giri, Swami 36
'Starman' 50, 51, 53–4, 55, 56, 96, 107, 232n44
'Stars (Are Out Tonight), The' 194
Station to Station (album) 74–80, 81, 83, 86, 87, 92, 98, 107, 132, 206, 212; *see also* 'Golden Years'; 'Wild is the Wind'; 'Word on a Wing'
'Station to Station' (song) 74–7, 79, 89, 126, 166, 171, 201, 218, 230n48
Stern, Howard 157
Stevens, Cat, 'Morning Has Broken' 227n8
Stooges 2, 86
Strange People (book) 11
Strauss, Richard 165–6; *Also sprach Zarathustra* 41; *Four Last Songs* 165, 172, 200
Stroumboulopoulos, George 172
Styrene, Poly 146–7
'Subterraneans' 91, 103
'Sue (Or in a Season of Crime)' 200, 213
Suede (band) 2, 143–4
Sukita, Masayoshi 94

'Sunday' 168–9, 238n4
'Supermen, The' 41–2, 80, 166, 239n19
Swift, Taylor 33
Switzerland 85, 100, 130, 141, 146

T. Rex 24, 148
'Take My Tip' (Davie Jones & the Manish Boys) 13
Talmy, Shel 13
tarot 37, 65, 67, 77
Taylor, Vince 49
Temple, Julien 240n5
Tennant, Neil 56
Terry, Sara 134
Tesla, Nikola 182
Tevis, Walter, *The Man Who Fell to Earth* 72
That'll Be the Day (film; 1973) 72
'There is a Happy Land' 14–15, 224n13
Thin White Duke (character) 73, 74–5, 76, 81, 83–4, 98, 138, 218
'This Is Not America' 126
'Thursday's Child' 175
Tibet 17–18, 20, 21, 24, 35, 99, 122, 155, 166, 218
Tibetan Book of the Dead 23, 68
Tillich, Paul 91, 96, 103, 110–11, 231n16
Time (magazine) 52
'Time Will Crawl' 129–30
Tin Machine 134–6, 139, 143, 159, 164, 238nn10–11
Tintoretto 161
Tiomkin, Dimitri 80
"Tis a Pity She Was a Whore' 213
Today (radio programme) 184
Tokyo 100
Tolworth, London 51
Tonight (album) 120–5, 126, 129; *see also* 'Blue Jean'; 'Loving the Alien'
Tonight (television programme) 12
'Too Dizzy' 131–2, 193
Top of the Pops (television programme) 34, 55–6, 152, 232n44

Townshend, Pete 23
Toy (album) 21
Tree of Life (Kabbalah) 71, 75, 76, 83, 87, 209, 210
Tretchikoff, Vladimir 120
Trident Studios, London 46
'Tryin' to Get to Heaven' 159
Turner, Robin 184
Turner, Tina 2

U2 2, 131; *Achtung Baby* 139
Übermensch, idea of 41, 44
UFOs 35–6, 38
'Under Pressure' 106, 113, 120, 139, 140, 194
'Underground' 127
Underwood, George 8, 12, 38, 46, 59, 72, 141, 228n22, 231n20, 233n10

Valentine, Penny 34
'Valentine's Day' 189, 208
van Hove, Ivo 205–6, 207, 208, 209, 239n19, 239n23
Vandross, Luther 66, 127
Vaughan, Stevie Ray 108
Velvet Goldmine (film; 1998) 232n2
Velvet Underground 2, 119
Victoria & Albert Museum, London 199
video games 159–60
Visconti, Tony 22, 24, 33, 38, 39, 46, 65, 86, 93, 100, 164–5, 168, 169, 187, 188, 238n9, 239n30
'Voyeur of Utter Destruction (As Beauty), The' 152

Waite, Arthur Edward 77
Wakeman, Rick 39, 46
Walker, Johnnie 174
Walker, Scott 227n9
Walsh, Enda 204–5, 207, 209
Ward, Brian 50, 228n22
'Warszawa' 89–91, 200
Washington, Ned 80
Waterhouse, Keith, *There is a Happy Land* 224n13
Waugh, Evelyn 189, 237n8
'Wedding, The' 144
'Wedding Song, The' 145, 170

Wells, H.G. 146, 234n17
Wembley Stadium 139–40
West, Mae 36
'What in the World' 88
Wheeler, Rosina Doyle 44
'When I Met You' 208
'When I'm Five' 14–15
'When the Wind Blows' 127
'Where Are We Now?' 181, 184–6, 187, 188–9, 221
White Dragon (magazine) 84
Who, The 23
Wicca 36
'Width of a Circle, The' 40–1, 42, 236n22
'Wild is the Wind' 79–80, 182
Wilson, John 170, 172
'Win' (song) 30
Winstanley, Alan 237n7
'Wishful Beginnings' 152
witchcraft 36, 67–8, 80
Witter, Simon 142
Woodmansey, Mick 'Woody' 40, 50
'Word on a Wing' 78–9, 80, 108, 162, 218
Wyatt, Robert, 'Shipbuilding' 189

X-Ray Spex 146

Yeats, William Butler 36
Yentob, Alan 65
'Yet-San and the Eagle' 24
'You Feel So Lonely You Could Die' 190, 193
Young Americans (album) 65–7, 74, 107, 125, 159; *see also* 'Somebody Up There Likes Me'; 'Win'
'Young Americans' (song) 66
'Your Turn to Drive' 30

Zanoni 226n33
Ziggy Stardust (character) 49–59, 63, 64, 121, 131, 165, 179, 218; *see also* Aladdin Sane
'Ziggy Stardust' (song) 54–5
Ziggy Stardust tour (1972–73) 51, 55, 58–9, 230n47

A NOTE ON THE AUTHOR

Peter Ormerod is a journalist and writer who has written extensively about culture and faith for the *Guardian*. Peter is also an arts editor for NationalWorld. He has a lifelong fascination with religion, having been raised in a clergy family.